Settlement and metalworking in the Middle Bronze Age and beyond

Sidestone Press

Settlement and metalworking in the Middle Bronze Age and beyond

New evidence from Tremough, Cornwall

edited by
Andy M. Jones, James Gossip and Henrietta Quinnell

Published by Sidestone Press, Leiden
www.sidestone.com

ISBN 978-90-8890-293-2

Lay-out & cover design: Sidestone Press
Photographs cover: Cornwall Archaeological Unit, Cornwall Council

Also available as:
e-book (PDF): ISBN 978-90-8890-294-9

Contents

List of figures

List of tables

Acknowledgements

The authors would like to thank the Tremough Development Vehicle for funding the fieldwork, archiving and final publication. The Performing Arts Centre (PAC) site was excavated with the assistance of Francis Shepherd and Tim Carter and the project was managed by Charles Johns. The Academy for Innovation and Research (AIR) building and Car Park 4 site were excavated by Francis Shepherd, Ryan Smith, Jay Brown, Christine Wilson, Scott Hedge, James Dean, Hannah Henderson and Chris Verran.

Thanks to Jane Read for illustrating the artefacts other than the moulds illustrated in chapter 5, which were drawn by Craig Williams of the British Museum. Thanks also to Francis Shepherd who produced the site plans and sections and Anna Tyacke who photographed the Bronze Age swords. Thanks to Carl Thorpe for photographing the copper-alloy ring.

Figure 5.25 is reproduced with permission of the Prehistoric Society.

Figure 11.22 is reproduced with permission of Royal Cornwall Museum.

The authors are grateful to Graeme Kirkham for commenting on the draft report, to Stuart Needham for information on the enclosures at Cliffs End Farm and to Ben Roberts for information on recent work on Bronze Age metalwork.

The Ordnance Survey mapping included within this publication is provided by Cornwall County Council under licence from the Ordnance Survey in order to fulfil its public function to disseminate information to a wider audience. Persons viewing this statement should contact Ordnance Survey if they wish to licence Ordnance Survey mapping for their own use.

Summary

This monograph reports on three archaeological projects at the Tremough campus, near Penryn, Cornwall, that were carried out over a two-year period between 2009 and 2011 by Cornwall Archaeological Unit. It also summarizes the results of evaluation trenching undertaken in 2008.

The first phase took place in 2009 and involved archaeological monitoring during the construction of a new Performing Arts Centre (PAC). Two pits of Early Neolithic date and two tree-throws, the infilling of which, is thought to be broadly contemporary with that of the pits, were identified. Over the last 14 years a number of other Neolithic pits and their associated artefact deposits have been excavated at Tremough, and these PAC pits have added to our knowledge of this practice; in particular there was evidence that their positions may have been marked by stones. Tree-throws are being increasingly recognised and investigated on prehistoric sites across Britain and the identification of these in a Cornish context has increased our understanding of these features. It has been suggested that the voids left by the fallen trees were used in a similar manner to the pits.

The second and third projects were carried out in late 2010 and 2011. On the site of the Academy for Innovation and Research (AIR) a small, sub-circular, post-built structure was radiocarbon dated to the first half of the second millennium cal BC. It is one of the first buildings in the South West region to be radiocarbon dated to the earlier Bronze Age, and one of only a few to be found in southern Britain.

On the site of a new car park (Car Park 4), investigations revealed a hollow-set roundhouse within which was a collection of stone bivalve moulds for the production of copper-alloy objects, which included ring-headed pins, socketed tools and chisels dating to the Middle Bronze Age, Taunton metalworking phase, *circa* 1500-1300 cal BC. A small number of copper-alloy objects were also recovered, which included a spiral finger ring and part of a pin. Analysis of the soil samples revealed that small droplets of copper-alloy were present and the geochemistry of the soils from several features identified high levels of copper and tin, which indicated that metalworking had taken place inside the structure. At the end of its occupation, the house was formally abandoned and infilled with material which included over 600 sherds of Trevisker Ware pottery as well as worked stone. The excavation of the roundhouse has been hugely significant because it represents the first 'metalworkers' house' to be investigated in England and provides a close set of radiocarbon determinations for the metalwork.

A second hollow-set Middle Bronze Age roundhouse was located immediately to the south west but this was not excavated and was buried in situ in order to preserve it. Cleaning above, however, revealed ceramics of Late Bronze Age date, which might suggest that the site had become used as a midden.

Nearby and to the north west of the roundhouses was a deeply cut curvilinear ditch, which formed part of a circular enclosure. This ditch surrounded numerous pits and postholes, a number of which formed rectangular structures. Large quantities of burnt stone were found in association with two pits, and these were possibly linked with cooking. Worked stone, pottery dating to the Late Bronze Age and the tip of a clay sword mould were also recovered from this enclosure, which is suggestive of small-scale metalworking taking place within the site. Radiocarbon dating places activity within the enclosure in the period *circa* 1000-850 cal BC. The enclosure represents the first of its kind in the South West and parallels have been drawn with sites found in the east of England and Ireland.

A second multi-ditched enclosure to the south was evaluated. This could not be securely dated, although later prehistoric or Romano-British pottery was recovered from an upper infill layer within the outer ditch. It is, however, possible that the site was contemporary with the Late Bronze Age enclosure and the possible links between the two enclosures are explored.

Chapter 1

Background to the investigations

Andy M Jones and James Gossip

Introduction

The plateau upon which Tremough Combined Universities in Cornwall (CUC) campus, Penryn, is located has proved to be one of the richest archaeological sites in Cornwall, with evidence for human occupation extending, at least intermittently, from Mesolithic flintwork through to the historic Queen Anne house and the modern university buildings which stand on the site today. Over the last 15 years several other archaeological interventions have taken place and the earlier stages have been fully reported in two publications (Gossip and Jones 2007; Gossip and Jones 2009-10).

In particular, large-scale excavations undertaken between 2000 and 2004 were focused on the investigation of an earlier fourth millennium cal BC Neolithic flint scatter and pits which were devoid of finds and a another pit group which contained a significant later Neolithic Grooved Ware assemblage radiocarbon dated to *circa* 2900-2300 cal BC. Five timber post-ring structures dated to the Early to Middle Bronze Age were uncovered and these appear to have been used for ceremonial purposes. Finally, a Late Iron Age enclosure and a small enclosed Romano-British settlement and field system were also investigated (Gossip and Jones 2007, 22-7).

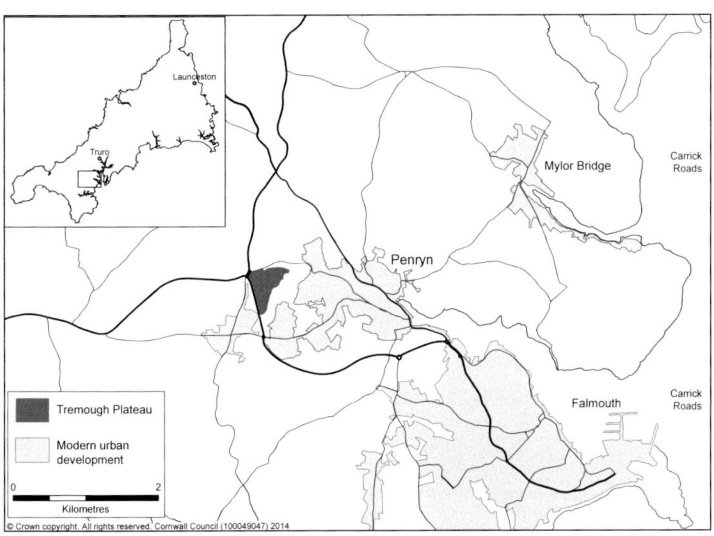

Figure 1.1 Location map showing Tremough.

This report covers three phases of archaeological recording carried out at Tremough by Cornwall Archaeological Unit, Cornwall Council, between 2009 and 2011. The first stage took place in 2009 at the site of the Performing Arts Centre (PAC). The second, at the Academy for Innovation and Research (AIR), and the third at Car Park 4 were carried out in 2010 and 2011. An earlier phase involving the evaluation trenching in 2008 of a multi-circuited enclosure will also be reported, as this site lay immediately to the south of the major sites discussed here and has not been published elsewhere.

Report structure

In the light of the very significant results gathered by the recent archaeological interventions relating to the Early Neolithic and Bronze Age occupation of the plateau at Tremough (Gossip and Jones 2007), it was decided that rather than reporting on the sites as separate entities in a series of journal articles, they should be drawn together into a single publication. This would include all the analysis undertaken on the component sites and consider them against the broader knowledge which has been gained over the last 14 years. Given the significance of the evidence for metalworking which was found in Roundhouse 1, and the lack of nearby comparanda for both Enclosure 1 and Structure 1, it was also decided to discuss these sites at greater length within a broader synthesis.

This resulting monograph is divided into four sections. The first (this section) outlines the background to the project and gives a brief overview of related sites and the programme of archaeological recording undertaken since 2008. It also describes the setting of the plateau and the geological background, and provides concise descriptions of each of the three investigated areas (PAC building, AIR building and Car Park 4).

The second section outlines the stratigraphical results from the major excavated sites, including the PAC pits, Structure 1, Roundhouse 1 and Enclosure 1. In addition, the evaluated Enclosure 2 is also described.

The third section contains detailed specialist reports on the artefacts, including reports on the ceramics, stonework, copper-alloy finds and the moulds. The reports on analysis of the environmental samples are also found within this section and these include the geochemical analysis of Roundhouse 1, the plant macrofossils and the charcoal. The results of the radiocarbon dating are also reported here.

The final section provides a synthesis which draws together the results from the analyses of the excavated sites and places them within their wider context with other excavated sites in Cornwall and beyond.

Terminology used in this report

Detailed records of all archaeological features were made, with each context being allocated a unique number. All cut features are shown with [ ], archaeological layers referred to throughout the report are shown within ( ) brackets. Structures are denoted by an unbracketed number, and the major excavated sites reported on in this volume are prefixed with a capitalized letter (for example, Roundhouse 1) to distinguish them from sites excavated elsewhere and from sites covered by earlier publications on Tremough. Details of the recording methodology and the project archives can be found in the grey literature (Gossip 2008a; 2009; 2011).

The probability distributions for the radiocarbon determinations (see chapter 10) have been calculated using OxCal (v4.1). The 95 per cent level of probability is used throughout this report unless otherwise stated. Where determinations from other sites are quoted in full they have also been recalibrated to OxCal (v4.1). Consequently they may differ from the original published sources, where earlier calibration curves were used.

Overview of work undertaken on the site

The Tremough plateau, which covers approximately 16 hectares, has proved to be one of the richest and most archaeologically important areas in Cornwall investigated to date (Figure 1.1). Several stages of archaeological investigation have revealed a picture of human activity which spans several millennia.

Geophysical surveys, archaeological assessments and fieldwork by Cornwall Archaeological Unit across much of the Tremough campus over more than a decade, have identified many significant prehistoric, Romano-British and medieval sites, including Early Neolithic pits, Late Neolithic pits associated with Grooved Ware, Bronze Age ceremonial post-rings, a rectilinear enclosure of Late Iron Age date, known as the 'Fort', Romano-British settlements and field systems (Gossip and Jones 2007; 2009-10), and a structure of earlier medieval date (Gossip, in preparation) (Figure 1.2).

Several of these sites were located close to and overlap chronologically with those reported on in this monograph. To the north of the PAC building, Early Neolithic pits, a ditch and a flint scatter were recorded in 2000; in 2002 (TRM 02 area) a number of Early Bronze Age pits and five post-rings of Early to Middle Bronze Age date were investigated to the south of the AIR building development and to the north of Car Park 4 (Gossip and Jones 2007, 6-22). These features will be drawn into the discussion of the site in chapter 11.

Closest to the PAC and Car Park 4 development sites, a multiple concentric-ringed enclosure (Enclosure 2) of at least later Iron Age - Romano-British date was revealed by a geophysical survey and recorded during evaluation trenching in 2008 (Gossip 2008a). The results from this trench are reported below in chapter 2.

The geophysical survey carried out in 2008 also revealed features suggesting prehistoric activity in the area of Car Park 4 (Archaeological Surveys 2008), including curvilinear features corresponding with Enclosure 1, which became the focus for excavation in 2011.

In the spring of 2009 a programme of archaeological recording was carried out in advance of the construction of a new Performing Arts Centre (PAC) (Figure 1.2). This work proved to be very significant as it extended the evidence for Early Neolithic activity across the plateau area, beyond where it had previously been encountered (Gossip and Jones 2007, 6), and expanded the range of activity identified on the site.

The work on the PAC site was followed in 2010 by archaeological recording on the site of the Academy for Innovation and Research (AIR) on the north side of the college campus. The results from this fieldwork also proved to be highly rewarding as they revealed a small circular post-built structure 7m in diameter (Structure 1) associated with Bronze Age pottery, which was subsequently dated to the earlier part of the second millennium cal BC. As such, it is significant because it is one of only a small number of earlier Bronze Age structures to have been excavated in southern Britain. It also provided the first hints of metalworking, a feature of the Middle and Late Bronze Age sites reported on in this volume.

An archaeological watching brief was undertaken in January 2011 during the construction of Car Park 4 and an adjacent area of temporary car-parking.

In the south-east portion of the stripped area, two hollow-set Middle Bronze Age roundhouses were uncovered. One of these, Roundhouse 1, was excavated and, although shallow, importantly it produced a collection of stone moulds used for casting socketed copper-alloy tools and pins. These represent the first

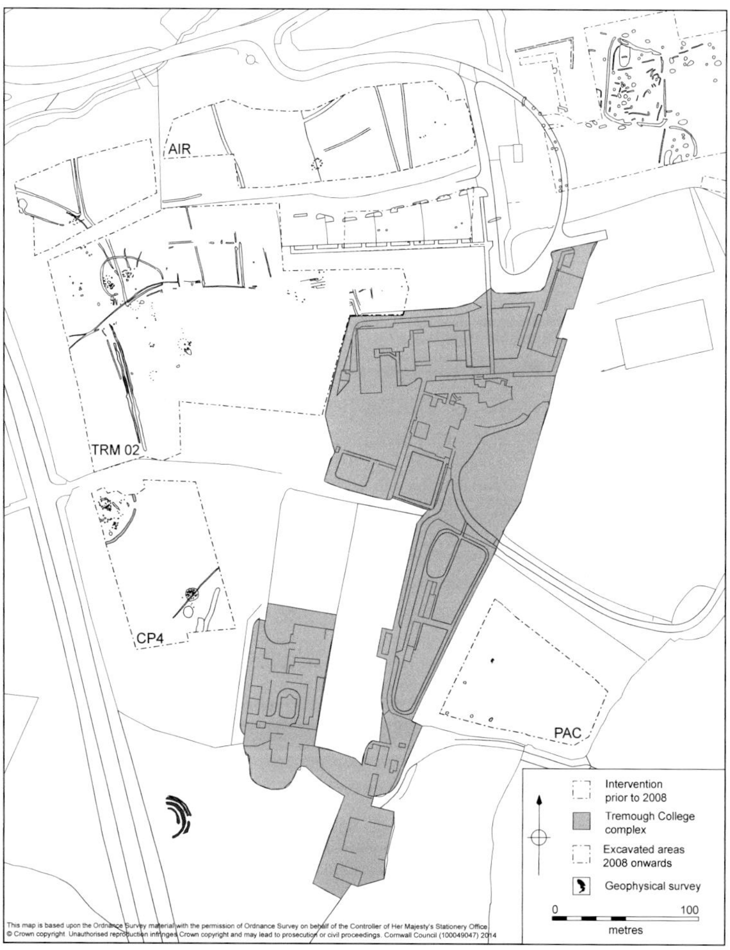

Figure 1.2 Location and areas of archaeological investigation at Tremough.

in situ evidence for metalworking within a domestic roundhouse to be recovered from Britain. The radiocarbon dating provides secure dating for Taunton-phase metalworking (*circa* 1500-1300 cal BC). The adjacent roundhouse, probably contemporary, was preserved *in situ*.

At the northern end of the Car Park 4 area an enclosure ditch was revealed surrounding structural remains dating to the early first millennium cal BC (*circa* 1000-800 cal BC). The excavated portion of the enclosure revealed no roundhouses or obvious dwellings, but there were at least two rectilinear structures, as well as features which may have been associated with structures and pits associated with fire-cracked stones. These were possibly associated with food preparation. Fragments of moulds were also found, indicative of small-scale metalworking. This site, Enclosure 1, is the first securely dated Late Bronze Age enclosure to be found in the South West peninsula, and the activities within it are to date unparalleled in the region.

Taken together, the excavations at Tremough described in this report have shed valuable light on the changing character of settlement activity over several millennia and on the character of metalworking over the span of the second millennium cal BC. This theme will be addressed in the following chapters.

In particular, the results of the investigation of sites within the car parking area are of national significance because they have revealed some of the best evidence to date for Middle Bronze Age metalworking within a settlement context in southern Britain. This aspect of the project is the focus of subsequent chapters.

Location and setting

The plateau

The excavated sites at Tremough are situated at the north-western and southern ends of an elongated spur or plateau which lies at a height of 80-120m OD immediately north west of the town of Penryn (NGR SW 76741 34834) (Figure 1.1). The plateau covers approximately 16 hectares, and until recently much of the area was agricultural land adjacent to the existing Tremough University campus. There are good views from the site over the large area of tidal estuary known as Carrick Roads to the east and to the sea beyond. The Penryn River, which flows into Carrick Roads, lies some 2 kilometres to the east of the investigated area and it is likely that these waterways formed important communication routes in prehistory.

To the west and north of Tremough lies the elevated undulating granite plateau of Carnmenellis while the landscape around Tremough is dominated and strongly influenced by the Fal Ria. This comprises a series of interlocking tributary creeks flowing into the River Fal, widening into the large estuary of Carrick Roads with the sea beyond. To the east and north lie gentle undulating hills dominated by arable and pasture fields.

The Tremough place-name is of early medieval origin and prior to the development of the University campus the site was farmland characterised as 'Anciently Enclosed Land' (Cornwall County Council 1996). 'Anciently Enclosed land' is made up of farming settlements documented before the seventeenth century AD and field patterns of medieval origin. The medieval and post-medieval farming landscape was, however, extensively altered in the later eighteenth and nineteenth centuries following the construction of the present Tremough house. During this period the field layout was reorganised to make larger rectilinear fields and an ornamental landscape was laid out around the house (Gossip and Jones 2007, 1).

Investigations across Cornwall have demonstrated that Anciently Enclosed Land has high potential for buried archaeology dating to the prehistoric and Romano-British periods (for example, Jones and Taylor 2010, 3), and it was for this reason that, despite having few known archaeological sites in 2000, the area was first targeted for investigation in 2000.

Geology

Geologically the excavated sites are at the junction between the igneous granite of Carnmenellis and the Devonian Mylor Beds. The exposed Tremough bedrock is categorised as metamorphic, with visible quartz veining, frequently contorted metamorphosed slates and mudstones (Geological Survey of Great Britain 1974) – known locally as killas – and granites and other igneous rocks occurring.

The underlying natural subsoil in the area of the PAC Building comprised a granitic yellow clay, known locally as rab, becoming paler at the base of the field slope. In the area of Car Park 4 the natural clay subsoil ranged from a bright pale yellow to a deep rusty orange across both sites with abundant weathered stones present in the subsoil. The overlying soil-type across the excavated areas has been classified as Stagnogley soils and Rankers (Soil Survey of England and Wales 1983).

PAC building

The PAC development site at Tremough was located on the lower slopes of a hill on the south-eastern side of the CUC campus (centred on SW 77049 34536), at a height of approximately 85m OD (Figure 1.2). Inland views are restricted to the north and west by rising ground. There are more extensive views to the south and east, and in the immediate area lower lying ground has been developed as a modern retail estate. Beyond this the land rises up towards Penryn College, the site of recently identified Late Neolithic Grooved Ware pits and Romano-British settlement activity (Gossip 2008b).

The tithe map for the parish of Mabe, *circa* 1840, shows the field much as it was prior to the development. Arrows pointing downslope on the north-eastern edge and along the south-western boundary hedge suggest that water drained along these routes.

Most recently the area of the PAC development has been in pasture but the geophysical survey (Archaeological Surveys 2008) found that much of the area was masked by a deposit of modern overburden and could not therefore be reliably surveyed.

Topsoil stripping confirmed that there had been significant ground disturbance in recent years both as a result of drainage improvements and adjacent development. Evidence of post-medieval attempts to drain the field effectively was most noticeable on the lowest part of the slope where regularly spaced linear trenches lined with stone formed a series of land drains aligned north west – south east. Ceramic land drains were also recorded close to the eastern edge of the site running parallel with the access road. The growth of reeds along this side of the field prior to stripping suggested that poor drainage was a recurrent issue. However, some archaeological features, in the form of pits were found to survive.

AIR building and Car Park 4

The AIR building (centred on SW 76848 34868) and Car Park 4 (SW 76787 34606) sites are located at the north-western and southern ends of the elongated spur which forms the plateau (Figure 1.2). The AIR site is located on a gradual north-facing slope, less than 50m to the south of a break of slope above a stream valley followed by the old road descending to Penryn. The site had much less extensive views than those from the PAC area or Car Park 4.

Prior to the development the AIR site had become covered with rough scrubby vegetation and trees planted in about 2000 had impinged upon it. No geophysical survey had been undertaken in this area but it was topsoil stripped because of the significant results from the excavations immediately to the south in 2002 (Gossip and Jones 2007) and to the east in 2009 (Gossip, in preparation). The potential of the area was confirmed by the discovery of Structure 1.

The Car Park 4 site was situated at the top of an even, gentle, south-facing slope, from which there were extensive views to the east and south east over the river Fal estuary. The tithe map again shows that there had been little change to the field layout in the area of Car Park 4 and until the time of the investigations it was down to pasture and had been used for grazing.

Geophysical survey of the fields around the Car Park 4 site (Archaeological Surveys 2008) suggested that archaeological potential was high in this area, identifying both Enclosure 1 and Enclosure 2. As a consequence, controlled topsoil stripping was undertaken in 2011. This revealed a large number of generally well-preserved buried archaeological features of later prehistoric date.

Chapter 2

Results from the excavations

James Gossip

This section focuses on the stratigraphical results from the excavated features. These are presented by site, that is to say the PAC building, AIR building and Car Park 4, and by period, from the Early Neolithic through to the Late Bronze Age. Finally, the results from the 2008 evaluation trenching of a multi-circuit enclosure dating to the later prehistoric period are presented.

PAC building

Topsoil and subsoil together averaged 0.8m in depth, but were up to 1.5m deep in places. These layers were mechanically stripped to the level of natural which comprised grey or yellow degraded granite and clay known locally as 'rab', becoming more orange in colour upslope. Large quantities of modern debris were found in both topsoil and subsoil indicating that the natural ground profile had at some point been cut away and backfilled with material before being sealed with a layer of topsoil.

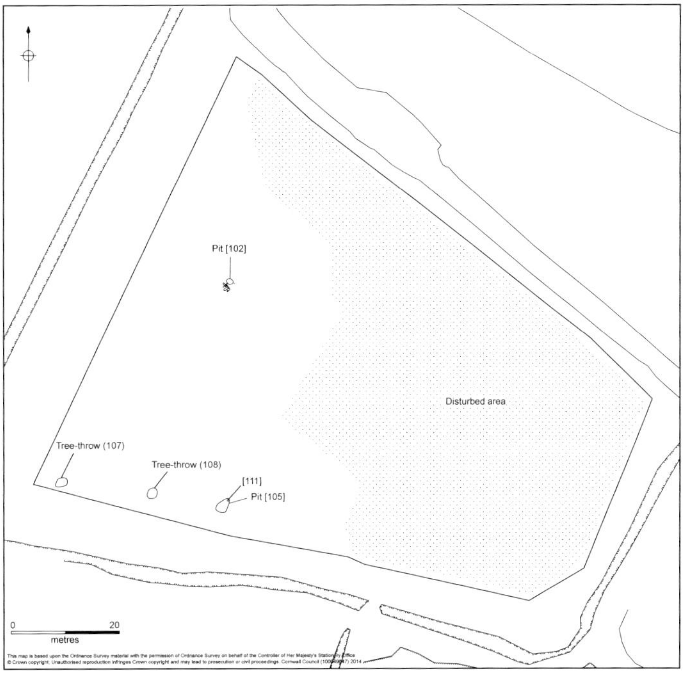

Figure 2.1 Plan showing Early Neolithic features in the PAC area.

The PAC pits had a discrete set of context numbers and these overlap with those issued in the 2011 excavations.

Early Neolithic pits

Two pits (Figures 2.1, 2.2 and 2.3), largely undisturbed by modern activity, were revealed beneath the topsoil (110), cutting into the natural.

Pit [102] was a raggedly circular bowl-shaped pit cut into the natural (109), 1.1m in diameter and a maximum of 0.3m deep. The pit was filled with densely packed granite and killas stone much of which showed evidence of burning. The fill (100) surrounding these stones was a dark reddish-brown silty clay containing a large proportion of charcoal made up of oak, small hazel roundwood, hazelnut

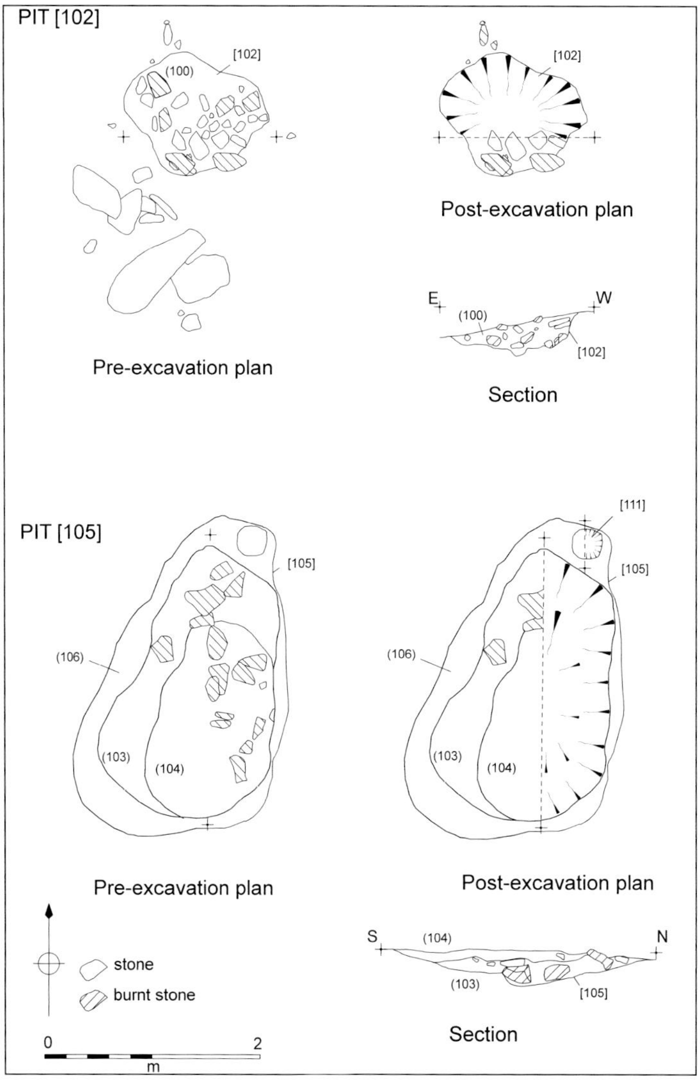

Figure 2.2 Plans and section drawings of pits [102] (top) and [105] (bottom).

Figure 2.3 Photograph of pit [102] showing stones within and beside it.

shell and hawthorn. A radiocarbon determination of 4750±40 BP, 3640-3378 cal BC (SUERC-29387) was obtained from a charred hazelnut from this feature. A total of 53 sherds of Early Neolithic pottery, from six vessels (**PP1**-**PP6**) (Quinnell, chapter 3) and three flint pieces were recovered from this fill. The flints comprised pebble waste, an arrowhead and a broken but used tool (**L1** and **L2**) (Lawson-Jones, below). A group of large granite rocks found above the natural subsoil nearby to the south may have been placed, possibly acting as markers for the backfilled pit.

Pit [105] was located close to two tree-throws on the south side of the development area. This was less regular than pit [102] but generally oval in shape, measuring 2.5m long and 1.6m wide, with a concave profile up to 0.25m deep. It was cut into natural subsoil (106). The primary pit fill was a black-grey charcoal-rich silty clay (103) 0.1m deep containing three pieces of flint – a piece of waste, a core tool and a probable broken leaf-shaped arrowhead **L3** – together with a sherd of Early Neolithic pottery (**PP1**). The charcoal was dominated by hazel, including hazelnut shell, which gave a radiocarbon determination of 4750±40 BP, 3640-3378 cal BC (SUERC-29383). Within this deposit were large numbers of granite, killas and quartz stones up to 0.3m in length, many of which had either been burnt or showed evidence of heat fracture. Above this deposit was (104), a compact greyish-brown silty clay containing burnt stone and three sherds of Early Neolithic gabbroic pottery, including one from vessel **PP8**.

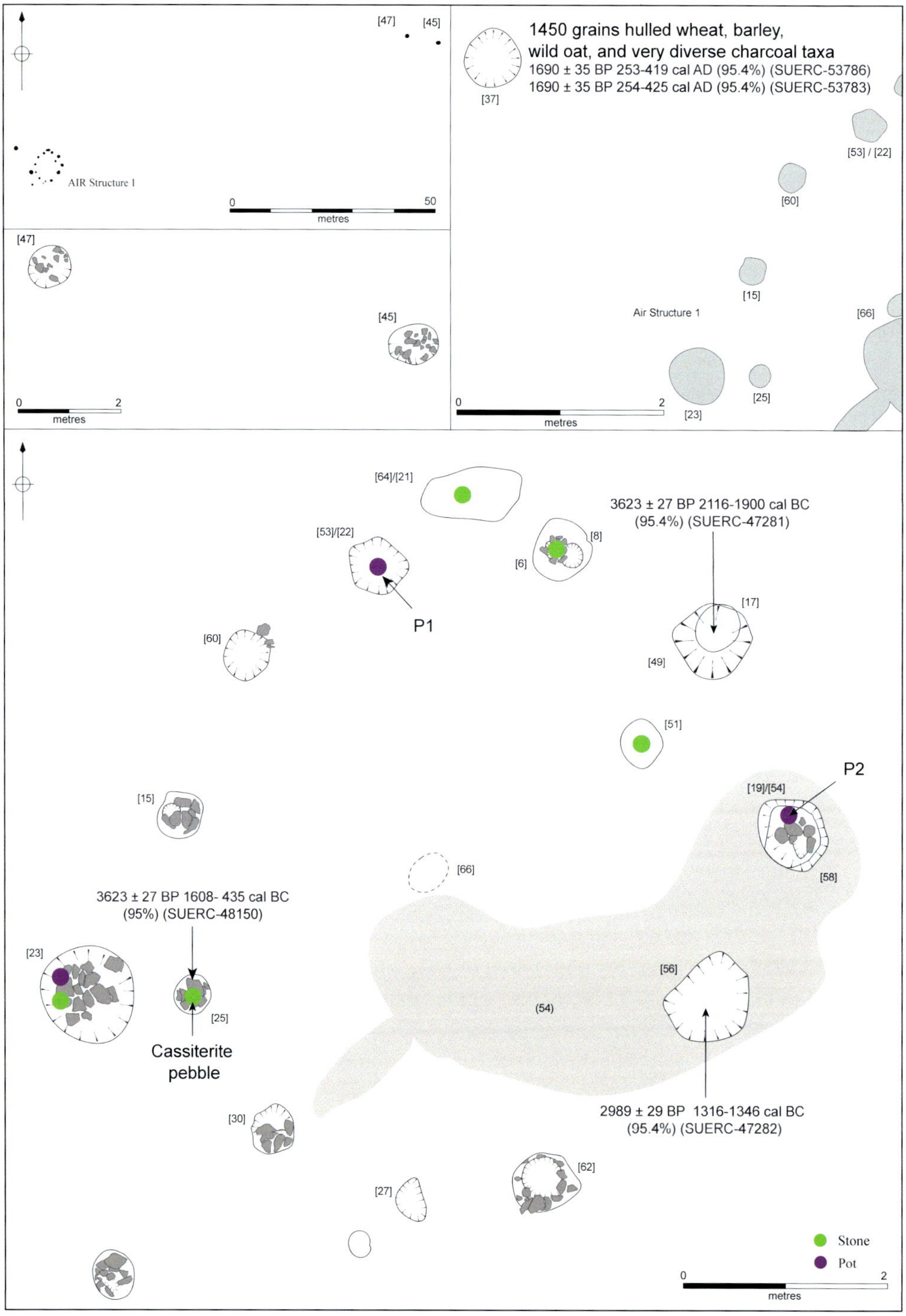

Figure 2.4 Plan showing Structure 1 and adjacent features.

A loosely-filled hollow [111] 0.2m deep and 0.3m in diameter immediately to the north of the pit represents a possible posthole and contained stones that may have been packing material.

The grey clay subsoil (106) was locally very pale and gritty and was thought either to be a natural variation or to have been affected by activity around the pit, perhaps the result of intense heat.

Prehistoric 'tree-throws'

Two other features, (107) and (108) (Figure 2.1), were recorded close to the southern extent of the development area. These were both irregular oval hollows between 0.2m and 0.3m deep, measuring 3m by 2.2m and 1.15m by 0.8m respectively, with irregular profiles, each filled with a dark grey or black charcoal-rich silty clay and frequent stone, including burnt granite and killas. The edges of the hollows in the natural rab were disturbed in several places by root runs. Hollow (107) also appeared to have suffered animal disturbance. Both features have been interpreted as the hollows left by tree-throws. A single piece of flint debitage was retrieved from tree-throw (108).

AIR building

The AIR building and associated car parking cover an area of just over 1 hectare, all of which was monitored during topsoil stripping. Features exposed in the natural (approximately 0.3m below surface) included some relating to an Early Bronze Age structure, a Romano-British hearth and isolated pits of unknown date.

Structure 1

The principal area of interest was an arrangement of 11 features, mostly postholes, forming a slightly elongated sub-circular shape measuring approximately 7m in diameter (Figure 2.4). It partially cut through a buried soil of brown stony clay (54)/(28) which covered an area of approximately 4.5m by 1.5m overlying the natural. This deposit was located in part of the eastern half of the structure and was cut by pit [56] and posthole [19]/[58]. Within the buried soil were 23 sherds of Bronze Age pottery, including vessel **P2**, suggestive of small storage or cooking vessels or those used for eating and drinking (see Quinnell, chapter 3).

The postholes had been cut into the natural stony subsoil to varying depths, with most 0.4-0.6m deep, and were largely circular in plan. Generally, fills were homogenous friable mid-brown silty clays, often with charcoal flecks present.

The majority had near vertical edges and flat bases, with *in situ* stone packing evident in [6], [17], [15], [19], [25], [30] and [62]. This might suggest the gradual rotting of posts, leaving the post-pipes intact; however, several contained sherds of unabraded pottery (chapter 3), which probably entered the postholes after the posts had been removed (chapter 11). In other postholes, packing stones were present but had collapsed into the fill, and only two [53]/[22] and [27] were devoid of stones.

Figure 2.5 Photograph of Structure 1 taken from the south-east, with stakes marking the positions of posts.

Posthole [6] had been cut by adjacent posthole [8] and the fill (7) contained two sherds of Bronze Age pottery, fragments of a greenstone cobble and a saddle quern. Postholes [17] and [19]/[54] were set within wider, shallower, more concave cuts [49] and [58]. Deposit (48), the fill of [49], contained two sherds of Bronze Age pottery and charcoal which gave a radiocarbon determination of 3623±27 BP, 2116-1900 cal BC (SUERC-47281).

Postholes [22]/[53] and pit [23] (located just to the west of the structure) contained joining sherds of Bronze Age pottery from vessel **P1**, although the features were not adjacent. Pit [23] also contained a beach cobble rubbing stone, re-used as a hammerstone. It was a shallow concave cut 1m in diameter and 0.15m deep, filled with stone (10) in a reddish clay and brown clayish silt matrix (11) with occasional charcoal. Deposit (11) contained a total of 39 sherds of pottery, including the joining sherd.

Posthole [21]/[64] produced a possible Bronze Age sherd and a possible beach cobble pestle, and posthole [25] a pebble utilised as a rubbing stone and a cassiterite pebble. Cereal grain from fill (24) in posthole [25] gave the radiocarbon date 3237±30 BP, 1608-1435 cal BC (SUERC-48150).

Posthole [27] produced a charcoal assemblage almost entirely of oak, and charcoal from internal posthole [66] was also dominated by oak with some hazel. Pottery was also found within postholes [27] and [30] (chapters 3 and 9).

Postholes were fairly evenly spaced, around 1m apart, with a far wider gap of 3m on the south-eastern side between postholes [19] and [62]. The location centrally within this gap of shallow pit [56], a possible hearth or burnt hollow, suggests it may have been deliberately placed within the area of the entrance. The pit was 0.9m in diameter and only 0.18m deep, concave and bowl-shaped, containing deposit (55), a mid-brown silty clay with frequent charcoal lumps and flecks and tightly packed angular granite stones, some of which showed signs of having been burnt. The charcoal-rich fill included oak charcoal which produced a radiocarbon date of 2989±29 BP, 1371-1126 cal BC (SUERC-47282). However, this posthole was located in an area which had been disturbed and the charcoal may have been from intrusive material. Within the structure, internal posthole [51] contained a whetstone with evidence of secondary use as a hammerstone.

Additional features

Pit [37], 5m to the west of Structure 1, produced the most diverse charcoal assemblage from this site, comprising oak, hazel, poplar / willow, hawthorn and holly. This was a shallow concave feature, 0.1m deep and 0.9m in diameter, filled with very dark, greyish-brown charcoal-rich silty clay. The edges cut into the natural subsoil were coloured red, presumably a result of *in situ* burning, suggesting that the feature was a hearth. Fill (106) also produced a rich charred cereal assemblage totalling 1450 grains, much of which was hulled wheat with less common barley, including some hulled barley. Oat grains were also abundant, together with weeds typically associated with arable habitats. However, radiocarbon dating of oat grains and wild radish returned near identical determinations: 1690±35 BP, cal AD 253-419 (SUERC-53786) and 1680±35 BP, cal AD 254-425 (SUERC-53783). The pit was therefore of later Romano-British date and considerably post-dated Structure 1. It was possibly related to settlement activity of this period revealed during earlier work in the vicinity (Gossip and Jones 2007, 40-41).

A group of pits and postholes were revealed some 80m to the north east of Structure 1. These included circular concave pits filled with dark clays and burnt granite, close to which were three possible postholes or small pits which formed a slight arc about 4m long. Surface pottery finds were undiagnostic and therefore the features cannot be assigned to any particular phase.

Car Park 4

Topsoil stripping in the Car Park 4 area extended over a total of 0.72 hectares. Recording work in the north-west corner of the stripped zone revealed a curvilinear enclosure ditch with pit and posthole structures of Late Bronze Age date within the enclosed area (Figure 1.2). Features were cut into the natural, below the topsoil, which was some 0.3-0.4m thick. Pit fills often contained large quantities of burnt stone and at least two rectangular post-built structures were identified, where deep postholes contained intact stone-packing. A pit filled with burnt stone also contained fragments of metalworking moulds.

Close to the south-eastern extent of the stripped area were the remains of two hollow-set roundhouses. Roundhouse 1 was excavated and found to contain a well-stratified collection of stone moulds for casting metal tools and pins (chapter 5), dated to the Middle Bronze Age. An adjacent structure, Roundhouse 2, which had perhaps been dumped over during the Late Bronze Age, was hand-cleaned, planned and then preserved *in situ*.

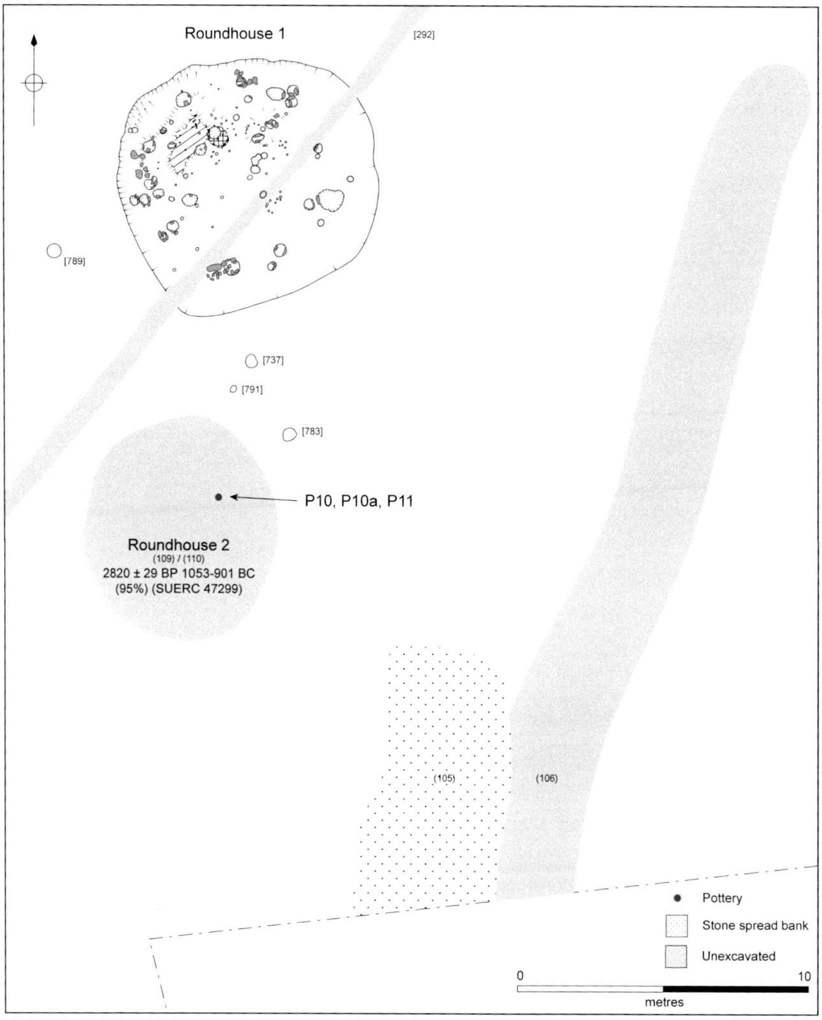

Figure 2.6 Plan showing Middle Bronze Age Roundhouse 1, Roundhouse 2 and adjacent features.

Roundhouse 1

Topsoil stripping revealed a circular area of dark brown silt approximately 9m in diameter, visible against the reddish-brown clay of the natural. Pottery recovered from the brown deposit suggested the presence of a hollow-set Bronze Age roundhouse. The area was cleaned by hand and various finds were recovered. It was then divided into four quadrants for excavation. Initially 0.25m wide baulks were left in place to create longitudinal sections through the roundhouse deposits.

Excavation of the north-west and north-east quadrants (1 and 2) revealed that the roundhouse was set within a concave hollow [796] cut to a depth of approximately 0.3m, into the base of which postholes and other features had been cut. The southern half of the structure, quadrants 3 and 4, was less well-preserved, having been truncated by later agricultural activity. Within the quadrant 1 cut of

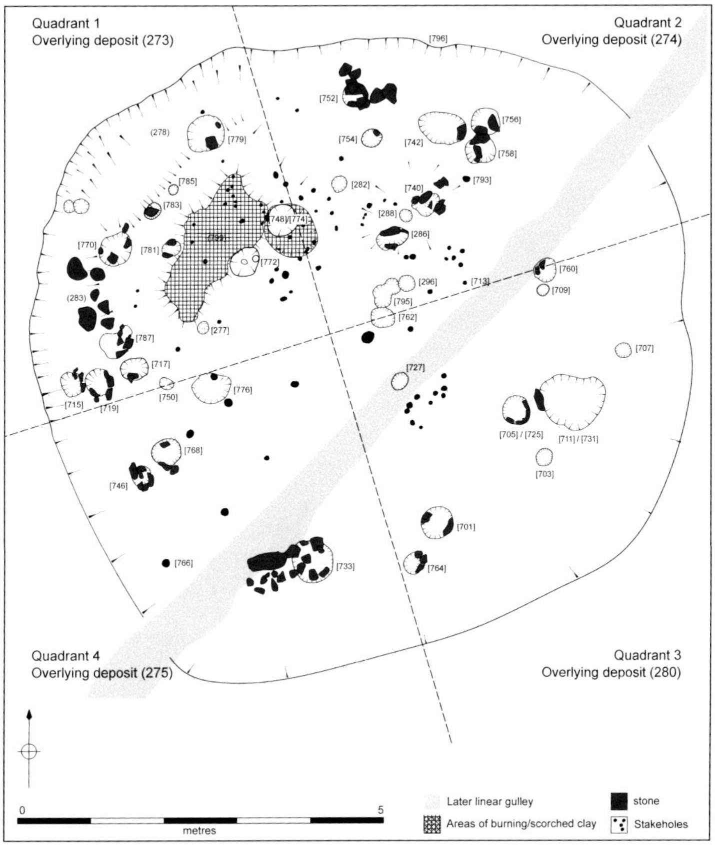

Figure 2.7 Plan showing features within Roundhouse 1.

the roundhouse was a 'gully' 0.05m deep filled by a mid-brown silty clay (278). Several angular granite stones (283) sat along the base of the south end of the gully, and it is possible that these were the last remnants of a wall which had lined the inside of the house hollow.

A number of artefacts were recovered from the gully fill (278). These included a relatively small assemblage of Trevisker pottery and four beach cobbles which had been used as pestles or hammerstones, most notably a cobble derived from the Budleigh Salterton area in south-east Devon and the pestle or hammerstone **S4** (chapter 4). In addition there was one metalwork find, SF400, a curved fragment from a copper-alloy artefact with a rib on one side.

A circle of ten outer postholes with a diameter of approximately 6.7m was set within the roundhouse hollow (Figures 2.7 and 2.8). They were generally regularly spaced about 1.25m apart, with the exception of postholes [768] and [733] (south-west quadrant 4,) and [756] and [760] (south-east quadrant 3), which at 2m were slightly further apart. Additional postholes had been cut adjacent to some of those in the main ring: posthole [746] next to [768], [758] and [742] either side of [756], [715] and [717] (possibly part of the main post-ring) next to [719], [764] close to [701] and [709] immediately adjacent to [760]. These postholes may have

Figure 2.8 Photograph of Roundhouse 1 taken from the south.

been added to the principal post-ring as a means of strengthening or renewing the structure. Charcoal from postholes [701] and [705], both on the southern arc of the principal ring, returned radiocarbon dates of 3109±29 BP, 1441-1407 cal BC (SUERC-47293) and 3065±31 BP, 1415-1252 cal BC (SUERC-47297).

Postholes [770] and [779] were both cut through the edge of the surviving inner gully represented by fill (278) in quadrant 1, although the significance of this in terms of phasing is uncertain. Postholes ranged in depth from 0.2-0.45m and were 0.1-0.55m in diameter; many contained the remains of stone packing. A group of small postholes or stakeholes was recorded close to the main post-ring in quadrant 1, comprising [750], [781], [783] and [785]. Postholes also occurred immediately outside the main post-ring in the south-east ([707] and [703] in quadrant 3), and it is possible that these were associated with an entrance to the roundhouse. Posthole [750] produced **S1,** a composite tool made on a cobble from Budleigh Salterton, Devon (chapter 5).

Internal features were concentrated in the northern half of the roundhouse in quadrants 1 and 2, but this may reflect better preservation in this area. Features comprised stakeholes, pits and postholes. There was little coherent pattern to the rather jumbled group of stakeholes in quadrants 1 and 2, although there was clearly a concentration around the hearth [748]/[774]. These had been cut through a baked clay floor surface (799), and they are therefore likely to have been linked to hearth activity, perhaps metalworking (chapters 5 and 11). Stakeholes tended to be 0.08m or less in diameter and 0.1-0.2m deep, usually vertical but occasionally driven into the subsoil at angles of up to 30 degrees.

Hearth [748]/[774] was a concave bowl-shaped cut measuring 0.8m in diameter and 0.15m deep, filled with a dark brown silty clay (747)/(773) with some charcoal flecks. Adjacent to the west was a similar possible hearth pit [772] filled with a charcoal-rich silty clay with patches of burnt clay. Both hearths showed extensive scorching on the base where they had been cut into the natural subsoil.

To the north west of the hearths was the baked clay floor surface (799), which had perhaps become a hardened surface as a result of prolonged proximity to the hearths. The surface consisted of a layer of clay no more than 0.06m thick above the natural subsoil, its surviving extents measuring approximately 2m long and 1m wide. It is possible that it had originally spread further but had been worn away.

An arrangement of postholes predominantly in the northern part of the structure comprised postholes [776], [277], [282], [754], [740], [286], [288], [296], [762], [795] and [727] may have formed a division within the roundhouse. These were generally smaller features than those of the outer post-ring, with diameters ranging between 0.15m and 0.35m (except [776], 0.44m in diameter) and up to 0.4m deep. Post-packing was largely absent, with the exceptions of [286] and [740], and they were filled with homogenous grey or reddish-brown silty clays. This group of postholes may indicate an internal structure or subdivision within the roundhouse. Posthole [286] gave the determination 3169±29 BP, 1501-1400 cal BC (SUERC-47292).

Copper-alloy artefacts recovered from the postholes comprised two lengths from a possible pin shaft (SF413) from the fill of posthole [785] (quadrant 1) and a spiral finger ring (SF403) found within posthole [705] in quadrant 3 (chapters 5 and 11).

The roundhouse hollow had been infilled by a single deposit of mid brown silty clay-loam soil. This was numbered (104)/(273) in quadrant 1, (274) in quadrant 2, (280) in quadrant 3, and (275) in quadrant 4. The infilling contained numerous finds. In quadrant 1 (104)/(273) contained pottery including sherds from **P4**, **P6**, and **P7**, (274) over quadrant 2 contained a sherd from vessel **P8** and (275) over quadrant 4 contained sherds from **P3** and **P5**. Stone finds included **S2**, a whetstone, and **S3**, a pestle or hammerstone, from deposit (273) (chapters 3 and 4). Vessel **P9** was also recovered from quadrant 1 (104)/(273). This is of Late Bronze Age date (chapter 3, below) and is indicative of later activity over the site.

The most significant artefacts from the floor of the roundhouse were the remains of nine stone mould fragments for casting metalwork, including ring-headed pins, a socketed axe and a chisel (chapter 5). The moulds were retrieved from quadrants 1 and 2 at the bottom of infill layers (273) and (274), directly on the floor of the roundhouse, with a clear concentration around the area of hearth [748]/[774] and baked clay floor surface (799).

Charcoal from deposit (280) in quadrant 3 gave a radiocarbon determination of 3091±27 BP, 1429-1297 cal BC (SUERC-47298).

Outer ring posthole [760] and the house hollow had been cut by a later linear gully, [292], which ran north east – south west across the roundhouse. The gully was 40m long, running from the eastern extent of the excavated area and terminating 15m south-west of the roundhouse. The date of the gully is uncertain, although clearly later than the roundhouse.

Roundhouse 2

Removal of topsoil immediately south-west of Roundhouse 1 revealed a second circular spread of darker brown silty clay measuring 7m in diameter, suggesting the presence of another hollow-set roundhouse (Figure 2.6). Preliminary hand cleaning of this deposit produced sherds of Late Bronze Age Plain Ware pottery from layer (109)/(110), including **P10**, **P10a** and **P11** and other sherds that may all belong to these vessels (chapter 3). Radiocarbon determination 2820±29 BP, 1053-901 cal BC (SUERC-47299), was obtained from residue on pottery, noticeably later than dates from the adjacent Roundhouse 1. This may indicate that the site of Roundhouse 2 had been used as a midden dump during the Late Bronze Age, the activity broadly contemporary with Enclosure 1.

Following initial cleaning, the decision was made to bury the roundhouse without further excavation below layers of geotextile membrane, fine excavated subsoil and sand (Gossip 2011).

Stone spread/bank and buried soil/old land surface

To the south east of Roundhouse 1 was a stony spread, or bank (105) aligned north east – south west (Figure 2.6). This spread comprised a mass of tightly-packed granite stones, measuring 5.5m wide and 9m long. The feature is thought to represent an eroded, ploughed down boundary which had marked the edge of a field system.

To its east was a linear band of dark clayey soil (106), 30m long and 2m wide, perhaps representing a buried soil or possibly a shallow ditch associated with (105) (Figure 2.6). More than 100 sherds of pottery were recovered from both deposits. These were generally of Trevisker type and the assemblage included decorated rims and body sherds from incised and cord-impressed vessels (chapter 3). The material is probably broadly contemporary with that from Roundhouse 1.

Enclosure 1

Enclosure 1 comprised a substantial length of ditch which, if projected beyond the investigated area, is likely to have enclosed an area roughly 60-65m in diameter (Figure 2.9). Approximately one-third to half of the probable interior was uncovered, and numerous pits and posthole structures were identified within this space.

The enclosure ditch [160]/[170]

A curvilinear enclosure ditch [160]/[170] ran from the western extent of the stripped area in an arc towards the north. The ditch was up to 1.7m wide and up to 1.35m deep, with very steep sides and a slightly rounded base throughout its visible extent (Figure 2.10). The ditch circuit was broken on its eastern side by a 5.5m wide entrance into the enclosure. The ditch terminals on either side of this were almost square-ended in plan, with vertical sides. The ditch was sampled by the excavation of six sections totalling 40 per cent of the exposed length. Although

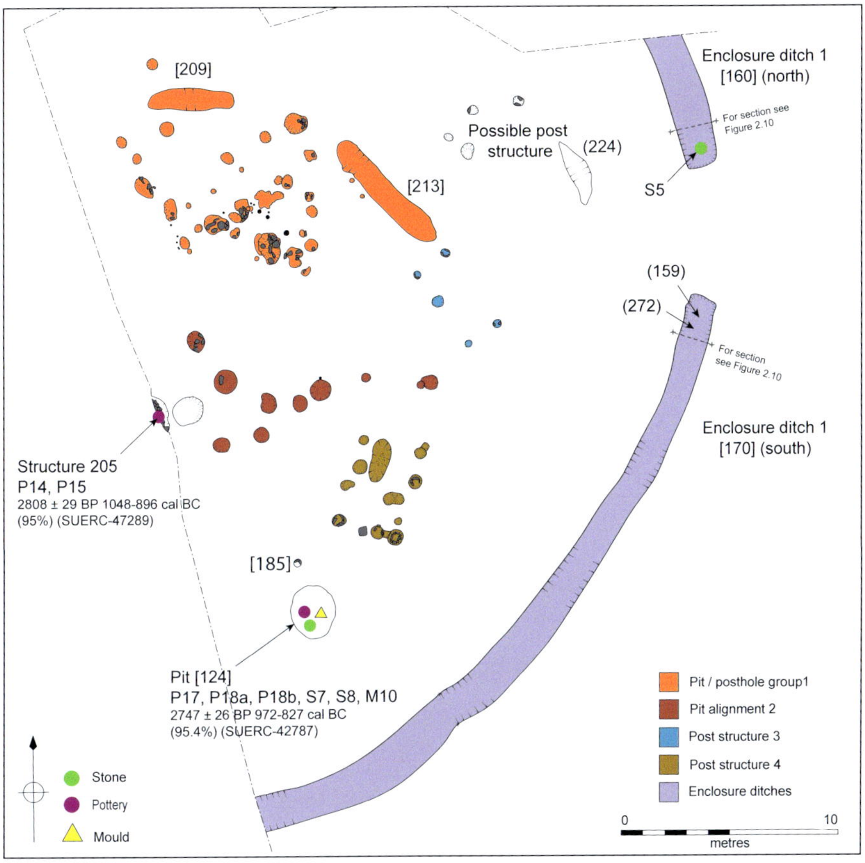

Figure 2.9 Plan showing Late Bronze Age Enclosure 1 and internal features.

it is likely that there was a bank and there was space for one within the enclosure, there was no indication of the position of one, either on the inside or the outside of the enclosure ditch, and the tip-lines in the ditch fills were inconclusive. However, the quantity of large granite stones recovered from the ditch filling might have derived from a stone revetment facing such a bank.

The basal fill (267)/(798) along the southern arc of the ditch comprised a dark greyish-brown silty clay with flecks and fragments of charcoal. This was overlain by a succession of dumped or eroded silty clay deposits, (266), (265) and (264),

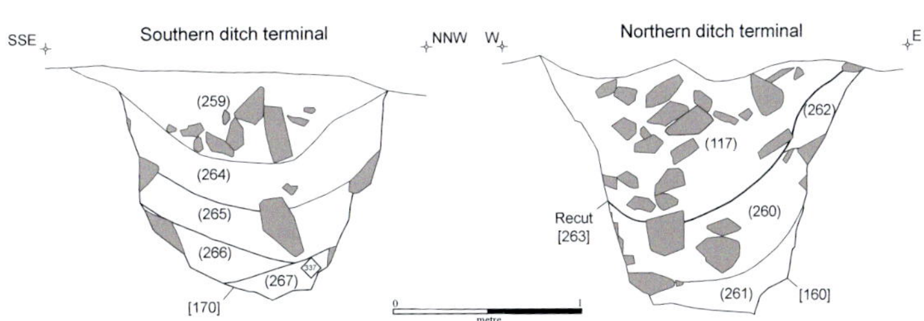

Figure 2.10 Sections across Late Bronze Age Enclosure 1 ditch [160].

containing a moderate amount of granite stones. Uppermost deposit (159)/(107)/(259)/(165), forming the top 0.4-0.55m of ditch fill in all excavated sections, was a dark brown silty clay containing large quantities of angular granite stones (mostly fist-sized and larger) and occasional flecks of charcoal. South terminal fill (159) contained a fragment of carinated bowl. Deposit (272), also in the southern arc of the ditch and located near to the base, contained two small fragments of burnt bone and produced a rim from a shouldered jar and a flat-topped bowl rim. Both of these ceramic forms belong to Late Bronze Age Plain Ware (chapter 3) and are consistent with a radiocarbon date from (798), a basal fill in the southern length of the enclosure ditch, of 2782±29 BP, 1006-843 cal BC (SUERC-47283).

The northern terminal of the ditch revealed a similar sequence of deposits to that found in the southern terminal. The ditch had been hewn from the bedrock with vertical sides (in contrast to the southern section which was less rocky), with a basal fill (261) comprising gritty silty clay probably derived from erosion of the sides and base soon after excavation. Above this was (260), a friable light brown clay with frequent large granite stones. A re-cutting of the ditch [263] was also evident, cut through the earlier deposits. This recut was filled with a dark clay deposit (117) containing very frequent granite stones 0.1m to 0.25m in length (Figure 2.10).

Pit / Posthole Group 1

A dense cluster of features, which have been grouped together as Pit / Posthole Group 1, was revealed in the northern part of the enclosure. Initially appearing rather random, it is very possible that these features, comprising mainly postholes but also pits containing burnt stone, represent a structure or perhaps a series of structures, probably rectangular, built successively in this area over time. Within this group of features were several components, including an 'L-shaped' setting, an amorphous group of pits and two shallow linear depressions.

Possible L-shaped structure

Two linear arrangements of features – postholes [244], [240], [158] and [144] and pit [114] on a north-west – south-east alignment and postholes [255], [177] and [211] aligned south west – north east – seem to form an L-shaped structure or two sides of a sub-rectangular structure measuring approximately 6m by 7m (Figure 2.11). Pottery from pit [114] had internal residue which produced a radiocarbon date of 2822±30 BP, 1071-899 cal BC (SUERC-47288). This determination was the earliest to be obtained from a feature inside the enclosure. Pits [164], [249] and posthole [171] lay on or close to the south-west - north-east alignment and may have been associated with it, or could possibly have been part of a structure described below. The fill (170) of posthole [171] contained two stone mullers, **S5** of quartz greisen and **S6** of granite. All of the pits contained burnt stones and moderate to frequent amounts of charcoal in their fills, [249] producing the richest charcoal sample of the group with taxa comprising oak,

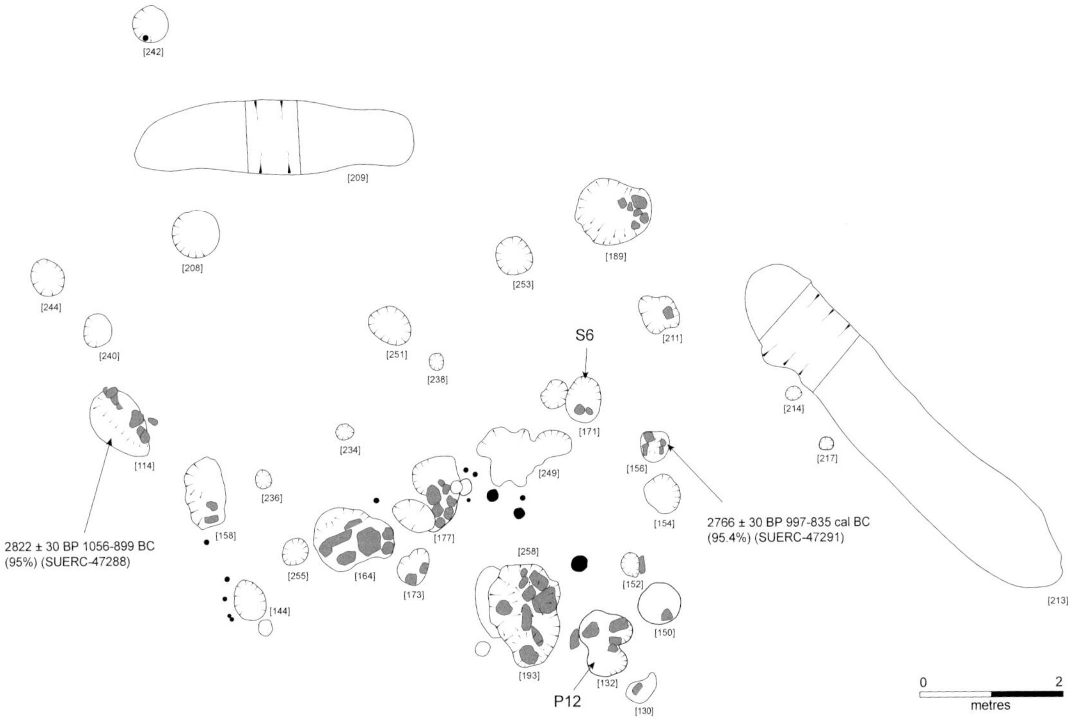

Figure 2.11 Plan showing Pit / Posthole Group 1.

hazel, blackthorn, hawthorn and broom or gorse (chapters 8 and 9). Of particular note is posthole [144], the fill of which contained clay metalworking mould fragments A-D, which are similar to those from pit [124] (below and chapter 5).

Parallel to the south-west – north-east alignment was a line of three small postholes, [236], [234], [238], which may have formed a structural subdivision within a building. Three larger postholes, [251], [253] and [189], were offset to the north of the line of small posts and may represent a separate structure.

A further posthole [242] was revealed containing fill (241), a dark brown silty clay. The posthole was 0.5m in diameter and 0.3m deep with steeply sloping sides and a flat base. A stakehole 0.4m deep was evident in its southern edge. Posthole [208] measuring 0.3m in diameter and 0.26m deep was recorded between [242] and [251]. The fill (207) comprised dark brown silty clay with a moderate amount of charcoal.

The majority of cut features were circular in plan with steep sides and flat bases; burnt stones were often present but did not form intact post-packing. Posthole size varied, with the outside edge postholes 0.16-0.4m in diameter; depths were more consistent, in the range 0.2-0.3m. The small inner post alignment ([236], [234] and [238]) comprised small postholes 0.1m in diameter and between 0.1m to 0.2m deep. The north-easternmost posthole [189] was notable as it was larger, measuring 0.3m in diameter and 0.8m deep.

A separate structure?

A further group of pits and postholes lay immediately to the south of the L-shaped structure. It is unclear whether these formed part of the same structure or were part of a separate phase. The group was made up of postholes [173], [258] (in pit [193]), [130], [132], [150], [152], [154] and [156], and possibly pit [164] (Figure 2.11). These features formed a rough triangle approximately 3m in size. Postholes [171] and [177] were also possibly associated with this group and produced oak, hazel, blackthorn, hawthorn and broom or gorse charcoal (chapter 9).

Most of these features also had vertical or near vertical profiles with flat bases and are likely to have been structural, measuring 0.15-0.25m in diameter and 0.25-0.4m in depth. Postholes [173], [258], [132], [154] and [156] all contained burnt stone, possibly representing collapsed post-packings, although the reason for the burning is unknown. In [154] a distinct post-pipe was revealed in the centre of fill (153), while pit [193] had a 0.05m deep layer of charcoal lining the base, with taxa comparable to those from [249]. A posthole, [258], was cut through the northern edge of the pit. Pit [164], 0.9m in diameter, 0.5m deep and sub-circular in plan, contained a dark brown compact silty clay containing large quantities of angular granite stones, many of which had been burnt.

Direct dating evidence was limited. Residue on pottery from posthole [156] gave a radiocarbon determination of 2766±29 BP, 997-835 cal BC (SUERC-47291), which is a little later than that from the L-shaped post-setting described above. Vessel **P12** was recovered from feature [132].

A wind-break or screen?

Shallow cut / deposits [209] immediately to the north and [213] to the east are likely to have been associated with the groups of pits and postholes described above. Measuring only 0.05m deep, it is possible that they represent the shallow remnants of buried soil deposits. However, it is also possible that the depressions were formed by linear structures, such as screens or windbreaks; features such as stakeholes may have been located in the unexcavated portions. Comparable features have been found within other Late Bronze Age enclosures, as, for example, at Mucking North Ring, where during the first phase a screen was erected between the roundhouses and the entranceway (Bond 1988, 14-19).

Pit Alignment 2

An alignment of features was recorded on a 10m long east-west axis in the central area of the enclosure (Figure 2.12). This comprised pits [202], [200], [126], [136], [123], [138], and postholes [140] and [142]. The pits were more or less circular with steep sides and flat bases or more bowl-shaped profiles. They were shallow, none of them exceeding 0.3m in depth. Diameters ranged from 0.4m to 1.8m. Pits [134] and [128] lay to the north of the alignment at its western end, angled towards the north-west. Pits generally contained single deposits of mostly dark greyish-brown silty clays, with some containing burnt stones; notable examples were [128], [134] and [140]. Charcoal was limited to oak from pits [126], [134]

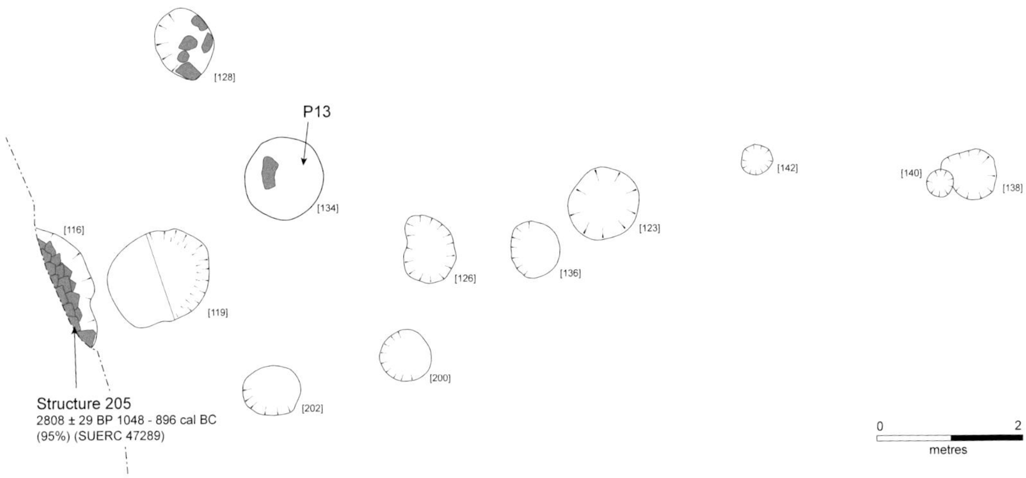

Figure 2.12 Plan showing Pit Alignment 2.

and [136], with [128] also containing traces of hazel (chapter 9). Pits [202], [126] and [123] incorporated some charred plant remains, including occasional wheat grains and glume bases, an oat / grass grain, occasional weeds, a charred hazelnut fragment and an oak bud, while pit [128] produced a larger assemblage of macrofossils including 22 hulled wheat grains (chapters 8 and 11).

The artefactual assemblage from this group included sherds from a thin-walled biconical vessel **P13** found in pit [134].

Postholes [140] and [142] at the eastern end of the alignment were clearly different to the other features and more evidently functioned as postholes, with vertical sides, flat bases (0.4m and 0.35m deep, 0.25m and 0.3m in diameter) and with the lower edges of their cuts lined with granite packing stones. The two postholes perhaps represented a stand-alone structure. Some maintenance or re-use of the structure was suggested as posthole [140] was cut through (137), the fill of pit [138].

Structure 205 and pit [119]

At the western end of Pit Alignment 2 was a large circular pit [119] measuring 1.25m in diameter and 0.3mm deep (Figure 2.12). The inside edge of the cut had a groove cut into its base within which was deposit (203), a light brown silty clay 0.05m thick, sealed by (118), a dark greyish-brown silty clay containing frequent pieces of charcoal, 0.25m deep.

To the west was a shallow depression or hollow cut [116], over which was stone Structure 205, comprising a carefully built cairn of granite stones, circular in plan, with an overall diameter of 1.6m and a height above the base of [116] of 0.5m (Figure 2.13). Many of the stones were cracked or scorched, indicating that they had been burnt. The structure was built within a shallow circular, concave cut into the natural subsoil 0.25m deep. Above the stones lay a large flat sub-rectangular stone approximately 0.5m wide, 1m long and 0.25m thick. This large stone was

Figure 2.13 Photograph showing Structure 205, from the east. Note its careful construction and the flat-laid stone on top.

lifted to reveal a mid brown silty clay filled core, the outer visible stones of the 'cairn' forming a coarsely constructed circular 'wall' 0.25m wide and 0.5m high on which the slab had been laid. The clay fill (115)/(103) contained sherds of pottery from Late Bronze Age vessels **P14** and **P15**, a large stone muller and a muller fragment (chapter 3). Residue on pottery from (115)/(103) returned a radiocarbon date of 2808±29 BP, 1048-896 cal BC (SUERC-47289). Plant macrofossils recovered from (115)/(103) included wheat and barley, a hazelnut fragment and a small arable weed assemblage (chapter 8). The charcoal was dominated by oak with a small collection of birch, blackthorn and gorse.

Deposit (270)/(271) from below the stones had a greasy texture and contained small oak fragments and a single hulled wheat grain. The finds from this area are problematic as they purportedly included a sherd from Late Iron Age imported vessel **P19** and a sherd of glazed post-medieval pottery (chapter 3). There was, however, no sign of disturbance to the stones of the cairn and the remaining ceramic assemblage associated with Structure 205 was all of Late Bronze Age date. It is therefore probable that the sherd from vessel **P19** and the post-medieval glazed sherd are both from adjacent layers (perhaps the topsoil), as layer (270)/(271) was first exposed during machine stripping and its extent not recognised at the time. The finds are therefore likely to have been wrongly assigned to this context number.

It is probable that Structure 205 represents burnt mound material which had been carefully arranged after use, with the adjacent pit [119] used as a cooking pit which may have been lined, hence the groove. The possible function(s) of this feature are discussed in chapter 11.

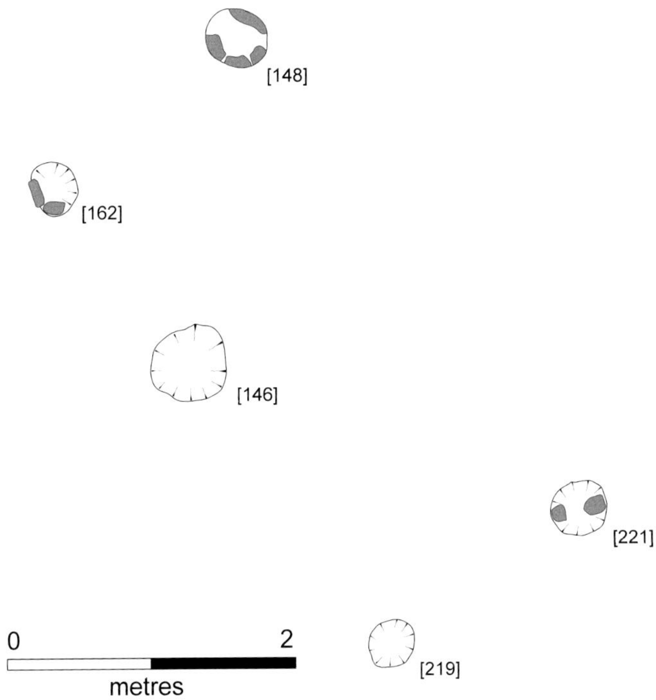

Figure 2.14 Plan of Post Structure 3.

Post Structure 3

In the eastern area of Enclosure 1 was a group of five postholes apparently forming a rectangular structure 4.2m long (north west – south east) and 2m wide (north east – south west) (Figure 2.14). The postholes forming the structure had consistently vertical sides and almost flat bases, were regular in diameter, ranging from 0.12m to 0.15m, and varied in depth between 0.2m and 0.45m. The deepest postholes were at the northern end of the structure.

Fills comprised dark greyish-brown silty clays, with postholes [221], [162] and [148] containing post-packing stones. Those in posthole [148] were particularly well-preserved, with stones lining the vertical cut of the feature. The intact nature of the postholes suggests that posts rotted *in situ*.

No artefacts were recovered from this structure, and none of the constituent postholes produced any charred plant macrofossils. Only a few flecks of charcoal were present and it was not possible to date this building. It is, however, likely, given its size and form, that it was broadly contemporary with Post Structure 4 (below).

Post Structure 4

Lying south of Pit Alignment 2 was a group of postholes forming a rectangular structure measuring 4.5m long and 3.5m wide aligned south west – north east along its long axis (Figure 2.15). Each long side comprised three postholes, ([181], [187], [169] on the north-west side, [179], [198] and [269] on the south-east side), with two additional postholes slightly off-set from these lines: [175] on the north-west side and [191] (with adjacent [247]) on the south-east side. The south-western shorter edge also had posthole [183], a deep vertical-sided stone-lined posthole immediately adjacent to [179]. A shallow elongated pit [167] measuring 2m by 0.8m was positioned inside the structure close to its northernmost corner, filled with a large quantity of burnt granite stones in a dark greyish-brown silty clay.

Postholes [179], [183], [181] and [198]/[121] on the south and eastern sides of the structure had intact stone-packing lining vertical cuts into the solid natural subsoil. The postholes contained single deposits of greyish or reddish-brown silty clays; all were circular with flat or slightly rounded bases. Some were particularly deep: [181], [175] and [198]/[121] were 0.7m, 0.8m and 0.9m deep respectively. The remaining postholes (with the exception of shallow posthole [196]) ranged in depth between 0.4m and 0.6m with a mean depth of 0.5m. Diameters were remarkably consistent and had a range of 0.15-0.25m. North-eastern corner posthole [269] appeared to have been maintained as it was part of a double posthole with [136] (probably the later re-cut); posthole [191] also had another, [247], immediately adjacent, perhaps to provide additional support. The south-eastern corner post [179] may also have been strengthened by the addition of posthole [183] along the southern edge. Beyond the south-west corner of the structure

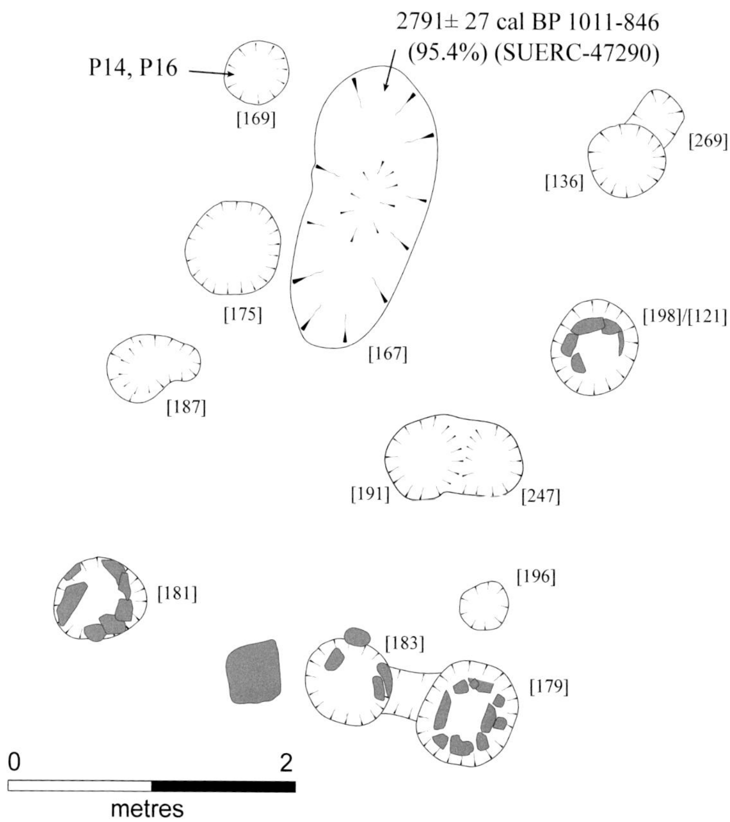

Figure 2.15 Plan of Post Structure 4.

posthole [185] was another steep-sided posthole with intact stone packing but this appears to be an isolated feature or was possibly associated with pit [124].

Many of the features produced fragments of pottery, with posthole [169], (fill (168), containing **P16**, and pit [167], (fill (166), containing 72 sherds of pottery, including a sherd similar to **P14** (Structure 205). Residue from pottery from (166) gave the radiocarbon date 2791±27 BP, 1011-846 cal BC (SUERC-47290). Postholes [191] and [198]/[121] contained stone mullers and [198]/[121] and posthole [185] part of a saddle quern (chapter 3). Posthole [181] contained a few tiny fragments of burnt bone.

Plant macrofossils included barley and wheat, with a single oat awn from [167] (chapter 8). Postholes [198]/[121], [175], [179], [181] and pit [167] produced large quantities of oak charcoal (chapter 9). Posthole [187] presented only a few fragments of oak charcoal, but a larger quantity of hazel. Overall, the structure produced a diverse range of species including birch, alder, hazel, blackthorn, hawthorn, broom or gorse, holly and ivy.

Pit [124]

Approximately 3m to the south of Post Structure 4 was circular pit [124], 2m in diameter and 0.55m deep with steep concave sides and a flat base. There was a single fill (112)/(108) of mid-brown silty clay rich in charcoal fragments, which formed the matrix for a densely packed deposit of largely fist-sized angular granite stones, amounting to approximately 75 per cent of the total deposit (Figure 2.16). All the stones were cracked or scorched, indicating that they had been heated. Stones were also seen above the level of the natural subsoil during the topsoil

Figure 2.16 Photograph showing pit [124], half excavated. Note the burnt stones in its fill.

stripping stage in the area of pit [124] and these may have been part of a stone cairn. As with Structure 205, it is possible that the pit was associated with a mound of burnt stone, or with activity linked with one (chapter 11).

Charred plant macrofossils were limited to only single examples of a wheat glume base and spikelet fork, with a ribwort plantain and grass caryopsis. A tiny amount of burnt bone was noted. The artefactual assemblage from pit [124] comprised more than 50 sherds of pottery, including vessels **P17**, **P18a** and **P18b**, slate lid **S8**, a fragmented muller and a rubber. Interestingly, a cushion or finishing stone **S7**, was recovered which may have been associated with metalworking. It was one of only two from the site, the other **S9** being unstratified. Also within fill (112) was Mould 10, the tip of a clay mould for a leaf-shaped sword, with 13 other small fragments of moulds. These included fragment C, possibly part of a ribbed socketed axe mould, D, part of a possible chisel mould and other socketed axe mould fragments G, H and J. Residue on pottery gave the radiocarbon determination 2747±26 BP, 972-827 BC cal BC (SUERC-47287). This deposit is likely to have been associated with an episode of structured deposition (chapters 5 and 11).

Possible post structure

An irregular group of four postholes 8m to the west of the entrance to Enclosure 1 may represent a small structure 3.6m long and 2.7m wide (Figure 2.9). Three of the postholes were sub-circular and steep-sided, between 0.25m and 0.35m deep and 0.4m in diameter. The exception was [226], which was an oval cut 0.7m by 0.5m, with a circular posthole cut on its southern edge. Fills comprised homogenous brown silty clays with occasional charcoal flecks. The two easternmost cut features ([230] and [232]) both contained packing stones, indicating that the postholes had a structural function. There were, however, no artefacts from any of the features associated with this possible structure.

Spread (224)

A very shallow linear spread (224), measuring 0.05m deep by 5m long and 0.4m wide extended towards the enclosure entrance to the south east of the possible post structure. It comprised a mid reddish-brown silty clay with no inclusions and may represent a remnant of buried soil. There were, however, no associated artefacts, and its date and origin are uncertain.

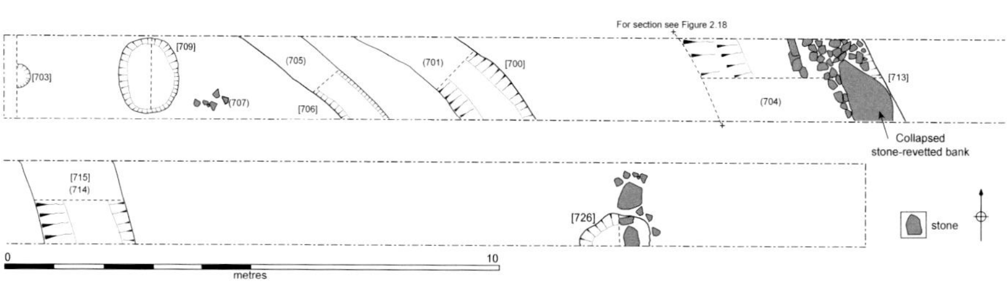

Figure 2.17 Plan showing evaluation trench across Enclosure 2.

Area south of Car Park 4: Enclosure 2

Located approximately 175m to the south of the Late Bronze Age Enclosure 1 was a multi-circuit ditched site, Enclosure 2, which is largely known from the results of a geophysical survey (Archaeological Surveys Ltd 2008), although an evaluative trench was excavated across it (Figure 11.24). It is discussed both here and in chapter 11 because of its proximity to the excavated remains in Car Park 4, and particularly because of its potential relationship with the Late Bronze Age Enclosure 1, described above.

In 2008 a programme of evaluation investigations included trenching to the south of Car Park 4 (Gossip 2008a). A single 38m long by 1.5m wide, east-west aligned trench was excavated to evaluate four concentric curvilinear ditched anomalies occurring to the east of a large linear magnetic anomaly indicating the position of a large service trench.

The excavation revealed a series of ditches, a pit and a posthole, sealed beneath topsoil (721) up to 0.1-0.15m deep) and its underlying colluvial subsoil (722) up to approximately 0.45m deep (deeper towards the eastern end of the trench). All the features clearly cut the natural rab subsoil (723). These features are described below, starting at the western end of the trench, within the interior of the enclosed area.

The evaluation on the multi-circuit feature had a discrete set of context numbers and these overlap with those issued in the 2011 excavations.

Cut [703], fill (702), was a circular posthole 0.2m in diameter and 0.1m deep. The top of the cut was overlaid by a deposit of very compact redeposited natural, thought to be derived from the excavation of the large adjacent service trench. A large sherd of pottery from a Late Iron Age or Romano-British Cordoned Ware storage jar was recovered from fill (702).

Cut [709], a large oval pit 1.7m to the east of [703]. It measured 1.45m long by 1.3m wide and 0.95m deep (Figure 2.17). The pit had near vertical edges and a flat base. Top fill (708) comprised mid brown friable silty clay 0.8m thick containing large quantities of granite stones up to 0.3m in length and a decorated sherd of Iron Age or Romano-British pottery. This sealed primary fill (717), a dark brown, compact silty clay, with occasional granite stones up to 0.15m long.

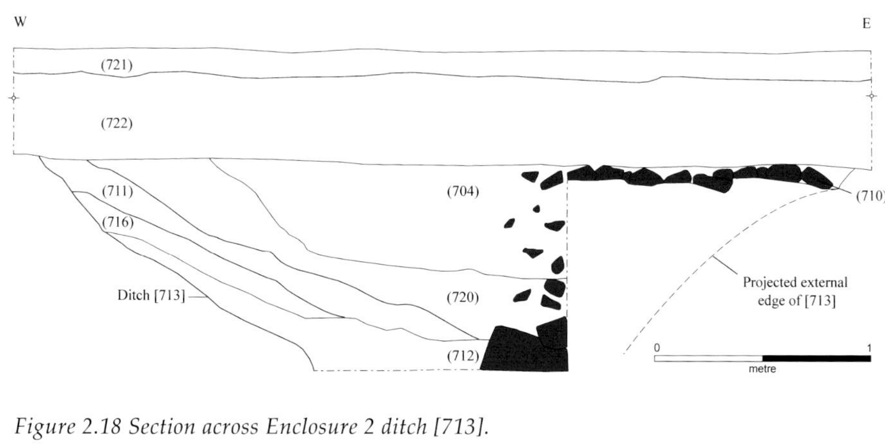

Figure 2.18 Section across Enclosure 2 ditch [713].

To the east of [709] was a curvilinear gully [706] measuring 0.55m wide by 0.2m deep. The profile was concave with a gently rounded base. The fill comprised (705), a mid greyish-brown silty clay.

Situated 0.9m to the east of [706] was concentric curvilinear ditch [700], 1.5m wide and 0.55 deep. This had a very steep north-eastern edge, a more concave south-western edge and a flat base. Stones found on edge at the base of the south-western edge may have been deliberately set. The top fill (701) comprising mid greyish-brown silty clay contained two sherds of Late Iron Age or Romano-British pottery. Below this was primary fill (724), a gritty, light brown silty clay with stony inclusions on the eastern side.

Located 3.6m to the east of [700] was [713], the cut of a large curvilinear ditch (Figures 2.18 and 2.19). The inner, west side of the ditch had a 45-degree concave edge cut through natural subsoil / bedrock, with a break of slope visible 0.9m below the top of the cut. The ditch was excavated to a depth of 0.95m below topsoil and subsoil but working constraints on the trench meant that it could not be fully excavated. The uppermost fill (704) comprised a compact mid reddish-brown silty clay, containing frequent stone on the eastern side and including a layer of rubble (710). Layer (710) included a large boulder and a dense layer of smaller stones within the eastern side of the ditch cut, presumed to have collapsed from a stone-revetted bank on the eastern, external side. Finds recovered from the upper fill (704) included eight sherds of Late Iron Age or Romano-British pottery. Below this were a series of deposits: (720) was a gritty, light brown silty clay with stony

Figure 2.19 Photograph showing Ditch [713] and outer stone bank, taken from west.

inclusions on the eastern side; below this was (711), a friable light reddish-brown silty clay with occasional charcoal and a sherd of Iron Age or Romano-British pottery; this overlay (716), a dark reddish-brown silty clay and basal fill (712), a gritty light yellowish-brown silty clay, with moderate small stone inclusions. All of these deposits beneath (704)/(710) were clearly deposited or infilled from the western side of the ditch.

Cut [715] was a curvilinear ditch 3m to the east of [713], occurring 0.6m below present ground level. The ditch had steep concave sides and a flat bottom. It was 0.7m deep, 1.8m wide at the top and 0.6m wide at the base. The top fill (714) was a light brown compact silty clay, with occasional granite fragments and occasional charcoal flecks; a small rim sherd of Late Iron Age pottery was also recovered from this layer. Below (714) was layer (718), a mid reddish-brown silty clay with occasional degraded granite and occasional charcoal flecks and, beneath this, primary fill (719), a light yellowish-brown friable and gritty silty clay.

Close to the eastern end of the trench and sealed beneath 0.6m of topsoil (721) and colluvium (722) was [726], a sub-circular pit approximately 1m in diameter and 0.25m deep with a concave profile and rounded base. The fill (725) comprised light brown silty clay with stony inclusions on the eastern side. Large stones were recorded on the adjacent subsoil surface.

The gully and the three concentric ditches ([706], [700], [713] and [715], which were revealed in the evaluation trench corresponded with the anomalies that were indicated by the geophysical survey (Archaeological Surveys 2008). The conjectured overall diameter of the outer circuit of the enclosure is approximately 50m, enclosing a space with an area of 1900 square metres. The innermost ditch [706] would have a diameter of approximately 22m and enclose an area of 380 square metres. The size of ditch [713] and the associated external stone-faced bank are particularly interesting and suggest a site of some significance (chapter 11).

The multi-circuited ditched form of the enclosure is very unusual in Cornwall and it may represent a ceremonial monument. Unfortunately, the primary phase of the moment could not be dated, and diagnostic pottery from the enclosure is limited to a few sherds of Late Iron Age or Romano-British pottery from the upper layers of the ditches. This indicates that the latest phase of use dates to the latter prehistoric period. However, given the proximity of Late Bronze Age Enclosure 1 it is possible that its origins were earlier. The possible character and date of this site are discussed below (chapter 11).

Chapter 3

The prehistoric ceramics

Henrietta Quinnell, with petrological comment by Roger Taylor

Introduction

This report covers the pottery recovered from the 2009 and 2011 excavations. In 2009 two small pits were identified as being of Early Neolithic date, and these produced the first substantive assemblage of pottery of this date to be recovered from Tremough.

The 2011 excavations of an earlier Bronze Age structure, a Middle Bronze Age roundhouse and a Late Bronze Age enclosure led to the recovery of a significant ceramic assemblage spanning much of the second millennium cal BC.

Early Neolithic pottery from the PAC building

Details of the assemblage

The assemblage consisted of 59 sherds, weighing 346g, representing a minimum of eight vessels. None of the vessels give sufficient indication of form to merit illustration. Sherds of all the vessels have been examined microscopically by Roger Taylor (below). Twenty-five sherds (135g) were of gabbroic fabrics, 34 sherds (211g) of granitic fabrics. On sherd numbers, therefore, 42 per cent of this small assemblage is composed of gabbroic fabrics, 39 per cent by weight; the percentages for granitic fabrics are 58 per cent on sherds and 61 per cent on weight.

All sherds, except those that were unstratified, appear to have been deposited in a fresh condition with areas of abrasion due to ground water and bioturbation.

Context (100), pit [102]

Context (100), the fill of pit [102], contained 19 sherds of gabbroic fabric weighing 69g 34 of granitic fabric (211g), and included vessels **PP1**-**PP6**. Vessels **PP4-6** show clear overlap of coils used to build vessels. All sherds from this feature may come from the six vessels described below.

PP1 Two joining sherds (6g) from small bowl or cup, smoothed surface, fabric 4-5mm thick, oxidised 5YR 4/6 yellowish-red; simple pointed rim with diameter approximately 160mm. Compare P115 and similar vessels from Carn Brea (Smith 1981, fig 71).

Petrology: Gabbroic. *Feldspar* – soft white altered angular grains, 0.05-2mm, but mainly less than 1mm, also a few less altered translucent cleaved grains, 0.5mm. *Mica* – a scatter of muscovite cleavage flakes, 0.1-1.2mm, sparse biotite, medium to pale brown cleavage flakes, 0.3-0.6mm. *Amphibole* – sparse white, fibrous, elongated grains, 0.2-1.1mm, and a fibrous aggregate, 2mm. *Magnetite* – black sub-angular magnetic grains, 0.1-0.4mm. *Quartz* – sparse transparent to translucent colourless angular grains, 0.5-0.6mm and one opaque rounded grain, 3.2mm. *Composite* – feldspar/biotite mica fragment, 0.5mm. *Matrix* – silty/finely sandy with fine feldspar, quartz and mica.

Comment: A relatively fine-grained gabbroic fabric with sparse inclusions and a silty sandy matrix, with a scatter of included larger mica flakes. These are unusual but not impossible in Lizard-sourced gabbroic clays, with granitic gneisses occurring on the flanks of the gabbro. However, the matrix and low quartz content is similar to **PP4** and **PP5** and the mica could have come from a source local to the site. This would indicate that the gabbroic component had been transported to the area of the site and mixed there with other materials.

PP2 Two joining sherds (10g) from small bowl or cup, smoothed surface partly burnished, fabric 5-6mm thick, 5YR 4/1 reduced dark grey on exterior, as **PP1** otherwise; simple pointed rim with diameter approximately 140mm, slightly inturned. Compare P113 from Carn Brea (Smith 1981, fig 71).

Petrology: Fine-grained gabbroic fabric with sparse inclusions, but no component indicates movement of clay.

PP3 Rim (4g) from straight-sided vessel, smoothed surface, fabric 5-6mm thick, reduced grey 5YR 5/1; rim rounded with slight external beading but diameter not determinable.

Petrology: Fine-grained gabbroic fabric with sparse inclusions, but no component indicates movement of clay.

PP4 Two joining sherds (43g) from thick base of bowl, exterior surface smoothed and oxidised 5YR 5/6 yellowish-red, interior burnished and reduced 5YR 5/1 grey. A further 30 sherds (119g) appear to be from this vessel on fabric. Thick-walled, 11-15mm.

Petrology: Granitic with sparse inclusions. *Rock fragments* – granitic, quartz feldspar and biotite mica, internal grain size up to 1.2mm, as fresh angular fragments, 1-7mm; quartz/muscovite aggregates, angular fragments, 1-2mm; doleritic greenstone, slightly foliated feldspar and dark green amphibole, a cluster of sub-angular fragments, 4.5, 5 and >10.6mm. *Quartz* – a scatter of translucent colourless angular and abraded sub-angular grains, 1-2.5mm. *Mica* – sparse biotite cleavage flakes, up to 0.5mm. *Feldspar* – sparse soft white angular grains dispersed in the matrix, 0.1-0.2mm, rarely 3mm. *Limonite* – a scatter of soft dark reddish-brown rounded grains, 0.2-3mm. *Matrix* – abundantly finely sandy/silty and micaceous.

Comment: Vessels **PP4** and **PP5** have a very similar granitic fabric with fragments obtained by crushing granite rock. The thickness and finish are also similar, suggesting that the sherds could be from vessels potted at the same time from the same clay source. The clay appears to be an alluvial clay deriving some mineral content from granite weathering. The greenstone fragments are sub-angular to sub-rounded and abraded and also appear to be an incidental component of the clay. Greenstones are mapped close to the margin of the Carnmenellis granite to the north of Penryn, pointing to potential source areas for the clay.

PP5 Two joining sherds (48g) from angle of carinated bowl, both surfaces burnished, interior reduced dark grey 5YR 5/4, exterior oxidised 5YR 5/6 yellowish-red. Thick walled approximately 15-18mm. Very much at the thick end of fabrics used for Neolithic bowls; compare Carn Brea P54 (Smith 1981, fig 68).

Petrology: Granitic with sparse inclusions, same as **PP4**.

PP6 Two joining sherds (65g) from bowl, both surfaces smoothed and oxidised, 5YR 5/6 yellowish-red. Approximately 8mm thick.

Petrology: Gabbroic fabric with moderate inclusions.

Context (103), the lower fill of pit [105]

This fill contained a single vessel, **PP7**.

PP7 a bowl sherd weighing 32g, both surfaces smoothed and oxidised, 5YR 5/6 yellowish-red. Approximately 10mm thick.

Petrology: Gabbroic with approximately 10 per cent added granitic-derived sand. *Feldspar* – abundant off-white altered angular to sub-angular grains, 0.05-1.5mm, translucent greyish and white cleaved unaltered sub-rounded grains, 3.2, 4.1 and 5mm; simple twinning suggests these grains are orthoclase feldspar from granite. *Quartz* – colourless to pale grey translucent, angular to sub-angular grains, 1-7mm. *Rock fragments* – granitic, quartz/feldspar biotite an angular fragment, 8mm; quartz/biotite 0.8 and 8mm, quartz/muscovite, 0.8mm. *Mica* – biotite cleavage flake, 0.8mm. *Magnetite* – sparse black sub-angular, magnetic grains, 0.15-1mm. *Tourmaline* – black glossy vitreous sub angular grain, 0.5mm. *Plant* – impressions on the interior surface up to 13mm long. *Matrix* – much fine-grained feldspar and some quartz less than 0.5mm.

Comment: A gabbroic fabric with a gabbroic clay to which a coarse, mainly water-worn granite-derived sand has been added. The inclusions differ from those in **PP4** and **PP5** as the granitic content has not been prepared by crushing.

Context (104) upper fill of pit [105]

This fill contained vessel **PP8** and two other sherds.

PP8 Bowl sherd (26g), both surfaces smoothed and oxidised 5YR 5/4 reddish-brown. The overlap between two coils extends across the sherd and has resulted in a zone of reduction, almost sooty, 5YR 3/4 very dark grey, which extends across the sherd. Approximately 6-10mm thick.

Petrology: Gabbroic fabric with moderate inclusions.

Unstratified

Four unstratified sherds weighing 8g were of a gabbroic fabric with no distinguishing features.

Comment on the PAC assemblage

Fills (100) in pit [102] and (103) in pit [105] produced identical radiocarbon determinations. Both dates calibrated to 4750±40 BP, 3640-3378 cal BC (SUERC-29383; SUERC-29387). These determinations confirm the identity of the pottery as Early Neolithic and are very similar to those obtained from a pit group at Portscatho, Gerrans (Jones and Reed 2006), and to those from the later pits in the group at Tregarrick Farm, Roche (Cole and Jones 2002-3). The only Early Neolithic sherd previously found at Tremough was an abraded gabbroic scrap from ditch [76] associated with a radiocarbon determination of 3944-3662 cal BC (AA-44604) (Quinnell 2007, 51), while the pit group with radiocarbon determinations from the earlier Neolithic produced no ceramics (Gossip and Jones 2007, 28).

The mean sherd size is 6g, much smaller than the 11.3g at Portscatho (Quinnell 2006) and 18g at Tregarrick Farm (Quinnell 2002-3). This small size argues against any special selection for deposition. The large wide-mouthed bowls which were very much a feature of Portscatho and Tregarrick Farm, and also of the pit assemblage from Wayland's, Tiverton (Leverett and Quinnell 2010) do not appear to be represented. There is also, in comparison to Portscatho and Tregarrick Farm (Quinnell 2006; Quinnell 2002-3), no evidence for the special selection of sherds such as rims, and nothing, except for the freshness of the material, indicates an act of deliberate deposition. There are several different forms represented at Tremough PAC, the range replicated at both Portscatho and Tregarrick Farm.

The pottery is important, however, for the complexity of its fabrics. Vessels **PP2**, **PP3**, **PP6** and **PP8** are made only of gabbroic materials; the latter two are coarser than the first two and the two pairs may be compared respectively to the fine and medium gabbroic fabrics identified at Carn Brea (Smith 1981, 162). However, **PP1** is made of gabbroic clay apparently transported to the area of the site and mixed with clay containing material deriving from the Carnmenellis granite. Vessel **PP1** may well have been potted close to the site of its deposition. Vessel **PP7** is made of gabbroic clay mixed with coarse, mainly water-worn sand from the Carnmenellis granite and again is likely to have been made on or near the site. While gabbro clay has now been demonstrated to have been moved and then mixed with other components from elsewhere during the Bronze Age, indeed at Tremough (Quinnell 2007, 59), there has been little evidence so far for this practice during the Neolithic. However, over 80 per cent of the Portscatho assemblage was made of gabbroic clay mixed with material found some 6 kilometres away from the gabbro zone in the Meneage area (Quinnell 2006, 7). Roger Taylor (pers comm.) considers that he is now (2010) picking up finer details of petrography than he did a decade ago, a comment, which in itself makes a case for a review of all gabbroic collections previously published. The granitic fabrics of **PP4** and **PP5** contain a mix of granitic and greenstone material which suggests a clay source located 1-2 kilometres to the north of the Tremough site. The overall picture is of the components for potting being brought together somewhere near the deposition site both from the gabbro some 15 kilometres to the south and more locally from the fringe of the Carnmenellis granite.

Finally, the suggestion has been made that vessels **PP4** and **PP5** are so similar in fabric and finish that they are likely to have been potted at the same time. Certainly neither of the pits contained ceramics that are likely to have been curated. The deposit of sherds from two pots made at the same time in one pit reinforces the impression of a very short time span for the material in the pits, enhanced by the similarity of the two radiocarbon determinations.

The pottery from the AIR building and Car Park 4

Introductory comments

Colour and oxidisation of fabrics

All of the ceramic assemblage is in gabbroic or gabbroic admixture fabrics, the second millennium BC Trevisker sherds being in both fabrics and the Late Bronze Age assemblage in gabbroic fabric without additional material. Sherds from a number of vessels have been examined under the petrological microscope by Roger Taylor and the identifications are included below under vessel descriptions. A small number of sherds were initially considered to be non-gabbroic but a comment that this was incorrect is included in Dr Taylor's archive report.

The sherds from the whole assemblage are generally oxidised, with surfaces, especially exteriors, generally reddish-yellow in shades centring on 5YR 6/6. Oxidisation, however, is sometimes patchy and frequently the centres of thicker sherds are reduced and sometimes the interiors. This reddish-yellow oxidised appearance is standard for gabbroic Trevisker Ware assemblages and appears also to be so in the limited number of Late Bronze Age assemblages that have become available for study. Surfaces, again as is usual in local assemblages of these dates, have smoothed rather than burnished surfaces.

Abrasion

Abrasion is based on the system devised by Sorenson (1996) for Bronze Age midden material at Runnymede with some modifications.

Very fresh	1; Sorenson Grade 1, hardly ever applicable.
Fresh	1/2; colour of core slightly patinated but unaltered surfaces with sharp corners and edges.
Moderate abrasion	2; core colour patinated, some definition in the sharpness of corners lost.
Abraded	2/3; core colour patinated, slight rounding of corners and slight erosion of surfaces.
High abrasion	3; core colour patinated, rounding of corners and of sherd outline, surfaces somewhat eroded.

Context	Description	Gabbroic
(18)/(54)	Fill of posthole [19]	23/190 **P2**
(13)	Fill of posthole [21]	1/5
(7)	Fill of posthole [6]	2/13
(48)	Fill of posthole [49]	2/3
(26)	Fill of posthole [27]	2/14
(29)	Fill of posthole [30]	2/5
(11)	Fill of pit [23]	39/635 **P1**
(12)	Fill of posthole [22]	1/13 **P1**
U/S	Unstratified	1/10
Totals		**73/888**

Table 3.1: Details of pottery from Structure 1 by sherd numbers and weight (g).

Structure 1

Description of the assemblage

Sherds in Structure 1 were in general fairly fresh or moderately abraded (Table 3.1).

P1 (Figure 3.1) Mostly from fill (11) of pit [23] and joining sherd from fill (12) of posthole [22]. A thin gabbroic fabric with sparse coarse – very coarse inclusions. Vessel rather irregular with slight neck below fairly upright rim with flattened top. Internal rim diameter approximately 150mm. Upper part of vessel untidily decorated with irregular horizontal lines impressed by cord in two parallel twists; the decoration is extremely untidy and the impressions overlap in places or form curves rather than lines. Most of the sherds join in groups of four, suggesting larger sherds were deposited and subsequently became fractured. Note that the two contexts containing sherds of **P1** were not adjacent to one another.

Petrology: Feldspar – altered soft white to pale grey angular to sub-angular grains, 0.1-2.5mm, rarely 5mm, some less altered translucent cleaved grains, 0.5mm. A*mphibole* – light-grey cleaved and bladed grains, 0.3-1.2mm. *Quartz* – sparse translucent colourless sub-rounded grains, 0.1-0.2mm. M*agnetite* – rare black glossy magnetic sub-angular grains, 0.2-0.5mm. *Matrix* – finely micaceous silty clay.

Comment: A standard gabbroic fabric.

P1 belongs with Parker Pearson's Group 5 of Trevisker Ware (1990, 10), small vessels suitable for eating and drinking but decorated with impressed cord. No close parallel is known for the untidy and unstructured cord-impressed decoration which may have extended well down below the girth; decoration appears to survive right down vessel **P1** as illustrated (Figure 3.1). The general shape of the vessel, thin-walled with a slightly curved shoulder, is also without close parallel.

P2 (Figure 3.1) Fill (18) within posthole [19]/[54]. Gabbroic fabric with moderate very coarse inclusions. Flattened, everted rim with internal rim bevel. Internal rim diameter approximately 170mm. Band of untidy deeply incised criss-cross lines beneath rim partly survives; a second non-joining sherd (not illus) from further down the vessel suggests a possible second criss-cross band. Many of the other sherds from layer (54) could come from this vessel.

Petrology: A standard gabbroic fabric (detailed petrology with the project archive).

P2 is best described as a small version of Parker Pearson's Group 3/4, either small storage or cooking vessels or wares for eating and drinking, decorated with incised lines. There appears to be no parallel for the suggested double band of criss-cross decoration (if this interpretation is correct).

Comment on other, non-illustrated, sherds

All the sherds appear to be gabbroic without admixture and represent at least another four vessels. Posthole fill (7) has two non-joining rim sherds, with a slightly smoother profile than **P1**; both have a line of double parallel twist cord beneath the rim and one has additionally two long fingernail slashes: both of these belong in size and decoration with Parker Pearson's Group 5 (1990). Posthole fill (29) has two different rim sherds from separate vessels; size is appropriate again for Group 5. Sherds from posthole or pit fill (11) are thick, approximately 17mm, and come from a large vessel of wide diameter with two cord-impressed lines running round the girth; each line is made by a double cord with opposed twist. This vessel had a diameter of approximately 340mm and belongs with Parker Pearson's Group 1 vessels (1990) with cord-impressed decoration, best interpreted as storage jars.

Comment on the Structure 1 assemblage

The distribution of pottery across Structure 1 shows no patterning. It is difficult to assess the significance of the presence of sherds of **P1** in two non-adjacent postholes. It is not known whether the sherds relate to initial post-packing or to tidying of the site after Structure 1 was no longer an upstanding building. Their generally fresh condition, might, however, suggest the latter (see discussion in chapter 11).

The radiocarbon dating from Structure 1 is rather broad. Fill (48) of posthole [49] produced a date of 3623±27 BP, calibrating to 2116-1900 cal BC (SUERC-47281), fill (55) of posthole [56] 2989±29 BP, calibrating to 1371-1126 cal BC (SUERC-47282), and context (24) from posthole [25] 3237±30 BP, calibrating to 1608-1435 cal BC (SUERC-48150). The problems these dates present are discussed in the section on dating (chapter 10), where it is concluded that the likelihood is that the earlier part of the time span indicated by the dates is more likely. If so, the structure is earlier, maybe by some considerable span, than the majority of circular houses which produce Trevisker assemblages (for example, ApSimon and Greenfield 1972; Nowakowski 1991; Jones and Taylor 2010).

While the dating can only be broadly assigned to the first half of the second millennium cal BC, the assemblage may be earlier than those known from Trevisker domestic sites that have been excavated across Cornwall (for example, Woodward and Cane 1991; Quinnell 2012). Trevisker ceramics appear in broadly funerary

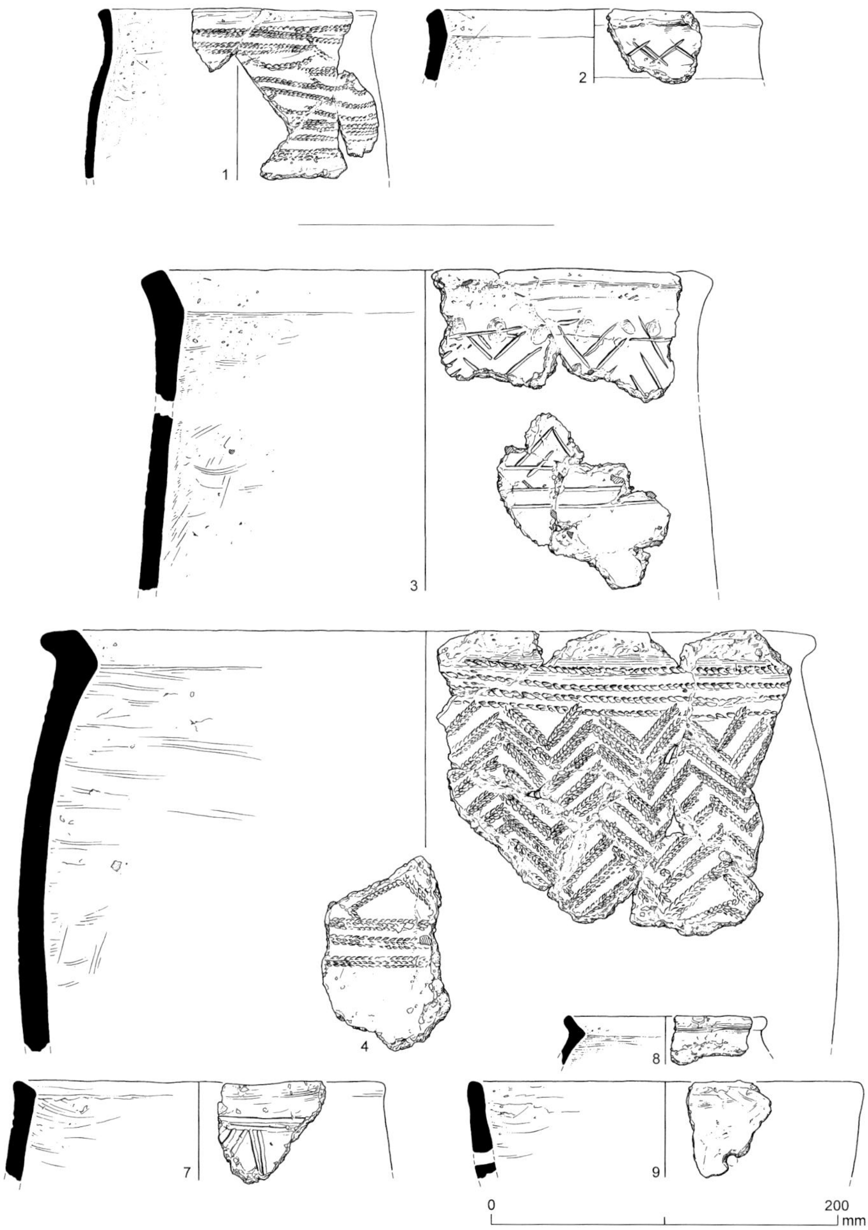

Figure 3.1 Earlier and Middle Bronze Age pottery. Vessels P1-2, Structure 1, AIR building. Vessels P3-9 Roundhouse 1 (Drawing by Jane Read).

contexts from around 2000 cal BC (Quinnell 2012, table 2) and about half of the vessels of which the petrology has been studied and shown to be of gabbroic fabric are of admixture (Parker Pearson 1990, 15). Gabbroic admixture fabrics were therefore in use in the earlier second millennium BC and the presence of gabbroic fabrics without admixture in Structure 1 contexts is not related to chronology. The presence of gabbroic fabrics only may be a matter of chance, particularly as so few (only six vessels) need be represented, or may have been specially chosen for reasons which cannot now be ascertained.

Four of the six vessels, including **P1**, are Group 5 (Parker Pearson 1990). The other vessels present belong to Groups 1 and 3/4 respectively. Woodward and Cane (1991, 126, fig 53) have shown that these small cord-impressed vessels appropriate for eating were rare on Middle Bronze Age sites, and totally absent from the large assemblage from Trethellan Farm, Newquay, but form around 10 per cent of those from Early Bronze Age funerary / ceremonial contexts. A distinctive small assemblage of Group 5 vessels with cord-impressed decoration came from activity from the seventeenth to fifteenth centuries cal BC over the site 2 cairn at Stannon Down, on Bodmin Moor (Quinnell 2004-5, 74-5); there the assemblage consisted only of Group 5 vessels. The Stannon data reinforced the suggestion that vessels for eating and drinking were considered appropriate for impressed cord decoration in funerary / ceremonial contexts in the Early Bronze Age; their place in the domestic assemblages of the Middle Bronze Age are taken by vessels of similar size but which either lack decoration or have fingernail or tip designs.

The presence of **P1** and the other Group 5 vessels indicates that Structure 1 is likely to belong in the earlier rather than the later part of the second millennium BC, and the unusual shape and decoration of **P1** may be related to this earlier date, for which there are so few comparanda. There is currently no evidence for the continuance of Group 5 cord-impressed vessels after *circa* 1400 cal BC. The pottery data, limited in extent though it is, supports a date earlier rather than later in the second millennium BC.

Roundhouse 1

Sherds from features in Roundhouse 1 (Table 3.2) are generally in a fresh condition but most of those from the infill layers have varying degrees of abrasion, suggesting that they were fresh when deposited but had suffered the effects of groundwater and bioturbation.

Sherds with illustration and / or petrology

P3 (Figure 3.1) Deposit (724), fill of posthole [725]. About 20 sherds, including a joining sherd from fill (745) in posthole [746] and decorated body sherd in infill layer (275). Large storage vessel, gabbroic admixture, sparse very coarse inclusions, flat-topped everted rim with internal bevel, untidy incised chevron pattern, with a single horizontal line above and three below. Internal rim diameter approximately 300mm. A row of slight fingertip impressions is present beneath the top of the decorated zone. Two rim sherds form conjoins, as do a separate group of four incised sherds from the girth, including the sherd from layer (745) in posthole [746].

The vessel forms a large example of Parker Pearson's Group 3/4 (1990). Untidy incised chevron designs occur on large vessels in the assemblages both at Trethellan Farm (Woodward and Cane 1991, fig 50) and Trevisker (ApSimon and Greenfield 1972, fig 15) but no exact matches appear to have been published.

Context	Description	Gabbro admixture	Gabbro	Total
(281)	Fill of posthole [282]	1/21		1/21
(297)	Fill of posthole [298]	1/9		1/9
(700)	Fill of posthole [701]	3/23		3/23
(730)	Fill of posthole [711], includes [704]	23/623 P3		23/623
(732)	Fill of posthole [733]	6/54		6/54
(745)	Fill of posthole [746]	3/22 P3		3/2
(747)	Fill of hearth [748]/[774]	13/812 P4		13/812
(775)	Fill of posthole [776]	2/4		2/4
(761)	Fill of posthole [762]	1/6		1/6
(784)	Fill of posthole [785]	2/23		2/23
(291)	Fill of gully [292]	6/39	1/5	7/44
(797)	Terminal fill of gully [292]		1/6	1/6
(104)/(273)	Infill layer in quadrant 1	507/10770 P4, P6	2/112 P7, 9	509/10882
(278)	Gully infill in quadrant 1	38/1257		38/1257
(274)	Infill layer in quadrant 2	10/332	1/13 P8	11/345
(279)/(280)	Infill layer in quadrant 3	18/130		18/130
(275)	Infill layer in quadrant 4	14/150 P3	1/49 P5	15/199
Removing baulks		10/106		10/106
Cleaning over Roundhouse 1		82/1577		82/1577
Unstratified		107/2484 P4	25/146	132/2630
Totals		**847/18442**	**31/331**	**878/18773**

Table 3.2: Details of pottery from Roundhouse 1 by sherd number and weight (g).

Petrology: Feldspar – soft white altered sub-rounded to sub-rounded-grains, 0.5-1mm, rarely 2mm, some less altered cleaved grains, 0.2mm. *Quartz* – a scatter of colourless to pale yellow stained, transparent to translucent angular to sub-angular grains, larger grains heat cracked, 0.3-3.5mm. *Amphibole* – a scatter of translucent pale, grey to light brown cleaved and fibrous grains, 0.2-0.5mm. *Rock fragments* – a scatter of black and black and white flecked, foliated amphibole/ feldspar 'greenstone' as angular fragments, 0.8-4.5mm, soft micaceous siltstone sub-rounded fragment 2.8mm. *Magnetite* – sparse black glossy sub-rounded and crystalline magnetic grains, 0.15-1mm. *Matrix* – finely micaceous with muscovite flakes and feldspar grains less than 0.05mm.

Comment: A fine-grained gabbroic admixture fabric with probable greenstone fragments.

P4 (Figure 3.1) About 600 sherds, mostly from the infill layers, but (747) the fill of hearth [748]/[774], contained two conjoining rim sherds and at least four body sherds. Large cord-impressed storage jar, gabbroic admixture, common very coarse inclusions. Rim, rounded and slightly expanded and everted, internal rim diameter approximately 400mm. Below rim four horizontal lines formed by single very thick twisted cord, overlapping in places; below this, a chevron cord-impression pattern made by much finer cord, 'plaited' with opposed twist, the lines impressed over each other so that a muddled impression of three-four lines of impression is produced. Triple lines of this 'plaited' cord border the base of the design. A possible sherd from the front of a perforated lug has impressions made by the same cord as below the rim. The vessel probably had two opposed large perforated lugs on its girth. While a large number of plain body sherds are present, there are no base angle sherds and no definite base sherds. About 80 per cent of the rim is present. About a third of the sherds have decoration but there are few that conjoin and sherds from the base of the decorated zone do not join sherds from the upper part. The small number of joins may be due to the very large vessel size, but it is possible that separate clumps of sherds were selected for deposition.

The vessel belongs to Parker Pearson's Group 1 storage jars (1990) on which plaited impressed cord decoration is usual. Chevrons are one of the common patterns on such vessels; the closest parallel to the nine untidy lines of chevrons on **P4** is the rather smaller Group 1 vessel found with a cremation at Largin Wood, Broadoak, in east Cornwall (Trudgian and ApSimon 1976). As usual with Trevisker ceramics, very close parallels for decoration are impossible to locate.

Petrology: Feldspar – white angular altered and some translucent cleaved grains 0.4-2.5mm. *Amphibole* – light brown to greyish angular cleaved grains, 0.3-1.2mm, some larger dark amphibole grains derived from the included rock fragments up to 5mm. *Magnetite* – sparse black glossy angular to sub-angular magnetic grains, 0.1-0.8mm. *Quartz* – a scatter of colourless transparent to translucent angular to sub-rounded grains, 0.1-1mm. *Rock fragments* – micaceous biotite hornfels fine-grained slightly foliated sub-rounded fragment 7mm, coarser granular angular fragment with distinct biotite flakes, 3mm, silvery muscovite schist, tabular and sub-angular fragments with rounded and sub-angular margins, 0.7, 1.1 and 4mm, amphibole/feldspar ('greenstone'), black and white altered feldspar/amphibole as angular fragments, 2-8mm. *Mica* – muscovite cleavage flakes mainly in the matrix but up to 0.1mm. *Matrix* – silty finely micaceous clay with grains of the main tempering minerals less than 0.05mm.

Comment: A gabbroic admixture fabric with fragments of contact metamorphic rocks from close to the granite margin, but with no evidence of granite-derived minerals. The composite amphibole/feldspar fragments are unlike most gabbroic composite fragments and may also be added components.

P5 (not illus), layer (275) infill within quadrant 4. Gabbroic fabric with very common coarse inclusions. A similar vessel to **P3** in form and decoration, but with a smaller internal rim diameter, approximately 270mm. The untidy incised chevron decoration, of which only that below the rim is present, has no bordering horizontal line. Parker Pearson Group 3/4 (1990).

Petrology: Feldspar – soft white altered sub-angular grains, 5.5mm, rarely 12.5mm. *Quartz* – a scatter of colourless transparent to translucent angular to sub-angular grains, 0.1-1.3mm. *Magnetite* – sparse black glossy sub-angular magnetic grains, 0.1-0.8mm. *Amphibole* – sparse medium grey angular cleaved grains and fibrous aggregates, 0.2-0.8mm. *Rock fragments* – incidental inclusions of dark, fine-grained, angular amphibole/feldspar fragments, 2.5mm. *Matrix* – finely micaceous slightly silty clay with some feldspar grains less than 0.05mm.

Comment: A gabbroic fabric.

P6 (Figure 3.2) infill layer (273) in quadrant 1. Gabbroic admixture fabric, common inclusions, some very coarse, fired in more reducing conditions than most of the other ceramics from Roundhouse 1. Exterior generally 5YR 5/2 reddish-grey, interior 5YR 5/3 reddish-brown. About 140 sherds (1390g), mostly approximately 9mm thick. Sherds present indicate a large vessel with a simple flat-topped out-turned rim and two simple vertical lugs with worn horizontal perforations, and decoration composed of cord-impressed lines which form a chevron design. Internal rim diameter approximately 200mm. The lines are made of three close-set parallel twist threads, unusually fine. Although so many sherds are present they represent only a small part of the vessel and the base is not present. The scrappy nature of the sherds prevents adequate illustration. Parker Pearson Group 2 (1990). A close parallel for this vessel, especially the fine cord impressions, cannot be located.

Petrology: Feldspar – soft white altered sub-angular to sub-rounded grains, 0.05-0.1mm. *Amphibole* – brown cleaved grains, 0.5-1mm. R*ock fragments* – amphibole/feldspar with dark green amphibole tending to form elongated crystals in a granular translucent to white feldspar matrix, unaltered angular elongated fragments 12.1mm and 0.5-6mm. *Quartz* – a scatter of colourless translucent sub-rounded grains, 0.3-0.8mm, a composite (sandstone) grain 2mm. *Magnetite* – a scatter of black glossy magnetic sub-angular grains, 0.1-1mm. *Matrix* – silty clay with grains of feldspar and sparse muscovite flakes less than 0.05mm.

Comment: A gabbroic admixture fabric with a relatively fine-grained (less than 0.5mm) and sparse original mineral content and with added feldspar/amphibole rock ('greenstone') fragments which resemble those in **P4**.

Figure 3.2 Middle Bronze Age pottery. Fine cord-impressed sherds from vessel P6 found within Roundhouse 1.

P7 (Figure 3.1) infill layer (104). Gabbroic fabric, moderately coarse inclusions. Poorly made vessel, flat-topped rim with slight expansion, poorly executed vertical and diagonal incised lines bordered on the top by a double line. Internal rim diameter approximately 190mm. Parker Pearson Group 3/4 (1990). Petrology as **P5** (in project archive).

P8 (Figure 3.1) infill layer (274). Gabbroic fabric, common coarse inclusions. Small thin walled vessel with everted rim with a concave internal bevel. Internal rim diameter approximately 110mm. Probably undecorated. Parker Pearson Group 6 (1990), in which the concave rim bevel and pronounced neck are unusual, although occurring in larger, decorated vessels. The petrology is similar to **P5** and **P7** (detailed petrology in project archive).

P9 (Figure 3.1) infill layer (104). Gabbroic, fine fabric with common coarse inclusions. Simple smoothed surface, fired in less oxidising conditions than Trevisker vessels, 5YR 6/6 reddish-yellow to 5YR 5/2 reddish-grey. Simple upright vessel with rounded rim and horizontal perforation made before firing. This is a stray Late Bronze Age Plain Ware piece incorporated into the top of the fill in Roundhouse 1.

Petrology: Feldspar – soft white variably altered angular to sub-angular grains, 0.05-1.5mm, rarely 2.5-4mm. *Amphibole* – sparse translucent light to medium grey cleaved angular grains, 0.1-1mm. *Quartz* – rare translucent colourless, sub-angular grains, 0.9-1mm. *Magnetite* – sparse black glossy sub-angular magnetic grains, 0.4mm. *Rock fragments* –rounded grey slate 0.8 and 2mm. *Matrix* – smooth clay with grains of the main tempering minerals less than 0.05mm.

Comment: A generally fine-grained gabbroic fabric.

Comment on non-enumerated sherds

Two rim sherds with cord-impressed decoration from vessels other than those enumerated come from infill layer (273) and were probably from Group 2 vessels (Parker Pearson 1990). Posthole [282] has an incised sherd and posthole [785] a cord-impressed sherd, which almost certainly come from the enumerated vessels described above, as indeed may a small rectangular lug from the initial cleaning over Roundhouse 1. This indicates that a minimum of eight Trevisker vessels are represented.

Comment on the Roundhouse 1 assemblage

Distribution and representation of vessels

There are a minimum of eight vessels represented, all of which occur in the infill levels which had been deposited into the abandoned house hollow (chapter 2). Five features contained sherds of vessels which principally occurred in the infill layers within the roundhouse.

Postholes [725] and [746], although widely separated, both contained sherds of **P3**, hearth [748]/[774] contained sherds of **P4** and posthole [785] a cord-impressed sherd probably from **P4**; posthole [282] contained an incised sherd probably from **P3**. Other features contained plain sherds (Table 3.2) which may come from **P3** or **P4**. These features with sherds from vessels in the infill are distributed around the circuit of Roundhouse 1 and in its hearth [748]/[774]. The greatest quantity of sherds in the infill came from quadrant 1, reflecting the distribution both of stone tools and of fragments of moulds for producing copper-alloy artefacts (below).

Only vessels **P3**, **P4** and **P6** are definitely represented by more than one sherd, the other five vessels need only have a single rim sherd. **P3**, **P4** and **P6** are unusual in that, although many sherds are present, the lower parts of the vessels are absent. Representation of **P4**, with the largest number of sherds, decreases moving down the vessel. About 80 per cent of the rim is present. The upper part of the decoration has a number of conjoins but the lower part, including the lower border, has none and few of the plain lower wall sherds join. The base is entirely absent. It is possible that this range of sherds represents deliberate selection, even possibly that sherds separated by gaps were deliberately selected and the remainder deposited elsewhere.

Dating

There are four radiocarbon determinations from Roundhouse 1: 3169±29 BP, calibrating to 1501-1400 cal BC (SUERC-47292), comes from posthole [286]; 3109±29 BP, calibrating to 1441-1307 cal BC (SUERC-47293), comes from posthole [701]; 3065±31 BP, calibrating to 1415-1262 cal BC (SUERC-47297), comes from posthole [705]; 3091±27 BP, calibrating to 1429-1297 cal BC (SUERC-47298) comes from layer (280), the infill in quadrant 3. Overall, these dates indicate activity in the house during the thirteenth and fourteenth centuries cal BC (chapter 10). The fourteenth century cal BC date from infill layer (280), in which all the vessels present are represented, is therefore that of the deposition of all the Trevisker vessels present in the roundhouse.

Fabrics

Vessels **P5**, **P7** and **P8** are gabbroic, the remaining five vessels gabbroic admixture, which all contain fragments of greenstone. This greenstone was not obtainable in the immediate area of gabbroic clays. Greenstones vary greatly in their detailed composition and outcrops occur across the Lizard a few kilometres to the north of the gabbro clays as well as in places around the periphery of the Carnmennellis granite, including in the broad vicinity of Tremough. The movement of gabbroic clays before potting, with the addition of inclusions often deriving from close to sites where the pots were used, is now well established through the petrological work of Roger Taylor (Quinnell 2012), and it seems likely that the Tremough Roundhouse 1 assemblage is yet another which resulted from this practice.

Other comment

There was a minimum of eight vessels present, from the infilling of the roundhouse hollow and the interior structural features. For such a large apparent assemblage this is a very small number of vessels. One of these vessels, **P4**, is a large storage vessel with impressed cord decoration (Group 1), three, **P2** and two not enumerated, represent smaller storage or cooking vessels with impressed cord decoration (Group 2), three, **P3**, **P5**, and **P7**, are all smaller storage or cooking vessels with incised decoration (Group 3/4), and one, **P8**, is a small plain vessel appropriate for eating and drinking (Group 6) (Parker Pearson 1990). The bias of the small vessel assemblage is storage and cooking, with limited provision for the consumption of food and drink; the Group 6 **P8** would have held several litres and is therefore a communal rather than an individual consumption vessel as was usual at this date. The use of gabbroic fabric without admixture belonged to vessels in the smaller sizes, **P5**, **P7** and **P8**, with gabbroic admixture used for the remainder which range from the large Group 1 **P4** down to **P3** Group 3/4. No useful pattern has so far been suggested for the reasons for the selection of these two gabbroic fabrics for different vessels in Trevisker assemblages. As commented above in the descriptions of the vessels, none have precise parallels in other published assemblages. However, as all the pottery discussed has connections with the abandonment and infilling phase of the roundhouse, the data it provides may have no relevance to the practices current when this was in use (see chapter 11).

Roundhouse 2

Illustrated vessels

P10 (Figure 3.4) (110) layer over Roundhouse 2. Gabbroic fabric, moderate coarse inclusions, smoothed surface, fired in less oxidising conditions than Trevisker fabrics, 5YR 6/6 reddish-yellow to 5YR 5/2 reddish-grey. Six conjoining sherds making up the whole profile of a simple Late Bronze Age Plain Ware vessel with one surviving small lug scar; some other sherds may come from this vessel. Internal rim diameter 215mm.

Petrology: Feldspar – soft white altered angular to sub-angular grains, 0.05-3mm, rarely 4.5mm, sparse less altered translucent cleaved grains, 0.2-0.8mm. *Amphibole* – dark brownish and greyish angular cleaved grains, 0.1-1.2mm. *Magnetite* – a scatter of black glossy sub-angular grains, 0.1-0.6mm, rarely 2mm. *Mica* – a scatter of muscovite cleavage flakes, 0.05-0.1mm. *Quartz* – rare colourless transparent angular, 0.8mm. *Rock fragments* – basaltic grey elongated sub-rounded 9mm shows aligned altered white feldspar laths in a dark matrix, mainly about 0.1mm up to 0.6mm long. *Matrix* – smooth clay with some grains of the main tempering mineral less than 0.05mm.

Comment: A gabbroic fabric. The rock fragment is probably from a source local to the Lizard gabbro.

Context	Description	Gabbro admixture	Gabbro	Totals
Roundhouse 2				
(109)	Soil over Roundhouse 2	4/53	27/359	31/412
(110)	Soil over Roundhouse 2		16/1015 P10, 10a, 11	16/1015
Cleaning Roundhouse 2		1/24	11/393	12/417
Other features				
(105)	Cleaning above stone spread	35/369		35/369
(106)	Soil layer	97/1044		97/1044

Table 3.3: Pottery from Roundhouse 2 and other features in Car Park 4 by sherd numbers and weight (g). Total assemblage from Roundhouse 2, 59 sherds 1844 grams, from other features 44 sherds 1413 grams.

P10a (Figure 3.4) layer (110), layer over Roundhouse 2. Gabbroic fabric as **P10**, with a similar diameter and firing, but finer. Small circular boss survives on vessel wall.

P11 (Figure 3.3) layer (110), layer over Roundhouse 2, Gabbroic fabric, very finely made and well-fired, but abraded. Two body sherds approximately 5mm thick, with decoration comprising blocks of finely incised lines in different directions, apparently infilling a design of triangles. A simple out-turned rim of the same thickness may be the rim of the same vessel; this is less abraded. There is no known parallel for these sherds in Cornwall and they may represent an elaboration of **P13** from Pit Alignment 2 (below).

Other sherds

All of the sherds in layer (110) may come from vessels **P10**, **P10A** and **P11** (Table 3.3). Layer (109) has a small abraded gabbroic admixture sherd with Trevisker-type cord impressions. The numerous gabbroic sherds from layer (109) include a small, thin, everted rim, which may be of Late Bronze Age type, and sherds from simple Plain Ware vessels as in layer (110). An abraded gabbroic admixture sherd came from cleaning over Roundhouse 2 and this context also has another Plain Ware vessel, as **P10** but with the scar of a large circular lug, and another sherd has a small squarish lug.

Comment on Roundhouse 2 material

The Trevisker-type gabbroic admixture sherds may derive from activity around the adjacent Roundhouse 1 or be contemporary with the occupation of Roundhouse 2.

Some six Late Bronze Age Plain Ware (LBAPW) vessels in gabbroic fabric are probably represented. These are likely to post-date use of Roundhouse 2 as they were found during cleaning and were not properly stratified (chapter 2). They may represent later activity over the house hollow.

Figure 3.3 Late Bronze Age pottery. Incised sherds from vessel P11, found over Roundhouse 2.

A radiocarbon determination of 2820±29 BP, calibrating to 1053-901 cal BC (SUERC-47299), was obtained on a sherd of pottery in layer (110) over the western edge of the Roundhouse 2 and relates to these vessels. Two recent sites have provided dated assemblages of Late Bronze Age Plain Ware (LBAPW): Higher Besore, Truro (Quinnell, forthcoming), and Scarcewater tip, Pennance, St Stephen-in-Brannel (Quinnell 2010a, 107). On both these sites the LBAPW material is generally gabbroic, but it lacks the admixture component present in the preceding Middle Bronze Age Trevisker vessels. The Tremough vessels are similarly gabbroic, without additional materials. The disuse of admixture fabrics at the start of the Late Bronze Age appears to be now reasonably well established.

At Higher Besore the LBAPW divided into two successive groups, the first consisting of simple slightly curved-sided vessels, the second of a variety of bowls and jars discussed below in relation to the assemblage from Enclosure 1. Some of the Higher Besore vessels were associated with part of a clay Wilburton-type sword mould, which dates to *circa* 1150-1000 cal BC, but without radiocarbon determinations. Others came from pits with determinations of 1050-890 cal BC (93.7 per cent) (Wk-21204), 1060-890 cal BC (Wk-21202) and 930-810 cal BC (Wk-21203); it is uncertain whether the last of these is aberrant. This earlier Higher Besore pottery is generally comparable to the Roundhouse 2 group, although the small lugs of this assemblage are not represented. It may be that we are seeing different minor features in separate sites. At Higher Besore there was evidence that the pottery was made locally and this may also have been the case at Roundhouse 2, Tremough.

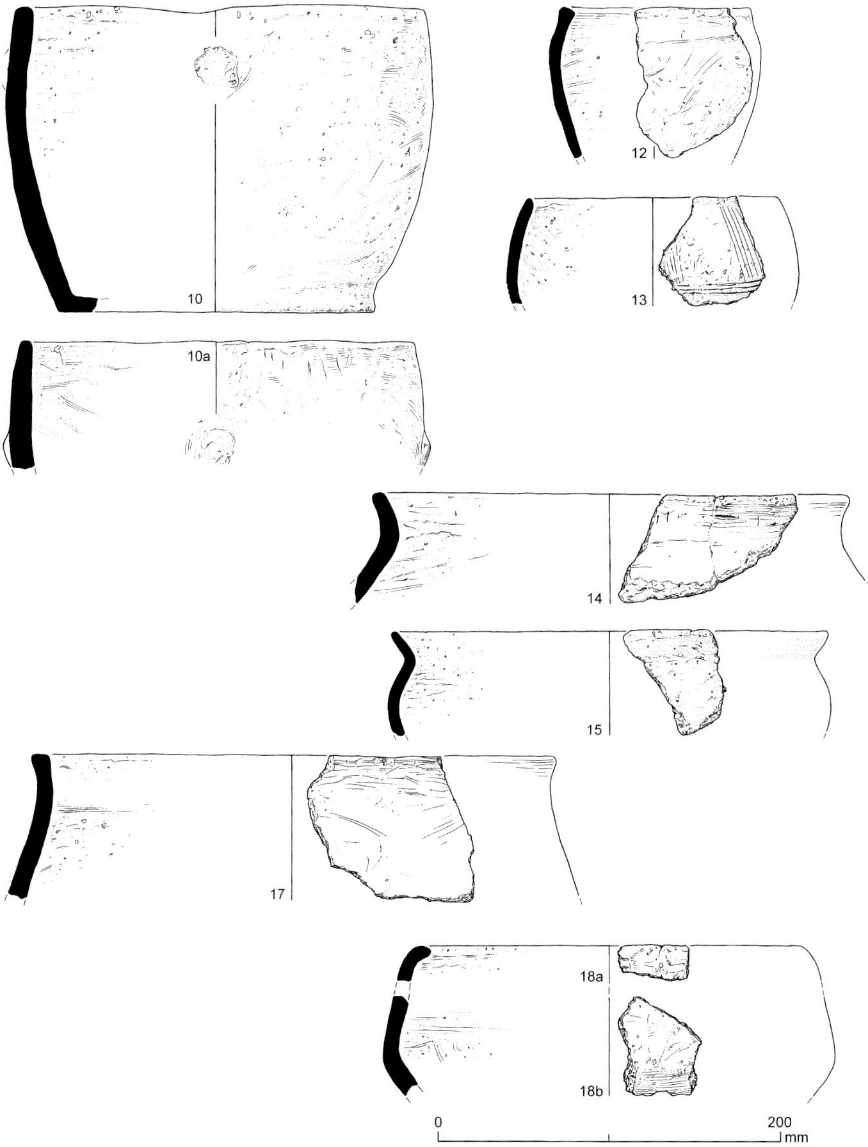

Figure 3.4 Late Bronze Age pottery. Vessels P10, P10a from Roundhouse 2. Vessels P12-18 from Enclosure 1 (Drawing by Jane Read).

At Scarcewater the assemblage was much smaller than at Higher Besore and the division between early phase simple curved-sided jars and later phase bowls and jars was less clear cut. Structure 3084 had early phase material and two radiocarbon determinations, 1120-920 cal BC (Wk-21449) and 1130-920 cal BC (Wk-21450). However, an isolated feature, pit [3402], produced a date of 1000-830 cal BC (Wk-21451) and both simple early phase jars and a small carinated vessel. It is probably true to say, on the basis of the three sites considered, Higher Besore, Scarcewater and Tremough Roundhouse 2, that early phase LBAPW dates

Context	Description	Gabbroic
Enclosure ditch [170]		
(117)	Fill of recut [263] north terminal	3/51
(159 = (107)	Top fill south terminal	2/27
(165) = (159)	Top fill south terminal	7/220
(259) = (159)	Top fill south terminal	13/83
(272)	Fill of southern ditch	7/106
Pit / Posthole Group 1		
(113)/(102)	Fill of pit [114]	7/43
(129)	Fill of posthole [130]	5/202 P12
(143)	Fill of posthole [144]	9/185
(149)	Fill of posthole [150]	1/12
(155)	Fill of posthole [156]	9/154
(170)	Fill of posthole [171]	2/6
(192)	Fill of pit [193]	13/110
(257)	Fill of posthole [258]	2/14
Pit Alignment 2		
(100)/(127)	Fill of pit [128]	1/5
(101)/(133)	Fill of pit [134]	5/100 P13
(201)	Fill of pit [202]	1
(122)	Fill of pit [123]	2
Structure 205		
(115)	Fill of hollow [116]	69/1168 P14, P19
(103) = (115)	Fill of hollow [116]	4/55 P15
(271)	Below Structure 205	1/29
Post Structure 4		
(120)	Fill of posthole [121]	6/93
(166)	Fill of posthole [167]	71/1245
(168)	Fill of posthole [169]	1/14 P16
(174)	Fill of posthole [175]	2/66
(178)	Fill of posthole [179]	1/43
(180)	Fill of posthole [181]	3/13
(190)	Fill of posthole [191]	4/63
Pit [124] with moulds		
(112)	Fill of pit [124]	49/1417 P17, 18a. 18b
(108) = (112)	Fill of pit [124]	55/774

Table 3.4: Details of pottery from Enclosure 1, contexts by sherd numbers and weight (g). Total assemblage: 355 sherds, 6089g.

to the eleventh and tenth centuries cal BC, and that refinement of dating should be expected as further sites with this material are found. The presence of the incised sherds **P11** in the soil over Roundhouse 2 is a reminder of just how little is really known about ceramics during this period.

Adjacent features

The ceramic assemblage from over the stone spread / bank (105) and soil layer (106) is generally Trevisker Ware and all gabbroic admixture, abraded or with moderate abrasion. Layer (105) had a sherd from a cord-impressed vessel and two rim sherds, one with incised decoration and one with deep grooving producing the effect of cordons (*cf* Trethellan P53, P64: Woodward and Cane 1991, figs 49-50). Context (106) had five different rim sherds, two cord impressed and three with incised decoration; small decorated body sherds may belong to these or other vessels. There is no radiocarbon dating from either of these contexts although they may be broadly comparable contemporary with Roundhouse 1.

Enclosure 1

Sherds from both the enclosure ditch infill and the internal features (Table 3.4) were generally either fresh or moderately abraded. Some sherds from both context groups have varied abrasion, suggesting that they were fresh when deposited but had suffered the effects of groundwater and bioturbation.

Enclosure ditch [170]

32 sherds, 487g

Ditch fill (159) had a piece of carinated bowl, possibly from the same vessel as **P15** from fill (115) in Structure 205 / Pit Alignment 2. Fill (272) had a rim from a shouldered jar as **P14** from fill (115) and also a flat-topped simple bowl rim. Carinated bowls and shouldered jars belong with the later group of Late Bronze Age Plain Ware (see below). A radiocarbon determination of 2782±29 BP, calibrating to 1006-843 cal BC (SUERC-47283), came from ditch fill (798).

Pit / Posthole Group 1

48 sherds, 481g

Illustrated sherd

P12 (Figure 3.4) fill (129) of posthole [130]. Gabbroic fabric, common coarse inclusions. Well-made jar with slight carination, flat-topped rim, internal rim diameter 95mm.

Petrology: Feldspar – white variably soft and altered angular to sub-angular grains, 0.05-1.8mm. *Amphibole* – a scatter of brownish grey cleaved elongated grains, 0.5-0.8mm. *Magnetite* – sparse black glossy sub-angular magnetic grains, 0.1-1mm. *Quartz* – rare translucent white sub-angular grains, 0.2-3mm. *Matrix* – smooth finely micaceous clay.

Comment: A standard gabbroic fabric.

Other sherds

Fill (143) within posthole [144] had parts including the base of a thin-walled vessel, some non-joining body sherds and a small everted rim with an apparent black coating. Fill (190) within posthole [191] has a finer version of rim **P14**. Fill (192) within pit [193] had a smaller and finer version of **P12** and also a flat-topped rim from a simple straight-sided vessel. Fill (257), within posthole [258], has a small sherd from a carination and a flat-topped rim from a vertical straight sided jar.

Dating

Two radiocarbon determinations were obtained: 2822±30 BP calibrating to 972-827 cal BC (SUERC-47288), came from (102), the fill of pit [114], and 2766±29 BP, calibrating to 997-835 cal BC (SUERC-47291), came from (155), the fill of posthole [156].

Pit Alignment 2

9 sherds, 141 grams

Illustrated sherd

P13 (Figure 3.4) (101)/(133) fill of pit [134]. Gabbroic fabric (petrology with project archive). Simple thin-walled biconical vessel, 145mm internal diameter. Fine incised line decoration around girth and sloping into diagonal blocks up to the rim. No parallel known for this vessel.

Other sherds

Fill (122) within pit [213] has sherds from a small jar with rounded shoulder and sharply everted short rim.

Dating

No radiocarbon dates.

Structure 205

74 sherds, 1252g

Illustrated sherd

P14 (Figure 3.4) from fill (115) of hollow [116]. Gabbroic fabric as **P12**. Vertical flat-topped everted rim, internal diameter 260mm, from a large storage-type jar flaring outward to a shoulder.

P15 (Figure 3.4) from fill (115) of hollow [116]. Gabbroic fabric as **P12**. Two highly oxidised joining sherds from the rim and shoulder of a jar or bowl with everted rim and rounded carination. Internal rim diameter 240mm.

Other sherds

Fill (115) within hollow [116], only partly excavated, contained rim sherds from some eight other vessels, either everted jar rim forms or from fairly straight-sided bowls and probably from a carinated bowl. Fill (115) within the hollow also contained a small 4g post-medieval sherd with internal glaze from sample 338 which must be intrusive or recovered from adjacent to the stones during the topsoil stripping. (See also Late Iron Age imported sherd **P19** below).

Dating

A radiocarbon determination of 2808±29 BP, calibrating to 1048-896 cal BC (SUERC-47289) was obtained from fill (115).

Post Structure 4

88 sherds, 1537g

Enumerated sherd

P16 (not illus) from fill (168) of posthole [169]. Gabbroic fabric (petrology with project archive), with medium inclusions, fine burnished finish on both surfaces. The shape is a slightly less everted version of **P14**, vessel wall 4-5mm thick.

Other sherds

Fill (166) within posthole [167] had a rim as **P14** and also a flat-topped rim from a simple open bowl.

Dating

A radiocarbon determination of 2790±27 BP, calibrating to 1011-846 cal BC (SUERC-47290), came from fill (167).

Pit [124] with moulds

104 sherds, 2191g

Illustrated sherds

P17 (Figure 3.4) from (112), the fill of pit [124]. Gabbroic fabric (petrology in project archive). Flat-topped rim from storage jar with slightly incurved closed neck, good outside burnish. Internal rim diameter approximately 300mm.

P18a (Figure 3.4) from (112), the fill of pit [124] Gabbroic fabric. Sharply inturned rim from a wide carinated bowl, roughly finished fabric. Internal rim diameter 210mm.

P18b (Figure 3.4) from (112), the fill of pit [124]. Gabbroic fabric. Sherd from angle of carinated bowl which would have had a small base; not the same vessel as **P18a** but illustrated together to give an impression of form. A large sherd with good interior dark burnish comes from another similar vessel.

Other sherds

Other sherds from pit fill (112) represent a more roughly made version of **P17**, a smaller necked jar and a vessel with a wall less than 4mm thick. Layer (108) had a rim as **P14** but with better burnish and also a thick straight-walled piece with a simple rounded rim, with the possible remnant of a squarish lug.

Dating

A radiocarbon determination of 2747±26 BP, calibrating to 972-827 cal BC (SUERC-47287), came from fill (112).

Comment on the Enclosure 1 assemblage

This assemblage contains large shouldered storage jars, bowls and jars with carinations and also biconical jars. The radiocarbon dates indicate the tenth and earlier ninth centuries BC. The forms, except for the unique biconical jar **P13**, are broadly paralleled by vessels in the second group of Late Bronze Age Plain Ware from Higher Besore, Truro, but these dating slightly later, in the ninth century cal BC (Quinnell, forthcoming). However, pit [3402] at Scarcewater (Quinnell 2010a, 107) produced, together with simple straight-walled jars, a carinated jar P26 and a date of 1000-830 cal BC (Wk-21451), a determination that is very much in keeping with the dates from Enclosure 1. The dates from Tremough and Scarcewater strongly indicate that these forms, broadly the later Late Bronze Age Plain Ware group in Cornwall, start in the tenth century BC. Tremough, Scarcewater and Higher Besore are the only sites with Late Bronze Age Plain Ware in good stratified contexts which have associated radiocarbon determinations.

Generally knowledge of ceramics in Late Bronze Age Cornwall is very limited. This paucity of knowledge extends into the first part of the Early Iron Age down to around 600 cal BC, a period which, for convenience, may be termed 'Earliest Iron Age'. Trevelgue Head cliff castle, Newquay, has produced shouldered jars and carinated vessels dated to the eighth century BC, and the publication of this material made it clear that these forms probably continued down to around 600 cal BC, when simpler smaller vessels called the 'Plain Jar Group' appeared (Quinnell 2011, 7.7, 7.8). Thus currently the second Late Bronze Age Plain Ware group appears to continue without any definite changes through the first two centuries of the Iron Age. It might be more realistic to term this material Late Bronze Age / Earliest Iron Age.

Two long-known sites, Bodrifty in West Penwith (Dudley 1956) and Nornour in the Isles of Scilly (Butcher 1978), have vessels belonging to the shouldered jar and carinated bowl and jar groups but their stratigraphy is less clear and not supported by modern radiometric dating. Other sites with contemporary ceramics have been discussed in the report on Trevelgue Head (Quinnell 2011, chapter 7). Overall, the amounts of pottery found on Late Bronze Age – Earliest Iron Age sites in Cornwall appear to be much less than those from the preceding Middle Bronze Age and from the subsequent Early Iron Age Plain Jar Group.

Two features of the Enclosure 1 assemblage deserve further comment. The average sherd size is large, 17.2 grams, as opposed for example to the 9.4 grams average for prehistoric sherds from Trevelgue (Quinnell 2011, table 7.1). Practices that this large sherd size might reflect are rapid rubbish disposal, allowing sherd sizes to remain substantial, and quite possibly deliberate deposition. It is likely that much of the pottery from structural features may have been stored prior to deposition and in some instances there is evidence for structured deposition (chapter 11). The other feature of the assemblage is the large size of some of the vessels, especially **P14** and **P17** and fragments of similar rims not individually numbered. This indicates a possible predominance on vessels for storage, or, perhaps, for large-scale communal cooking.

Late Iron Age imported sherd?

P19 (Figure 3.5) ostensibly from (271) in the area of the cairn associated with Structure 205 but almost certainly incorrectly numbered and probably from a topsoil context. Sherd weighing 29 grams from the lower part of a large vessel, well burnished inside and out. Double deeply grooved lines provide the impression of added cordons around the vessel. Both surfaces reduced 5YR 4/1 dark grey, interior oxidised 5YR 5/4 reddish-brown. Moderate fine inclusions. Probably wheel made and not part of the Cornish Cordoned ware repertoire.

Petrology: Feldspar – white to grey, angular to sub-angular grains 0.1-0.8mm, one grain shows twinning indicating plagioclase 0.05mm. *Quartz* – translucent to transparent colourless and white angular to sub-angular grains, 0.05-1.2mm, one rounded and polished grain 1.5mm. *Mica* - muscovite cleavage flakes 0.05-0.1mm, biotite dark brown cleavage flakes 0.05-0.1mm. *Composite* – rare quartz feldspar grains 0.8mm and 1.1mm. *Matrix* – silty clay with fragments of the main tempering minerals less than 0.05mm.

Comment: A granite-derived fabric, not obviously distinguishable from south-western British granite-derived fabrics; sodic plagioclase is a standard component mineral of most granites.

General comment:

Cornish Cordoned wares are all, as far as is known, made of gabbroic fabric. The general appearance of the sherd, both of its fabric and the double grooved lines, suggest that it is not local. The sherd has been examined by Lisa Brown (pers comm.) who agreed with the suggested Breton origin. The fabric matches those of some granitic fabrics from Late Iron Age Brittany, especially Fabrics B3.1-3 and B2.3 from Le Yaudet (Williams 2005), and the form would be accommodated amongst the imported rilled micaceous wares discussed for Hengistbury Head, Dorset (Cunliffe 1987, 310), but which occur widely across Late Iron Age sites in western Brittany (*ibid*, Ill, 223) and which also occur at Le Yaudet (Brown and Durham 2005; Cunliffe and Galliou 2005). These wares have only been found at Hengistbury, Hamworthy and Maiden Castle in mainland Britain (Cunliffe 1987, 310). Breton Iron Age imported wares known in South West Britain are restricted to two sherds from Mount Batten, Plymouth (Cunliffe 1988, 40, fig 27, P20, P36), which are both of black cordoned wares of amphibolic fabric, the

Figure 3.5 Late Iron Age pottery. Cordoned sherd from vessel P19.

commonest North French import at Hengistbury. If the identification of **P19** is correct, it is the first Breton sherd from Cornwall but of a different fabric to those from Mount Batten.

Baked clay weight and other material

Weight SF406 (Figure 3.6) from layer (273) infill in quadrant 1 of Roundhouse 1. A ceramic weight with flattish cross section, probably with much of the lower end crumbled off; 80mm across, 60mm+ long and 22mm thick. Top end flattened. Cylindrical perforation approximately 17mm across and not worn.

Petrology: Slate / slaty hornfels – bluish to silvery grey tabular grains predominantly aligned parallel, with a few fragments showing randomly orientated tilting; fragment margins are angular to sub-angular, 1-9mm. *Quartz and vein quartz* – colourless transparent to translucent and opaque angular and rare rounded grains, 0.5-2.5mm. *Sandstone and silty sandstone* – sparse grey sub-angular to sub-rounded grains, 1-2mm. *Mica* – sparse muscovite cleavage flakes, 0.1mm. *Feldspar* – rare soft white altered grains, 0.1-0.5mm. Clay with slate fragments less than 0.1mm.

Comment: The hole appears to have been made by drilling after firing. There is little disturbance of the layering of the slate fragments which might have occurred had the hole been made by moulding the clay round a rod or pushing a rod through

Figure 3.6 Middle Bronze Age ceramic weight SF406 from Roundhouse 1.

the clay while plastic. The layering of the slate fragments appears to be an original depositional structure. The clay and its mineral content have been sourced to the edge of the thermal aureole of the granite close to the site.

The fabric contains about 70 per cent slate. No parallel is known for this object. Those objects described as clay 'loomweights' from Bronze Age contexts in South West Britain are broadly cylindrical with perforations through their longest axis – for example, from settlements at Trevisker (ApSimon and Greenfield 1972, 341) and Trethellan (Nowakowski 1991, 140) – and are made of clay sourced very close to the sites; they contain very little temper. This ceramic object is unusual not only in its shape but in its manufacture and the material from which it was made. 'Loomweights' are perforated before firing this artefact has been drilled through after firing. Its material consists largely of slate with only sufficient clay to bond the slate together. Given the occurrence of metal-working moulds in the infill context from which **SF406** came, some connection with metalworking is possible.

Daub Several contexts had fairly formless lumps of material best described as baked clay or daub; they do not appear to be part of artefacts such as baked clay weights.

- *Structure 1* (11) fill of pit [23]. There are two abraded small lumps, weighing 6g, one with a fingernail impression.
- *Roundhouse 1* layer (274), infill layer within quadrant 2. There are four fragments weighing 85g.
- *Structure 3, Enclosure 1* (161) fill of posthole [162]. An assemblage comprising ten lumps weighing 780g.

The petrological examination of the daub fragments indicates that they are of a local clay with a granite-derived content.

Chapter 4

The prehistoric worked stone artefacts

Henrietta Quinnell, with petrographic comment by Roger Taylor

Dimensions are not given for fragments in the tables below unless over about 15mm in size. The term 'fresh' is used to indicate that objects were broken fairly soon before deposition and do not relate to excavation damage. If no comment is given on origin of rock this is local; that is to say from within 5 kilometres of the site; most granite is therefore local.

Structure 1

Comment

As with the 2000-2 excavations at Tremough (Quinnell 2007, 81), most of the stonework recovered was sourced locally, either in the immediate vicinity of the site or from the Carnmennellis granite within a short distance of it. Beach-derived material comes from the coastline outside the Fal estuary, a distance of some 5 to 6 kilometres. There are five sandstone beach cobbles and five chunks of granite but only one used. The cassiterite pebble probably comes from the alluvial gravels of the Carnon River some 7-10 kilometres to the north (Table 4.1).

The saddle quern fragment from (7), the rubbing stone fragments from (7) and (24), the rubbing stone fragment with pestle use from (13), the rubbing stone fragment from fill (11) in hearth [27] and the whetstone fragment from fill (50) in posthole [51] are all objects from the usual Bronze Age domestic repertoire. These artefacts are unusual because domestic structures of the earlier Bronze Age period are almost unknown in the South West peninsula (chapter 11). The artefacts from context (11) and from (50) have also been used as hammerstones. Such use can be domestic but would also be appropriate for the preparation of metal ores, something hinted at by the presence of the cassiterite pebble fragment. Middle Bronze Age structure 392, excavated in 2002, produced a cassiterite cobble (Quinnell 2007, 83).

All items were broken, shortly before deposition, except for two granite fragments which had been brought to the site but not used. This includes the cassiterite pebble. This universal breakage is unusual. While deliberate breakage as part of disposal and deposition practices is likely for the artefacts, the breakage of the pebble may have happened in the process of ore preparation. All the artefacts appear to come from contexts on the north side of the Structure. When comparing the broken nature of this small assemblage to the virtually unbroken material from

Context	Description	Stonework
(7)	Fill of posthole [6]	Small fragment of working surface from saddle quern, coarse muscovite granite, flattened surface with faceted quartz and feldspar grains, fresh break.
(7)	Fill of posthole [6]	Small fragment from large coarse greenstone beach cobble, surface glossy and at least one area polished from rubbing-type use, fresh break.
(13)	Fill of posthole [21]	Part of tabular aplite beach cobble, 90mm+ x 80mm x 17mm, with both flat surfaces worn smooth through use as rubbing stone, edges have striations from pestle type use, burnt with resulting pitting on surfaces, fresh fractures.
(50)	Fill of posthole [51]	Part of bladed fine silty sandstone beach cobble, 85mm+ x 45mm x 10mm, one side worn flat and very slightly concave through whetstone use, most of surface including edges worn to some extent, surviving end used as crude hammerstone, fresh breaks on edge also probably from hammerstone use.
(11)	Fill of pit [23]	Flat, fine-grained sandstone beach cobble, 48mm+ x 90mm+ x20mm, both surfaces smooth from some use as rubbing stone, detachment from surviving end from use as hammer, fresh break, possibly burnt.
(24)	Fill of posthole [25]	Broken alluvial cassiterite pebble with some quartz, 43g, fresh break.
(24)	Fill of posthole [25]	Broken aplite beach cobble, 50mm+ x 65mm+ x 28mm, fresh break, possibly burnt, just possibly used as rubbing stone.
(44)	Fill of pit [45]	Coarse non-megacrystic muscovite granite, flat surface a natural joint, no apparent use.
(44)	Fill of pit [45]	Granite fragment, fine-grained non-megacrystic, flat surface not apparently used and probably natural.
(46)	Fill of pit [47]	Two fragments of weathered surface lump of medium fine-grained biotite granite without megacryst, unused, burnt, recent fractures.

Table 4.1: Stonework from Structure 1.

the later Roundhouse 1, it is noteworthy that all pieces come from cut features and it is possible that they could relate to the erection rather than the demolition of Structure 1. From the 2000-2 excavations, Early Bronze Age structure 66 and pits produced no stonework and of the Middle Bronze Age post-rings only structures 392 (three) and 102 (two) produced stone tools; these were all probably parts of deliberately structured deposits (Gossip and Jones 2007, 34-5; chapter 11, below).

Roundhouse 1

Comment

Most of the stonework comes from the same range of contexts as that from Structure 1 (Table 4.2). However, the two cobbles from Budleigh Salterton, Devon, **S1** and one other, and two tabular stream cobbles, are from sources not represented in Structure 1. One granite muller fragment and an unused piece represent use of the local granite. Beach cobbles are represented by two of greenstones, one of sandstone and one of aplitic granite.

The muller fragment from posthole fill (724), the whetstone **S2** from infill (273), the end rubbing-stone wear on **S4** and the pestle from gully (278) may all relate to domestic use; the intensive use of **S2** is perhaps more appropriate to metal artefact production. All the other pieces, two, including **S1** of Budleigh quartzite, in posthole fill (749), the beach cobbles of greenstone **S4** and of sandstone, both in gully (278), and of aplitic granite **S3** in infill layer (273), are all heavy-duty pestle /

Context	Description	Stonework
(724)	Fill of posthole [725]	Pebble of medium-grained muscovite granite with coarse, unabraded surface, fractured end, not used.
(730)	Fill of pit [711]	Small surface fragment from contact area between fine and coarse aplitic granite, one smooth surface with facetted grains from use as muller of triangular cross-section.
(749)	Fill of posthole [750]	S1: composite tool, probably import from Devon.
(273)	Infill layer in quadrant 1	S2: whetstone, sandstone cobble.
(273)	Infill layer in quadrant 1	Fragment of white vein quartz, 40mm long, possibly recent fractures.
(273)	Infill layer in quadrant 1	White vein quartz beach pebble, 55mm x 38mm x 20mm.
(273)	Infill layer in quadrant 1	S3: aplitic granite beach cobble pestle / hammerstone.
(278)	Gully cut into natural in quadrant 1	S4: greenstone beach cobble pestle / hammerstone.
(278)	Gully cut into natural in quadrant 1	Beach cobble fragment (?), Budleigh Salterton quartzite, pale pinkish-grey with naturally glossy surface, 50mm+ x 98mm x 45mm, on one surface gloss worn away with abrasion, probably caused by grinding hard material, two small patches of pestle use on end, fresh break.
(278)	Gully cut into natural in quadrant 1	SF401: beach cobble of quartz-rich sandstone with muscovite, 102mm x 85mm x 35mm, both ends some use as pestle / hammerstone and some hammer use on one long edge.
(278)	Gully cut into natural in quadrant 1	Beach cobble, dolerite / basalt with small feldspar phenocrysts and paler greenish bands of alteration, 95mm x 70mm x 35mm, slight pestle use on one end.
(274)	Infill layer in quadrant 2	Tabular beach / river cobble of siltstone, 125mm x 37mm x 15mm, with one edge worn straight and slightly convex from use for grinding or as a whetstone.

Table 4.2: Stonework from contexts in Roundhouse 1.

hammerstones which have been used on hard materials such as the breakage of ore for metal processing. The rocks used have been selected as very durable for this purpose. However, there is no evidence for actual ore smelting on site. This appears to be the first recorded instance of probable Budleigh quartzite cobbles from east Devon occurring in Cornwall.

Almost all the stonework from the infilling deposits comes from north-west quadrant 1, with a single piece from north-east quadrant 2; however, two of three cut features with stonework were in south east quadrant 3 with only one beneath north-west quadrant 1. Unlike the objects in Structure 1, only the granite muller from (724) and a piece of vein quartz from infill layer (273) have fresh breaks. Virtually all the material comes from infill levels, with only three pieces, including **S1,** from cut contexts, possibly related to construction rather than abandonment. The apparent distributional bias of the stonework reflects that of the stone metalworking moulds (chapters 5 and 11).

Illustrated stonework

S1 (Figure 4.1) (749) the fill of posthole [750]. Tabular quartzite beach cobble 125mm x 104mm x 20mm, both flat surfaces have some possible use polish, slight anvil traces on one surface, most of edge has facets caused by use as pestle /

hammerstone. Brownish colour, glossy surface and quartzitic composition closely resemble material in the Budleigh Salterton Pebble Beds; possibly a coastal import from Devon.

S2 (Figure 4.1) (273) infill layer within quadrant 1. Silty fine-grained sandstone tabular stream cobble, triangular shape, damaged before use, 80mm x 43mm x 12mm; all surfaces and edges worn from whetstone use, two specially marked facets on longer edges, facet across wider end, similar use smoothing flat surfaces. Transverse striations on one long edge.

S3 (Figure 4.1) (273) infill layer within quadrant 1. Beach cobble of aplitic granite with some small feldspar / quartz phenocrysts, 50mm x 40mm x 35mm; broken after some pestle use, size subsequently heavily reduced by use as hammer / pestle, one end coarse hammerstone use, other pestle use.

S4 (Figure 4.1) (278) gully in quadrant 1, SF402. Beach cobble of doleritic greenstone, pestle, 130mm x 90mm x 55mm, pecked finger grips on both flat faces, one of which has been worn flat from rubbing-stone use, both sides with some rubbing-stone use. Both ends have heavy pestle use. Dolerite is relatively dense and therefore appropriately heavy for hammerstone use.

Enclosure 1 and associated structures

Comment

Most of the stonework is of the same materials and comes from the same local sources as that in Structure 1. This larger assemblage, however, also includes several examples of elvans, slate from surface outcrop **S8**, a foliated basic tuff beach cobble **S9**, talcose **S9** and unstratified lamprophyre which all can source to the local 5 kilometres or so around the site. The granites include several surface pieces as well as cobbles. Several pieces of granite and elvan were imported to the site but not apparently used (Table 4.3).

Saddle querns are represented by the fragment reused as a muller in posthole [121], Post Structure 4 and another piece also reused as a muller from pit [124]; both these are elvan as is an unstratified example. There is also a granite segment from an unstratified saddle quern. Mullers are represented by the greisen cobble **S5** from the enclosure ditch, granite cobble **S6** from Pit / Posthole Group 1, two weathered granite fragments for layer (115) in Structure 205, a granite and an elvan fragment from Post Structure 4, an elvan fragment from pit [124] and an unstratified granite fragment. There is a single broken whetstone using a tabular silty sandstone cobble from Pit Alignment 2. Rubbing stones, surprisingly, are not present and the pestle / hammerstone items so prominent on the other sites are not present either. The slate cover **S8** is another 'domestic' item not present on other sites. Overall this assemblage is far more representative of general domestic artefacts than those of the other sites. The unusual artefacts are the cushion / finishing stones **S7** and **S9**, from pit [124] and unstratified, the former being associated with clay mould fragments and so potentially with metalworking.

Context	Description	Stonework
Enclosure ditch [170]		
(117)	Fill of north terminal	Fragment of white vein quartz beach cobble, 65mm+ x 65mm+ x 35mm, recent fracture marks from deliberate breakage.
(117)	Fill of north terminal	S5 quartz greisen river cobble muller.
(159)	Fill of top south terminal	Glossy oval flint beach pebble, with chatter markings, maximum dimension 30mm.
Pit / Posthole Group 1		
(113)	Fill of pit [114]	Rough discoidal medium grained granite with muscovite and common black tourmaline, probably unused, 55mm x 55mm x 20mm.
(170)	Fill of posthole [171]	S6 granite river cobble muller.
(176)	Fill of pit [177]	Two joining piece of weathered block of aplitic granite with sparse feldspar phenocrysts and black tourmaline, natural tabular fragment, 120mm x 155mm x 33mm, apparently unused.
Pit Alignment 2		
(118)	Fill of posthole [119]	Broken whetstone, elongated rounded cobble of silty sandstone with muscovite, 65mm+ x 25mm x 12mm, two surfaces flattened by whetstone use, fresh fracture occurred when use worn cobble thin. Typical fine-grained material characteristically used for whetstones.
Structure 205		
(115)	Fill of hollow [116]	Muller fragment of fine-grained biotite muscovite granite from small naturally weathered fragment, 65mm+ x 105mm x 31mm, pronounced worn convex surface with no visible dressing, fracture fresh.
(115)	Fill of hollow [116]	Fragment of large muller, using naturally weathered surface fragment of medium fine-grained granite with muscovite, a little biotite and black tourmaline, 130mm+ x 115mm x 70mm, one worn convex surface with surviving dressing adjoining another possible surface at an angle, fresh fractures. No parallel known for two adjacent muller surfaces.
(115)	Fill of hollow [116]	Fragment of glossy elongated beach cobble, aplite with scattered quartz phenocrysts, 20mm+ x 40mm x 20mm, probably unused but possibly deliberately broken.
Post Structure 4		
(120)	Fill of posthole [121]	Fragment triangular sectioned muller, from surface block of microgranitic elvan with feldspar and quartz phenocrysts up to circa 10mm and some plates of altered biotite, 75mm+ x 114mm+ x 55mm. Made on fragment of former saddle quern of which part of concave working surface survives, slightly convex working surface with dressing striations, fresh probably deliberate breaks, possibly burnt.
(166)	Fill of pit [167]	Glossy white vein quartz beach pebble maximum dimension 42mm.
(180)	Fill of posthole [181]	Fragment of porphyritc elvan with parallel surfaces, 150mm+ x 85mm+ x 40mm, probably unused, fresh fractures.
(184)	Fill of posthole [185]	Block of biotite lamprophyre, not water worn. Corner of saddle quern, 80mm thick 130mm+ x 130mm+, surviving worn surface dished but no visible dressing, incipient fractures perhaps produced by burning, fresh breaks.
(186)	Fill of posthole [187]	Chunk of weathered surface fine-grained granite with small feldspar phenocrysts, 140mm x 120mm x 60mm, unused but shape suitable for muller.
(190)	Fill of posthole [191]	Muller, fine-grained granite with sparse small megacrysts and some black tourmaline, 96mm+ x 90mm+ x 60mm, part of convex muller surface with traces of dressing striations, probably made on fragment of surface granite.

Table 4.3: Stonework from contexts in Enclosure 1.

Context	Description	Stonework
Pit [124] with moulds		
(112)	Fill in pit [124]	S7 cushion / finishing stone, using foliated tuff beach cobble.
(112)	Fill in pit [124]	S8 large slate lid.
(112)	Fill in pit [124]	Fragment of muller, non-porphyritic elvan, probable surface fragment, 82mm+ x 78mm+ x 45mm, triangular cross section, convex worn surface with no surviving dressing, traces of slightly concave surface which may come from quern, fresh breaks.
(112)	Fill in pit [124]	Three white vein quartz pebbles, smooth and flattish rather than glossy, maximum dimensions 68mm, 52mm, 42mm.
(112)	Fill in pit [124]	Surface or river pebble with a contact between coarse granite and aplite passing through it, one probable worked flat surface on the aplite side, convex, probable small rubber, 58mm x 52mm x 34mm, fresh breaks.
Unstratified		
unstratified		S9 cushion / finishing stone, talcose.
unstratified		Fine-grained granite with small feldspar phenocrysts, probable surface fragment, also showing contact with coarse grained granite. Purplish centre and orangy surfaces suggest post-use burning. Muller fragment, slightly cheese-slice cross section, 150mm+ x 100mm+ x 45mm, surface worn flat, facetted crystals and traces of striations on the working surface, very fresh damage.
unstratified		Coarse non-megacrystic muscovite granite, probably a partly weathered surface fragment. Corner of saddle quern, 190mm+ x 190mm+ x 140mm, curved segment of dished worn surface survives, good facetted crystal on this surface: broken, possibly deliberately, on two sides.
unstratified		Porphyritic elvan with abundant small feldspar phenocrysts up to 10mm long, occasional quartz phenocrysts showing euhedral form in some cases, occasional plates of biotite. Surface weathered block. Segment of saddle quern with smooth dished working surface which is almost glossy but on which there are numerous small pecks which may be an attempt to roughen the surface; 400mm wide, 250mm+ long, 100mm thick. Partly burnt, one of the two principal breaks has an impact fracture which suggests that breakage was deliberate and post-burning.

Table 4.3: Stonework from contexts in Enclosure 1 (continued).

Two cushion / finishing stones with similar irregular facets to those from Tremough were found in Late Bronze Age pit [2009] at Higher Besore, Truro; S49 a small stone of easily worked serpentinite with numerous facets and S50 a fragment of a small stone using a siltstone river cobble, again with multiple facets. Both had been ground into shape and have smooth, very finely abrasive, surfaces. The pottery from this pit at Higher Besore belongs with the later Group of Late Bronze Age Plain Ware with dates centring on the ninth century BC. The classic examples of cushion stones are the cuboid objects from the Beaker period at Lunteren in Holland (Clarke *et al* 1985, plate 4.3) which are thought to have been used in the formation of small sheet metal artefacts. Identified examples appear rare in Britain and the only cuboid one similar to the Lunteren pieces from Cornwall is SF20 from Site 2 at Stannon Down: this, although not strictly stratified, probably belongs to the seventeenth to fifteenth centuries cal BC (Quinnell 2004-5, 74, fig 31). By the Late Bronze Age it is generally considered that small bronze anvils were used instead of stone blocks (for example, Eogan 1983, 193, 321) although small triangular stone blocks with ground and rounded angles were found in the

Dowris hoard (*ibid*, 295). The four cushion / finishing stones from Tremough and Higher Besore have similar multiple irregular ground facets at varying angles and are both of much the same date. However, they differ in shape from the earlier cushion stones. There is also no indication that they were used in the production of sheet metalwork, and it seems likely that their multiple fine-grinding surfaces were used in the finishing stages of the production of cast artefacts.

The Enclosure 1 assemblage is Late Bronze Age tenth to early ninth centuries cal BC in date. Chronologically comparable assemblages are those from Higher Besore, with 22 items (Quinnell, forthcoming), and Scarcewater with seven (Quinnell 2010b). Cereal preparation items form a significant part of the Higher Besore assemblage, as do rubbing stones, which are absent from Tremough. Generally there seems very little difference between Middle and Late Bronze Age domestic stonework assemblages in Cornwall, the largest of the former being that from Trethellan Farm, Newquay (Nowakowski 1991, 141-56).

None of the items in the enclosure ditch itself or in Pit / Posthole Group 1 appear to have been broken before deposition. However the whetstone from Pit Alignment 2, the three items from layer (115) in Structure 205, the three utilised items from Post Structure 4 and the two mullers from pit [124] have fresh breaks, as do the three muller or quern fragments (unstratified) and the saddle quern from posthole [185]. There appears to be no particular pattern in the position of features with stonework within the various structures.

Illustrated stonework

S5 (Figure 4.1) (117) the fill of the north terminal of enclosure ditch [160]. Triangular tabular muscovite quartz greisen river cobble, slightly waterworn, 130mm x 100mm x 40mm, one side worn flat through use as muller with traces of parallel dressing striations still visible. Convenient hand-held shape.

S6 (Figure 4.1) (170) the fill of posthole [171] in Pit / Posthole Group 1. Muller of medium-grained muscovite granite with some black tourmaline, possible stream cobble, some fracture on one edge, 150mm x 110mm x 30mm, one surface worn smooth and slightly convex, possible traces of dressing still visible.

S7 (Figure 4.1) (112) the fill of pit [124] with mould fragments. Complex hexagonal cushion / finishing stone, with some damage on one side; 120mm x 70mm x 45mm. All original surfaces worn smooth and glossy, with areas of earlier facets showing in junctions. Some small patches have striations / scratches which may survive from the shaping of facets. One face has possible impact fractures from hammerstone use. Foliated basic tuff, very fine-grained but not overly hard (scratches with steel point), mottled greyish-green. Possibly a cobble of Lizard origin.

S8 (Figure 4.1) (112) the fill of pit [124] with mould fragments. Greenish-grey tufaceous slate, natural cleaved fragment clearly edge-trimmed to rough triangle, 150mm x 151mm x 16mm; possible lid or cover. Fairly local to site but outside metamorphic aureole.

S9 (Figure 4.1) (unstratified). Soft greenish-grey talcose, almost certainly of Lizard origin. Multi-facetted cushion / finishing stone similar to **S7** from fill (112) but smaller, on a parallel sided block 102mm x 50mm x 22mm; six major facets but traces of earlier facets between them, facets worn smooth and glossy with blocks of scratches in different directions on most surfaces, some fresh damage.

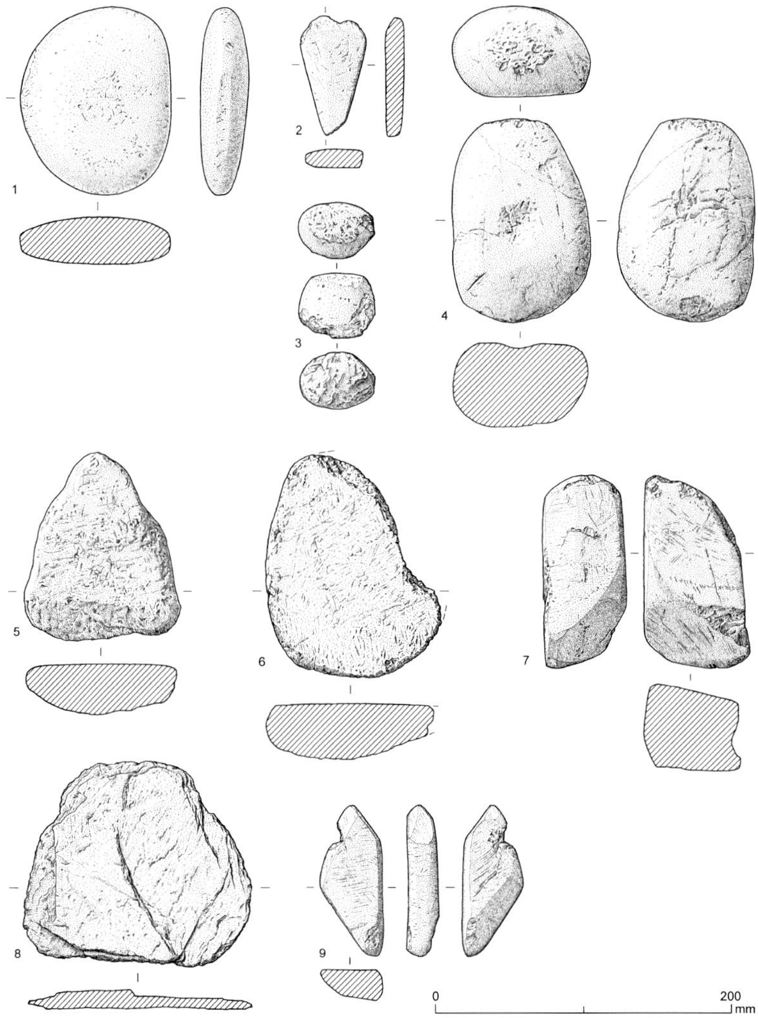

Figure 4.1 Middle and Late Bronze Age stone artefacts. S1-S4 from Roundhouse 1 contexts. S5-S9 from Enclosure 1 contexts (Drawing by Jane Read).

Chapter 5

The moulds and metalwork

Susan Pearce, with Henrietta Quinnell and Andy M Jones,
with petrographic comment by Roger Taylor

The moulds

The moulds from Roundhouse 1

Elements were considered from nine stone moulds for casting copper-alloy objects from Roundhouse 1, which has been radiocarbon dated to *circa* 1500-1300 cal BC. All these artefacts were found at the bottom of the infill layers, mostly around the area of the hearth [748]/[774], and are therefore associated with the early stages of abandonment of Roundhouse 1. Eight of the nine came from (273) an infill deposit in quadrant 1; Mould 7 came from the 'roundhouse cleaning layer' and a small clay mould fragment also came from the cleaning of the roundhouse.

Mould 1 (Figures 5.1, 5.2 and 5.3) SF 410

This is part of a bivalve (or multiple piece) mould with a matrix on each face. Surviving length 65mm, width 42mm, thickness 22mm; sides well dressed, end opposite break much rougher. Matrix 1a would cast the ring section of a ring- (or quoit-) headed pin 32mm across and of square section, 4mm by 2mm.

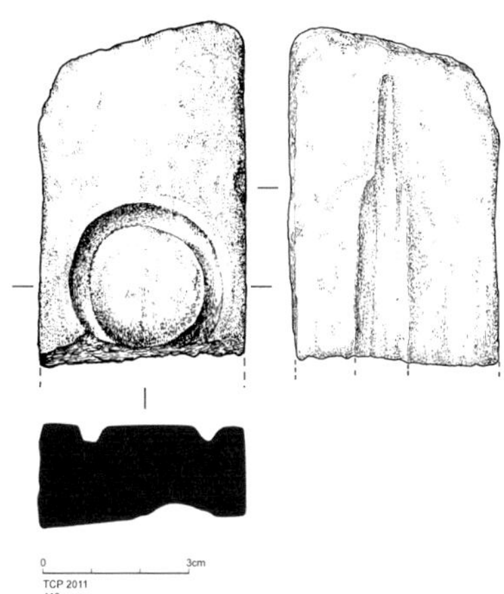

Figure 5.1 Mould 1 showing matrix 1a (left) and 1b (right) (Drawing by Craig Williams).

Figure 5.2 Photograph of Mould 1 showing matrix 1a.

Figure 5.3 Photograph of Mould 1 showing matrix 1b.

These pins are an insular type, and show considerable variation in size and in section, while some have incised decoration (Pearce 1983, 47). They are concentrated in Sussex and Somerset, in, for example, the hoards from Taunton Workhouse (Smith 1959 (ed)) which had parts of at least five, and Monkswood, Somerset (Smith 1959 (ed)), but part of an almost certain ring-headed pin came from the Tredarvah, Penzance, find (Pearce and Padley 1977). The pins were presumably used as dress fasteners, and were fashionable for a long period through the Middle Bronze Age. Matrix 1b is for part of a pin shaft. It has had substantial wear and in part is abraded and somewhat misshapen, but was probably originally square in section.

Petrology: Altered weathered non-porphrytic micro-granitic elvan. Widespread potential sources occur across Cornwall.

Mould 2 (Figures 5.4, 5.5 and 5.6) SF 407

Mould 2 is half of a bivalve mould, complete as it stands but possibly re-dressed. Length 82mm, maximum width 52mm, thickness 26mm. Exterior smoothly dressed but wider bottom edge rougher than the rest, possibly suggesting the piece in its present form had been re-dressed. It looks well worn, and the carving is of poor quality. The face carries two matrices side by side. Matrix 2a, on the viewer's

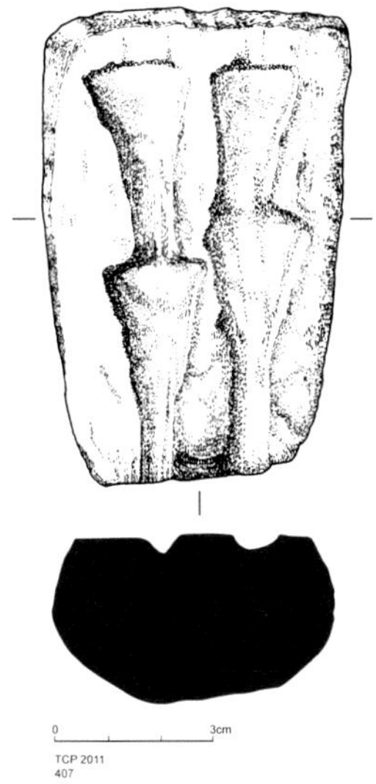

Figure 5.4 Mould 2 showing matrix 2a (left) and 2b (right) (Drawing by Craig Williams).

Figure 5.5 Photograph of Mould 2 showing back surface.

Figure 5.6 Photograph of Mould 2 showing surface with matrices.

right, would produce a small triangular blade 35mm long, 20mm wide at its widest, surmounted by a wide, clumsy collar 18mm across at widest, which narrows to a tang that merges into what appears to be the pouring funnel.

It appears to be a type of tanged and collared chisel. Such chisels are usually slimmer and longer and date to the Late Bronze Age, when they are common, but the chisel range is large, and it is possible that there are earlier types.

Matrix 2b is for a very similar piece, buts fits awkwardly on the mould beside matrix 2a, because there was not enough space to carve a matrix with an adequate collar and blade extension.

Petrology: Weakly foliated sedimentary rock, probably volcanic tuff. There are widespread potential sources, including Mount's Bay and possibly the Lizard.

Mould 3 (Figures 5.7, 5.8 and 5.9) SF 408

This is half a bivalve mould, with one side broken away, and it shows signs of wear. Length 114mm, width 40mm, thickness 37mm. Exterior roughly dressed. The matrix would produce a small but fairly substantial socketed tool 70mm long, 25mm width of blade at widest, with near-parallel sides and a heavy mouth moulding up to 25mm deep. Up to five irregular chevrons were cut (rather than properly carved) into the exterior face.

Socketed tools of various types appeared in the Middle Bronze Age, for example in the Taunton Workhouse hoard. Most of such pieces have side loops, but those from Soham, Cambridgeshire, and Barham, Norfolk, do not (Rowlands 1976, nos 1101, 1126, plate 34, 350, 353), and another example from Soham has a multiple chevron pattern on its face (Rowlands 1976, no 1079, plate 34, 347). A recent

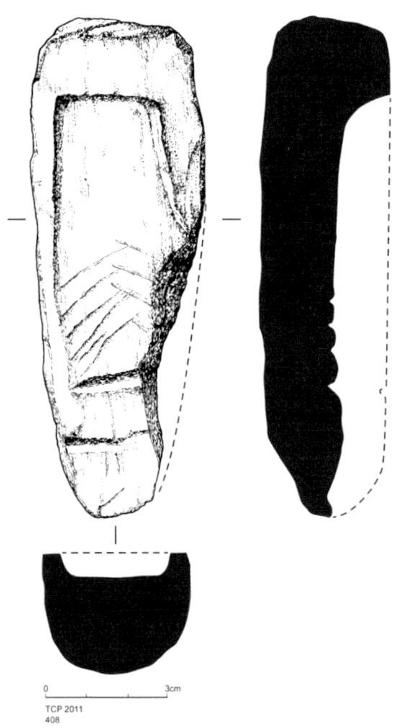

Figure 5.7 Mould 3 showing surface with matrix (Drawing by Craig Williams).

Figure 5.8 Photograph of Mould 3 showing surface with matrix.

Figure 5.9 Photograph of Mould 3 showing back surface.

find from Wrington, in north Somerset, has two palstaves and a socketed hammer, loopless but with a protruding spike on one side which appears to be an integral part of the tool, and has two ribbed chevrons on its face (Portable Antiquities Scheme PAS-9B2032). A Late Bronze Age find from Minster, Kent, has a tool with broadly similar dimensions, apparently no loop and a shield or chevron on its face (Turner 2010, no 20/18, illustration 107, 174). Again, the broad type had a long period of use.

Petrology: Altered very fine-grained non-porphrytic elvan. There are widespread potential sources across Cornwall.

Mould 4 (Figures 5.10, 5.11 and 5.12) SF 411

This is most of one half of a well-made and well-worn bivalve mould, with a matrix on each face. Surviving length 123mm, width 38mm, thickness 116mm. Exterior well dressed. Matrix 4a would cast a portion of a ring-headed pin, probably of square section, surviving length 77mm, external diameter across ring 40mm. Matrix 4b has the shaft of a pin, perhaps ground down, surviving length approximately 150mm. For discussion, see Mould 1, above.

Petrology: Altered weathered non-porphrytic micro-granitic elvan. Widespread potential sources are possible. It is virtually identical to Mould 3 (SF408) (above).

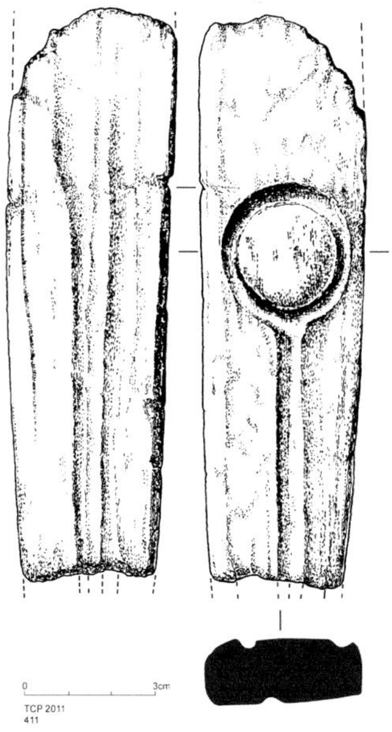

Figure 5.10 Mould 4 showing both surfaces (Drawing by Craig Williams).

Figure 5.11 Photograph of Mould 4 showing matrix 4a.

Figure 5.12 Photograph of Mould 4 showing matrix 4b.

Mould 5 (Figures 5.13, 5.14 and 5.15) SF 409

This mould presents some intriguing problems. It is half of a bivalve mould, shows considerable evidence of use, and is now in five pieces, apparently through cracking rather than breakage, possibly during use. Length 118mm, width 68mm, thickness 28mm. Exterior dressed to a smooth finish. It has two opposed casting vents. The lower part of the matrix would produce a relatively long and slender expanded blade 92mm long, 50mm at its widest, with an irregularly placed and poorly cut shield pattern on its upper face. A shield pattern on the blade occurs on a group of fairly late palstaves and these sometimes have similar blade shapes, like those from Arreton, Isle of Wight, or Birchington, Kent (Rowlands 1976, nos 567, 613, plate 30, 308, 312), but the similarities are not close. There is no sign of a side loop (unfortunately the area where traces of one might have shown is superficially damaged, but indications would probably have survived). The upper body of the casting would have been sub-rectangular in section, with a deep, strong mouth moulding, characteristic of some socketed axes, below the pouring funnel.

Overall, Mould 5 would have produced a slender but sizeable socketed tool, with a blade possessing some palstave-like elements, and no side loop; comparative material is cited in the discussion of Mould 3. It is possible that this mould was originally for a palstave and was cut down and altered to produce a socketed tool, but it is fully functional as it stands and does not require such an interpretation.

Petrology: Altered or weathered fine-grained greenstone; widespread west Cornwall sources.

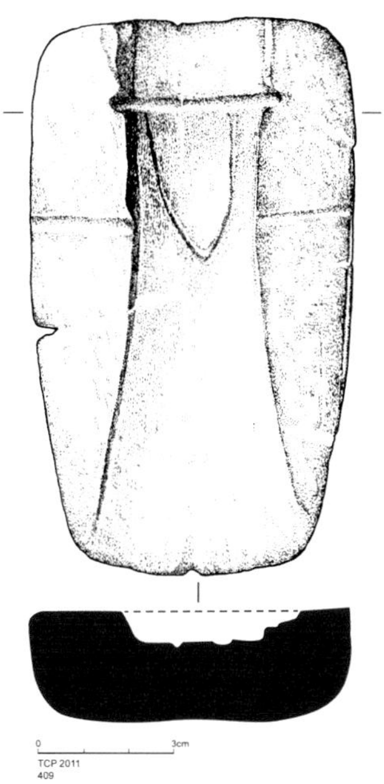

Figure 5.13 Mould 5 showing matrix (Drawing by Craig Williams).

Figure 5.14 Photograph of Mould 5 showing matrix.

Figure 5.15 Photograph of Mould 5 showing back surface.

Mould 6 (Figure 5.16) SF 414

This is half of a bivalve mould, well worn and broken at one end. Surviving length 84mm, width 42mm, thickness 26mm. Exterior sides well dressed. Its matrix would produce part of a pin shaft 83mm long, of lozenge section 10mm across. A darkened area on the back suggests that at some point there was a second matrix here.

Petrology: Altered weathered non-porphrytic micro-granitic elvan. Widespread potential sources for the stone are found across Cornwall. It is virtually identical to Mould 3 (above).

Mould 7 (Figure 5.17)

Surviving length 75mm, width 38mm, thickness 16mm. Exterior well dressed with clear longitudinal scratches on back. This is a well-worn part of half of a bivalve mould, the matrix of which as it survives would have produced a section of pin shaft of lozenge section 62mm long and 5mm wide.

Petrology: Altered weathered non-porphrytic micro-granitic elvan. Widespread potential sources of the stone are found across Cornwall. It is virtually identical to Mould 3 (for a discussion of this type of mould, see above).

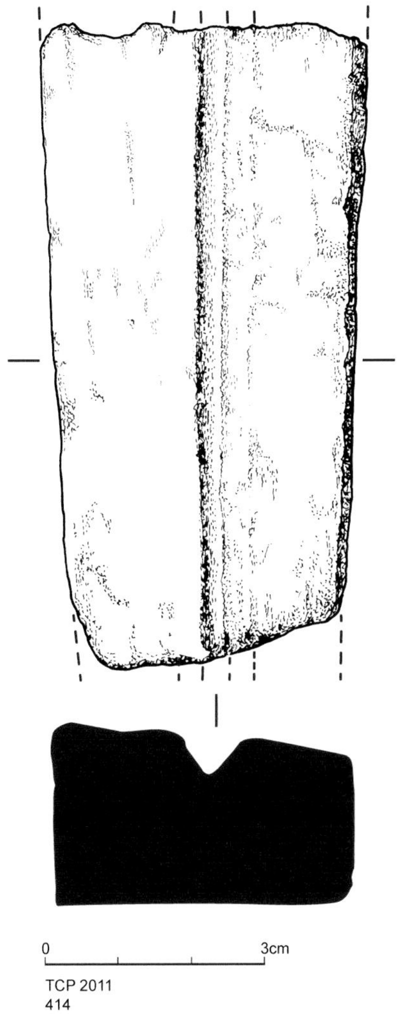

Figure 5.16 Mould 6 showing principal matrix (Drawing by Craig Williams).

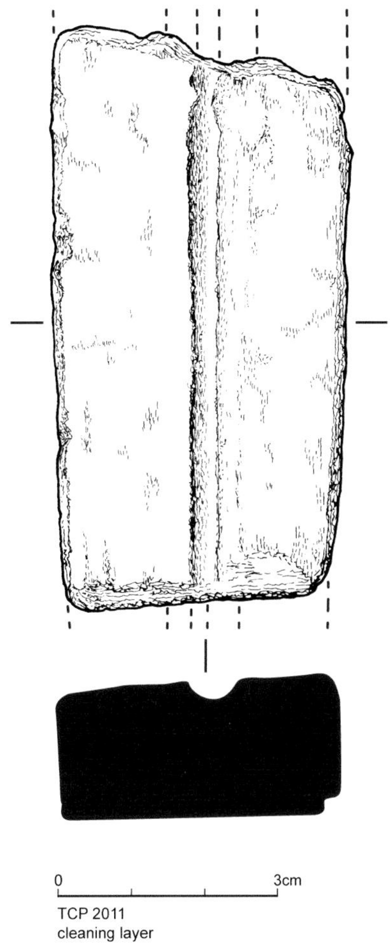

Figure 5.17 Mould 7 showing matrix (Drawing by Craig Williams).

Mould 8 (Figure 5.18) SF 412a

Surviving length 30mm, width 25mm, thickness 17mm. Original exterior well-dressed. Fragment of a well-used bivalve mould, carrying the corner of a matrix which possibly represents part of a blade approximately 24mm long.

Petrology: Very fine-grained non-porphrytic elvan, micaceous and probably kaolinised. Trace of darkened area on back suggests ground down from previous use. Multiple potential sources as any elvans in proximity to granites may be kaolinised. Trace of darkened area on back suggests that it had been ground down from previous use.

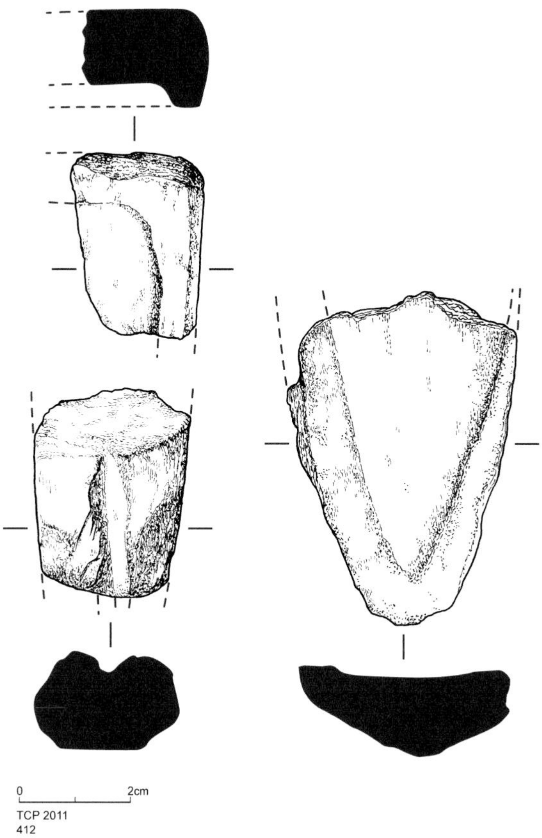

Figure 5.18 Moulds 8 (top left), 9 (bottom left) and 10 (right) showing surfaces with matrices (Drawing by Craig Williams).

Mould 9 (Fig 5.18) SF412b

Fragment of half of a well-used bivalve mould, with section of pin matrix approximately 25mm long, lozenge in section, approximately 8mm across. The other side may bear traces of a second pin shaft matrix.

Petrology: Very fine-grained non-porphyrytic elvan, as Mould 8 (above).

Clay mould fragment

Single abraded fragment, 18 grams. Micaceous clay with muscovite flakes up to 0.1mm, rare angular quartz up to 0.2mm, potentially from a kaolinitic source. Similar to the clays used in the Late Bronze Age mould fragment found in pit [124] (below).

Discussion

The radiocarbon determinations from Roundhouse 1 indicates that the moulds were deposited between *circa* 1500 and 1300 cal BC (chapter 10). As such they represent the most securely dated group of moulds from within a roundhouse settlement in southern England.

The nature of the rock used to make the moulds does not seem to have been important, just that it was soft and workable, and multiple sources were used for the moulds. These sources are, however, likely to have been found inland, as their softness and the weathering of material does not indicate that they were obtained from coastal locales (Roger Taylor, pers comm.).

The stone moulds all seem to have been deposited at much the same time, as part of the formal, final infilling of the roundhouse, although their location on the floor suggests that they were deposited early in this process. They are also likely to represent a significant element of the metalworking which had probably been carried out in the house (chapter 11). This might be consistent with the generally well-worn and fragmentary condition of the moulds, and the suggestion that some of them (for example, Moulds 6 and 9) had been reworked. If the moulds were nearing the end of their useful lives, it is likely that some of them would produce items which were ceasing to be fashionable, and this may apply to the ring-headed pins, of a type which falls comfortably within Middle Bronze Age copper-alloy working traditions. It is possible that these objects were part of the biography of the roundhouse, and this will be discussed in chapter 11 below.

Moulds 3 and 5 were intended to produce socketed tools of the very broad type which began in the Middle Bronze Age but continued into the Late Bronze Age. Mould 5 has a palstave-type blade used on a socketed tool, and is something of a hybrid. Both carry poorly carved V-shaped (shield and chevron) patterns on their faces, mould 3 particularly so. This links them with Mould 2, possibly already carrying a matrix of some kind, which was carved or re-carved to produce two tanged and collared chisels, with a degree of incompetence which would have rendered the mould more-or-less unusable. Speculation suggests that either a smith was experimenting with new forms or that an apprentice was trying his hand, in either case apparently using moulds near the end of their useful lives. The stone mould assemblage overall might be viewed as transitional between the standard forms of the Middle Bronze Age and those of the succeeding industry, and as such could fit into the later stage of the date range for the roundhouse infill suggested by the radiocarbon determinations, or just after this.

The clay moulds from Pit [124] in Enclosure 1

A small number of clay mould fragments associated with the Late Bronze Age Enclosure 1, dating from *circa* 1000 cal BC to 850 cal BC, were recovered during the excavations. Pit [124], fill (112), produced Mould 10 as well as 15 additional small fragments, A-O; details of the latter are given below when they are informative.

Mould 10 (Figures 5.18, 5.19 and 5.20)

Fragment of part of a clay mould, with matrix for the tip of a blade approximately 49mm long and approximately 34mm at its widest, probably the tip of a leaf-shaped sword, of uncertain type. Leaf-shaped swords of various types appear towards the end of the Middle Bronze Age and continued to the end of the Bronze Age. Clay

Figure 5.19 Photograph of Mould 10 showing matrix (Drawing by Craig Williams).

Figure 5.20 Photograph of Mould 10 showing back surface.

mould fragments used to cast leaf-shaped swords of uncertain type were found at Stoneycombe Quarry, Dainton, Devon, during excavation of a Late Bronze Age occupation site (Needham 1980; Silvester 1980).

Petrology: Off white 5YR 8/2, light grey burning 5YR 7/1. Very finely micaceous clay, probably kaolinitic. Probably a clay weathered from a kaolinised area, the nearest of which are Tregonning Hill and the St Austell granite; possibly kaolinisation on Carnmenellis granite but in small areas which have not been commercially worked. The apparent layering of wrapping of the clay shows no petrological difference.

Mould C (not illus)

Abraded fragment, 13 grams, reduced, outer surface 5YR 7/1 pale grey, interior surface 5YR 5/1 gray. Two-layer wrap clearly visible.

A possible fragment from a ribbed socketed axe mould. Inner surface fairly flat with V-shaped depression approximately 4mm across, possibly from a rib; possible edge of a depression from a second rib converging with the first.

Petrology: Micaceous clay with muscovite flakes up to 0.3mm, sparse angular quartz, probably from a kaolinitic source.

Mould D (not illus)

Abraded fragment, 12 grams, reduced, 5YR 5/1 gray. Rectangular piece approximately 40mm x 25mm x 10mm, bottom edge ragged; possibly inner wrap has split off.

The mould surface suggests an object with a straight edge 35mm+ across, deepening from 2mm to 4mm, possibly from an artefact such as a chisel.

Petrology: Rare angular to rounded quartz in very finely micaceous clay.

Moulds G, H, J (not illus)

Three fragments totalling 18 grams, two conjoin; abraded, pale fired oxidised 5YR 7/3 pink merging to 6/1 gray on interior, 7-8mm thick. Dimension of joined pieces 50mm x 30mm; concave suggesting just possibly a plain socketed axe.

Petrology: Angular translucent colourless quartz and quartzitic grains 0.2-2.1mm probably about 5 per cent in soft heavily abraded very finely micaceous clay matrix. Probably from a kaolinitic clay source.

Mould K (not illus) (112) the fill of pit [124].

Abraded fragment, 7 grams, oxidised 5 YR 6/8 yellowish-red, no sign of wrap, possibly from collar of casting gate, pointed at top, straight down on outside 26mm to a right-angle inturn suggesting seating; curve 50mm diameter.

Petrology Sparse angular quartz 0.1mm-2.5mm in micaceous clay matrix.

Clay moulds from other contexts in Enclosure 1

B (115) the fill of hollow [116]

Abraded piece of soft baked clay, 1 gram; clay identical to that of Mould 10 from pit [124].

A-D (143) the fill of posthole [144] in Pit / Posthole Group 1

Four abraded fragments totalling 12 grams; micaceous clay from sources similar to those in Pit [124].

Discussion

The clay used for these moulds has a very fine matrix and is very dense compared to the daub-type baked clay listed elsewhere (chapter 3). The matrices are generally soft and friable, which has led to their now abraded condition. All clays used appear to come from kaolinitic sources. Those not individually described are slight variants on G, H and J from Pit [124].

The clay sword-tip Mould 10 from Pit [124] fits with the radiocarbon date obtained from the pit infill, 2747±26 BP, 972-827 cal BC (SUERC-47287). The minimal features of the other clay mould fragments from the pit are broadly in accord with this (Henrietta Quinnell, personal observation).

Other than at Dainton (Needham 1980), evidence for Late Bronze Age metalworking has been quite sparse in the South West peninsula (for example, Skowranek 2007) and close dating is even less common, which makes the dating of the Tremough finds very important. The finds are, however, particularly significant as the mould fragments represent the first Late Bronze Age metalworking to be recovered from a contemporary enclosure site in the South West. Elsewhere in Britain some enclosures have stronger metalworking associations, albeit frequently on a small scale (Needham and Bridgford 2013), and the national comparanda for Tremough are discussed below (chapter 11).

The copper-alloy objects

Andy M Jones and Henrietta Quinnell

Copper-alloy objects from Roundhouse 1

SF400 (Figure 5.21)

Roundhouse 1, (278) fill of possible gully around part of quadrant 1. Curved fragment of copper-alloy artefact, maximum surviving dimension 20mm, with rib on one side; the slight protuberances shown on the other side are probably due to corrosion.

SF413 (Figure 5.22)

Roundhouse 1, (784) fill of posthole [785]. Two lengths of possible pin shaft 20mm and 25mm, one adhering to stone; 2-3mm across and with an apparent rectangular section. A further two short fragments 2mm across.

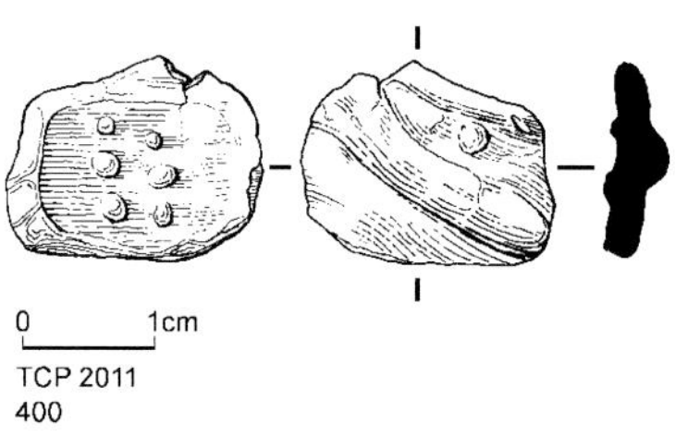

Figure 5.21 Copper-alloy object SF400 from Roundhouse 1.

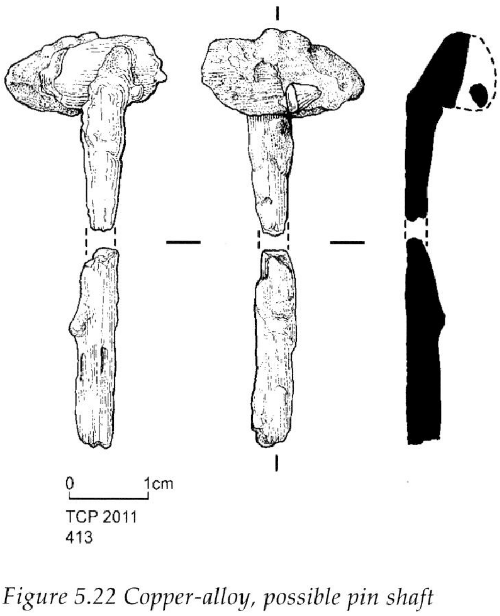

Figure 5.22 Copper-alloy, possible pin shaft SF413 from Roundhouse 1.

Spiral copper-alloy ring, SF403 (Figures 5.23 and 5.24)

Roundhouse 1, (704) fill of [705]. Spiral copper-alloy ring, at least five coils, each measuring approximately 2.5mm across. The ring is approximately 27mm in external diameter and 20mm high. The full size of the object is unknown, as examples can range from a single coil to more than five (Pearce 1983, 377; Drewett 1982, 361), and given that the find had been placed in the top of the posthole it is possible that one or more coils could have broken off.

The spiral ring was found in the top of a posthole. Both its location within a backfilled posthole and its almost certain high value as a personal ornament makes it unlikely to have been casually discarded, and it adds to the number of such items recovered from roundhouses in Cornwall (chapter 11, Table 11.2).

Spiral rings are known from the Taunton phase of metalworking, which is associated with an ornament horizon that includes gold bar-twisted torcs, earrings, pins and rings (Rowlands 1976; Gerloff 2007). The metalworking tradition lies within the Middle Bonze Age, *circa* 1400-1250 cal BC (Needham *et al* 2013, table 5.3). Most spiral rings are stray finds without context or are from metalwork hoards (for example, Portable Antiquities Scheme database finds Northumberland NCL-DA41F5, Norfolk NMS-300286 and North Yorkshire SWYOR-3FF370) which means that that they are not dated by any associations. Although none have previously been recorded in Cornwall, a number have been found in the wider South West peninsula, including one from Kent's Cavern in Devon, and in central southern England (Pearce 1974, fig 3; 1983, 377-8; Rowlands 1982, 362; Smith 1959; Anon 2014).

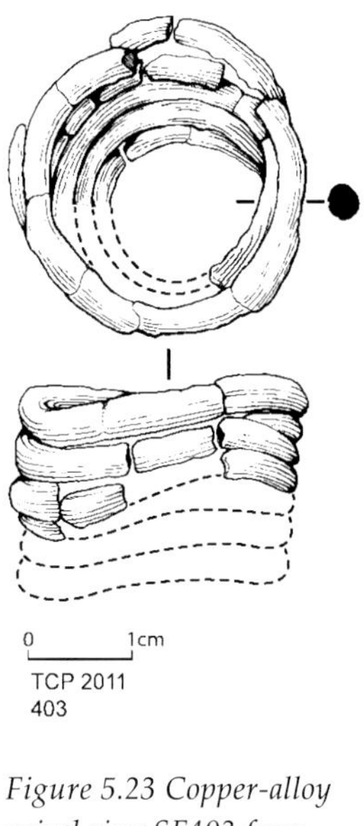

Figure 5.23 Copper-alloy spiral ring SF403 from Roundhouse 1.

Figure 5.24 Photograph of the copper-alloy spiral ring after conservation.

In particular, several spiral rings have been found in Sussex, notably in hoards, including Stump Bottom and Black Rock (Smith 1959; Tapper 2011), and recently eight were found within a hoard located near Lewes (recorded in Portable Antiquities Scheme database as SUSS-C5D042). Stratified finds are rare, although two were recorded from house 1 at Black Patch (Drewett 1982, 362) (Figure 5.25), which has been radiocarbon dated to *circa* 1400-1000 cal BC. These were found on the floor of the house and although the excavator suggested that they may have been hidden in the rafters, more recent interpretation has indicated that they may have been heirlooms and older than the house (Tapper 2011, 139). The radiocarbon determination from posthole [705] at Tremough, 3065±31 BP, 1415-1252 BC (SUERC-47297), therefore provides the closest date for this form of artefact.

Beyond southern England, Rowlands (1976, 97) drew attention to parallels to spiral rings from northern Europe, including from an urnfield at Wesselsheim Kr. Friedberg in western Germany and from a hoard at Villers-sur-Authie, Picardie, in northern France. As scholars such as Sabine Gerloff (2007) have noted, the Taunton phase of metalworking phase in Britain had strong links with northern France; large numbers of palstaves of French design have been found in southern Britain, for example, and other artefacts including several types of sword rapier, palstave and flanged axes are found on either side of the Channel (Muckelroy 1981; Talon 2012, fig 96), and the actual mode of transport has been demonstrated since the Dover boat was securely dated to the Middle Bronze Age (Clark 2004). Recent publication of metalwork from Salcombe, Devon, and Langdon, Bay, Kent (Needham *et al* 2013, 143), shows assemblages of copper-alloy artefacts transported across the Channel probably a little after the main Taunton phase. In addition to metalwork, other contact between France and the south West Peninsula in the later

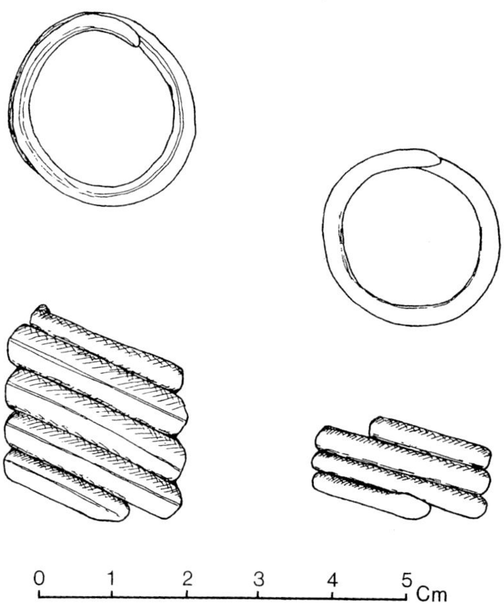

Figure 5.25 Copper-alloy spiral rings from house 1, Black Patch, Sussex (reproduced with permission of the Prehistoric Society).

second millennium cal BC is suggested by similarities between Trevisker ceramics and some assemblages found in Normandy (Marcigny *et al* 2007).

Also of relevance to this discussion is the recently discovered *racloir* mould from a Middle Bronze Age roundhouse at Trevalga, Cornwall, which indicated awareness of Continental forms of metalwork in the local production of a copper-alloy artefact of a type which was better known in France (O'Connor *et al* 2014, 64-5). The spiral ring, therefore, while not demonstrating direct Continental links, was associated with contemporary fashions in personal adornments that were found in southern Britain and northern France. It is likely to have been part of a complex set of contacts and exchanges around the southern coastal zone of Britain and the Continent which became more developed during the Taunton metalworking period (Needham 2009).

Chapter 6

Geochemical analysis of samples from Tremough

Will Marshall and Kevin Solman

Ten soil samples from Roundhouse 1 were analysed for their characteristic metals content using two main techniques, FP-XRF and ICP. The analysis was undertaken to help establish whether metalworking associated with the moulds had taken place within the roundhouse.

Preparation

Prior to analysis all soil samples were milled using a Pulverisette-5 Planetary Ball Mill fitted with zirconium oxide grinding bowls and balls. This was done to achieve a fine homogenous powder for subsequent chemical analysis. Samples were milled at 400rpm for 60 seconds.

Metals, for ICP analysis, were extracted from the soils using an acid mixture (*5.55%* HNO_3 *and 16.75% HCl (v/v)*) and microwave digestion following the method of Hassan, *et al* (2007). A MarsXpress microwave was used for the digestion of samples. This was run at 1600W with a ramp time of 10 minutes to 175°C and a hold of 30 minutes.

Samples for XRF analysis were prepared as powders using standard 32mm sample cups and 6µm polypropylene film.

Methods of analysis

1. FP-XRF: A Niton XL3T 980 X-Ray Fluorescence analyser was used to quantify the metals content of soil samples using fundamental parameters. Samples were placed in a test stand for analysis and Helium purging was engaged to allow the analysis of 'light elements'. The total firing time of x-rays was 180 seconds per sample. Three replicates were run for each sample and the mean result is reported here.
2. ICP-OES: A Varian 725-ES Inductively Coupled Plasma Optical Emission Spectrometer was used to analyse the metals content of the soil extracts. Three replicates were run for each sample and the mean result is reported here.
3. ICP-MS: A Thermo-Scientific X Series 2 Inductively Coupled Plasma Mass Spectrometer was used to analyse the metals content of the soil extracts. Three replicates were run for each sample and the mean result is reported here.

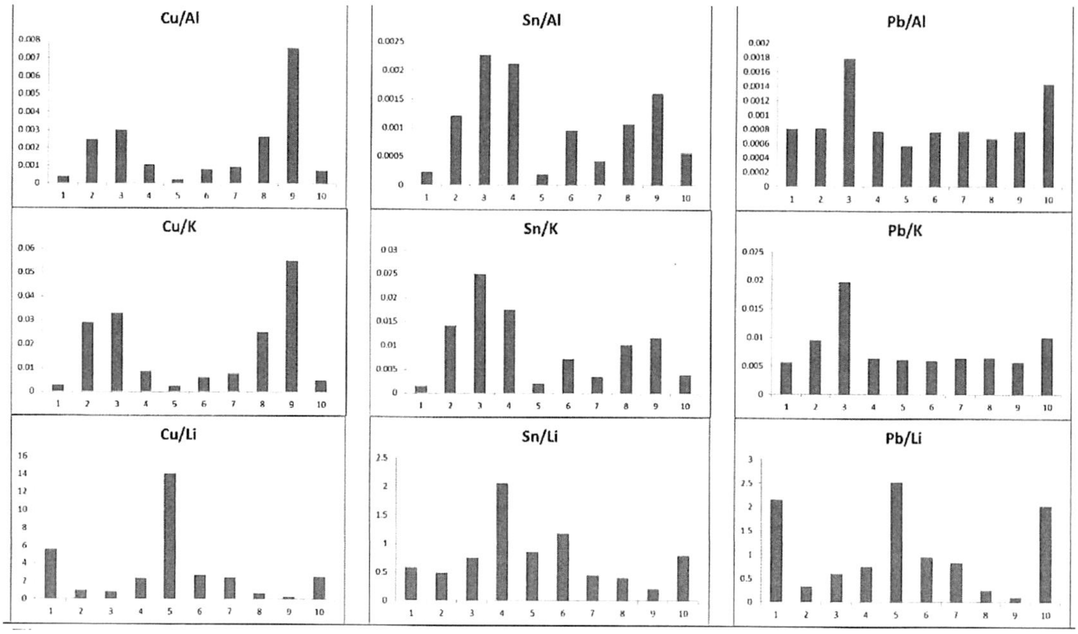

Figure 6.1 ICP-MS data. Copper (Cu), tin (Sn) and lead (Pb) concentrations normalised using aluminium (Al), potassium (K) and lithium (Li). Sample identifications are 1-10 as shown in Table 6.1.

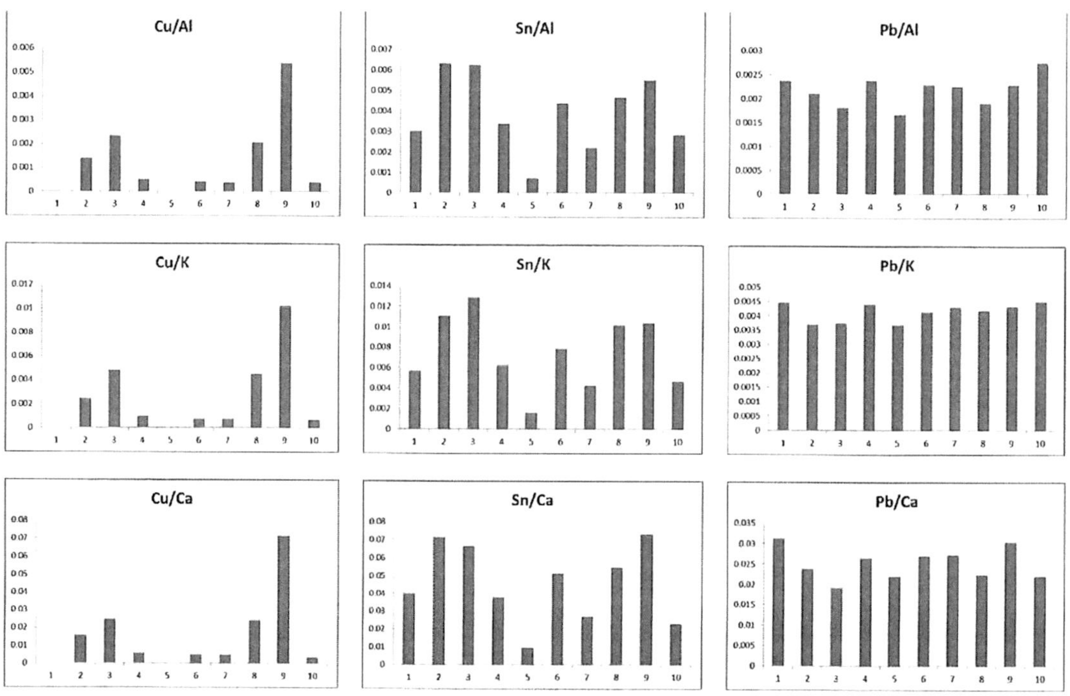

Figure 6.2 XRF data. Copper (Cu), tin (Sn) and lead (Pb) concentrations normalised using aluminium (Al), potassium (K) and calcium (Ca). Sample identifications are 1-10 as shown in Table 6.1.

Results and discussion

The full data set is contained in the associated spreadsheet forming part of the site archive report but selected data are presented in Table 6.1 below. Significant concentrations of copper and other metals were measured in several of the samples, notably 343, 344, 357 and 358, the latter of which is a hearth [748]/[774].

When the metals of interest to ancient metal workers (for example, Cu, Sn and Pb) were normalised against a number of conservative elements a trend emerged (Figure 6.1 and Figure 6.2). Normalising reduces sample matrix issues and grain-size bias (see, for example, Loring 1991; Shotyk *et al* 2001). Essentially it shows relative change between elements and can be used to highlight elemental enrichments as opposed to a simple increase in concentration. Al, K and Li were used for the ICP data. Li was not measured by XRF, and Ca was used instead. This manipulation confirms that a number of the samples were significantly enriched in copper and tin, relative to 000-B.

The values produced by the two analytical methods used here are not directly comparable, and the XRF results must be viewed as 'exploratory' because they are not calibrated to a certified reference material (CRM) specifically for XRF analysis. The XRF was used in 'prospecting mode', which produces a rapid indication of 'presence' and 'trends' in the material under the lens, but not within the body of the sample below. Furthermore, the methods used do not represent a 'total' rock analysis. They provide an indication of what is on the surface of the sediments and clay particles.

The initial results of these analyses are encouraging and would justify further work. Advanced statistics and ordination of these data could confirm and quantify the significance of the apparent relationships and further analysis using a sequential digestion of the samples, combined with isotopic analysis of the lead

		ICP-MS			XRF			
Analysis no	**Context no**	**Sample no**	**Cu**	**Sn**	**Pb**	**Cu**	**Sn**	**Pb**
1	(278) fill of gully	342	16.3	9.6	35.0	0.00	140.20	109.4
2	(295) fill of posthole [296]	343	131.4	64.5	43.5	71.50	325.54	108.7
3	(285) lower fill of posthole [286]	344	167.2	126.4	99.7	137.13	368.02	106.9
4	(284) upper fill of posthole [286]	345	41.5	85.2	31.2	24.16	155.43	108.9
5	(708) fill of posthole [709]	349	18.6	15.9	47.1	0.00	46.17	106.6
6	(273) upper infill layer in quadrant 1	353	39.4	46.6	37.4	20.21	207.93	108.8
7	(289) fill of posthole [290]	354	45.9	20.7	38.6	18.92	108.49	109.0
8	(761) fill of posthole [762]	357	192.0	78.0	49.3	117.86	264.90	109.0
9	(747) fill of hearth [748]/[774]	358	383.1	81.8	39.6	256.97	262.80	109.3
10	Background	000B	33.2	26.4	67.4	16.21	113.15	108.7

Table 6.1: Copper (Cu), tin (Sn) and lead (Pb) concentrations in the Tremough samples, as measured by ICP-MS and XRF. Presented as ppm. Note: XRF values only confirm 'presence' (see text) and are supplied only as 'additional information'.

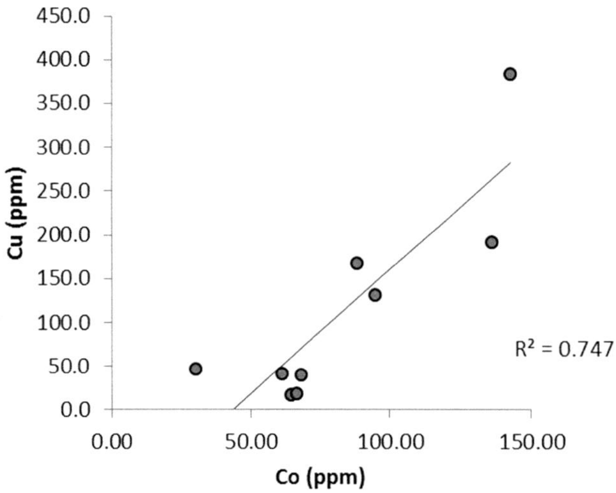

Figure 6.3 Tremough copper (Cu) and cobalt (Co) concentrations (ICP-MS data).

(Marshall *et al* 2009), could be used to try and determine the provenance of the material. Some information could potentially be obtained using the trace elements and 'contaminations' in the copper. For example, cobalt is found in some copper ores and these samples contain significant amounts of this metal. It was noted that the copper and cobalt concentrations have a strong linear relationship (Figure 6.3). A number of Cornish mines apparently produced amounts of cobalt ore as a by-product during the eighteenth and nineteenth centuries; for example, nineteenth-century finds of cobalt associated with copper lodes from Wheal Trugo, near St Columb Major, and Wheal Sparnon, near Redruth (De la Beche 1839, 614-5).

Chapter 7

The lithics

Anna Lawson-Jones

This report covers the lithics recovered from fieldwork in 2009 and 2011. In 2009 two small Early Neolithic pits were investigated and a small but significant number of flints recovered from within them; further unstratified pieces were recovered across the PAC building area. During the 2011 excavations of a Middle Bronze Age roundhouse and a Late Bronze Age enclosure in the Car Park 4 area, a small flint assemblage was recovered. These flints appear to have been residual and not directly associated with the sites where they were found.

Flint from the PAC building, including Early Neolithic pits [102] and [105]

This small assemblage consists of 18 pieces, 11 of which were unstratified, six came from shallow pits [102] and [105] and one from a tree-throw (108) (Table 7.1). The unstratified finds are considered with those from the pits because they were found in close proximity.

Both the pits produced Early Neolithic pottery, charcoal and burnt stone. Tremough has in recent years produced an array of Neolithic finds and features (Gossip and Jones 2007, 28-30), including pottery, worked flint and chert, part of a greenstone axe, a series of radiocarbon dates spanning the Early through to the later Neolithic period, plus a number of different types of features, including pits, structures, hearths, flint scatters and remnant old land surfaces, including at least one flint-knapping floor (Lawson-Jones 2007, 92-5).

Raw material sources

This assemblage consists of a mix of beach pebble flint, nodular flint and a single piece of Portland chert. The pebble flint is almost certainly of local beach origin, consisting most frequently of mottled, predominantly grey coloured flint. Its quality is very variable, frequently with faulting. Flint and chert pebbles can form

Table 7.1 (following two pages): List of all pieces within the PAC building flint assemblage. The above table presents the results of a piece-by-piece analysis. It should be noted that all comments regarding use-related wear are based on macroscopic analysis only.
Key: Prim. refers to 'Primary' (51-100 per cent surviving dorsal cortex); Sec. refers to 'Secondary' (1-50 per cent surviving dorsal cortex) and Tert. refers to 'Tertiary' (0-1 per cent surviving dorsal cortex). 'L' denotes illustrated pieces (Figure 7.1).

Context no.	Pebble, Nodular or Chert	Primary, Secondary, Tertiary	Retouched, Use-wear, Broken	Heated, Fresh, Abraded	Date, Form	Descriptive comments
Unstratified	? Pebble	Tert.	Snapped	-	? Probable engraver	A probably deliberately broken or snapped engraver on a thick, lumpy piece. Hard- and soft-hammered production. Slight, probably deliberate hinge removal intersecting with snapped edge. Uncertain piercing use of pointed end. Grey with white flecks.
Unstratified	? Pebble	Tert.	Use-wear along edge running up to the point	Heat damage	? Piercer	A chunky, fire damaged piece with soft- and hard-hammer removals. The bulbar end was removed during the production of this chunky, comfortable to hold piercer. The break is covered with small heat blisters, suggesting either that it was exposed to the hottest part of the fire, or that as the thinnest part of the tool it was the most susceptible to heat damage. The tip of the point has blistered off. Much of the remaining surface is covered in hairline crazing. Distal end also snapped off to form forefinger hold. Suggestion of lateral use-wear running up towards the broken point. Mottled or flecked grey.
Unstratified	Pebble	Prim.	Tip missing	-	Rejuvenation piece, and? piercer	Rejuvenation flake possibly used as a piercer. Very pale mottled, grey tan with frequent faulting. Platform preparation visible. Distal end has a break, possibly as a result of use as a lightweight piercer. One edge also shows tiny use-wear removals along its length. Fits well in the hand as a piercer.
Unstratified	? Nodular	Sec.	Retouched and utilised. Patchy dorsal gloss and focused abrasion.	-	Neolithic Ovate knife	L4 Slender, ovate, near discoidal knife flake. Small patches of dorsal glossing and short, concave area of use-wear (tiny, abraded removals or damage) on ventral surface. Gentle convex dorsal surface profile with thin flaked removals radiating out from oval, corticated thumb hold area. Cortex is thin and granular. Very dark grey with occasional small, pale flecks.
Unstratified	Pebble	Prim.	-	-	Waste	Tiny bulbous, primary flake – protrusion removed as a precursor to decortication. Dark grey-brown. Waste.
Unstratified	? Pebble	Tert.	Broken with ?slight retouch	-	Miscel. tool	Soft-hammered bulbar end of a flake, showing small breaks around periphery. Some platform preparation. Slight lateral abrasion and tiny removals, possibly the result of use as a small cutting flake. Slightly mottled, fine-grained, very dark grey.
Unstratified	? Pebble	Tert.	-	-	Waste	Small, narrow, slightly granular dark grey piece. Waste.
Unstratified	Pebble	Sec.	-	-	Cutting flake	Well-formed split pebble flake, with cortex running around three-quarters of its edge. Possibly unintentional scuffing of cortex has improved the hold for use as a cutting flake. Thin, sharp, uncorticated edge shows tiny removals indicative of slight, probable slicing wear. Mottled dark grey.
Unstratified	? Pebble	Sec. / Tert.	? Retouch Used	-	Neolithic ?Chopping / cutting tool	L5 A chunky, mottled grey piece, with possible smoothing across much of surface. Sharp, slightly jagged crescent-shaped working edge with bifacial removals caused during cutting / chopping use. May also have been preparatory retouch along this edge. Possibly not a modified core, but from a larger tool? Large flake removal produced a platform, one sharp side of which has been softened – probably via controlled crushing – to facilitate hand held use. A single thin flake has also been removed from the ventral face to create a better grip.

Context no.	Pebble, Nodular or Chert	Primary, Secondary, Tertiary	Retouched, Use-wear, Broken	Heated, Fresh, Abraded	Date, Form	Descriptive comments
Unstratified	?	Tert.	Used Polished	Heated	Neolithic Part of a probable polished axe	L6 Pale, dirty greyish-cream, uniformly heat discoloured flint with remnant polished surface, indicating that it has come from a larger polished piece, probably a broken polished flint axe. Long, slightly curved working edge with variable but bifacial use-related wear and removals. Opposing straight edges, although now short, run parallel to each other. Slight hair line crazing across surface.
Unstratified	? Pebble	Tert.	Platform retouch and broken	-	Waste	Small bulbar end of a broken / snapped bladelet-like piece, with retouched or modified platform preparation on the dorsal surface. Rejuvenation piece? / waste. Mottled, dark grey.
[102] / (100)	Pebble	Prim.	-	-	Waste	Initial flake removed from a pebble with a notably smooth and shiny outer surface, with slight cortical damage probably caused during its removal from pebble. Distal crushing, plus hammer damage on outer cortex, indicate anvil use. Pale, mottled greyish-tan.
[102] / (100)	Portland chert	Tert.	Very fine lateral retouch.	Abraded	- Triangular arrowhead?	L1 Small, thin, soft-hammered flake. Possibly an unclassified triangular arrowhead. Distinctive dark, fine-grained, smoky grey. Tiny removals focused all along one near straight edge and distal end. Opposing edge, although thin and uneven, is slightly abraded, the result of use-wear. Bulbar end is narrower and slightly thicker than the body of the flake, and fresh or unworn, suggestive of hafting.
[102] / (100)	? Pebble	Tert.	Broken	-	- Part of a miscel. tool	L2 Bulbar end of a long thin, triangular, soft-hammered flake. Miscellaneous utilised piece. Widest, distal end missing. Very narrow, tapered bulbar end, the result of careful core preparation. Long thin, delicate dorsal scars. Tiny possible post-depositional removals along one edge, but opposing edge shows slight abrasive wear. Dark grey with small pale mottles.
[105] / (103)	? Pebble	Tert.	-	Fresh	- Waste	Tiny piece of sharp, darkish grey debitage or waste from tool manufacture.
[105] / (103)	Nodular	Sec.	Slight use-wear	Fresh	Neolithic Core tool	A very sharp, near black, multi-platform core. Small flakelets still adhering. Slight cutting use wear focused along one sharp edge, with opposing cortex and flaked removal to facilitate hand-held use. Not a carefully reduced core, but a core tool.
[105] / (103)	?	Tert.	Bifacial retouch and broken	-	Neolithic Broken leaf shaped arrowhead?	L3 The bulbar end of a finely worked, soft-hammered piece – probable leaf-shaped arrowhead (rather than the butt-end of a knife, given its narrow profile). Dorsal surface shows near all-over thinning removals, while ventral face shows removal of larger thinning flakes. Possibly deliberately snapped, rather than broken during use. Mottled grey.
(108) Tree-throw	? Pebble	Tert.	-	Fresh	- Waste	Tiny piece of sharp, darkish grey debitage or waste from tool manufacture.

a substantial portion of any beach, up to 50 per cent according to Rogers (1923, 45), who was an early advocate of the study of Cornish beaches and interested in the sourcing and description of beach-derived material. The use of pebble flint to make tools occurred throughout the prehistoric period in Cornwall and is not in itself a datable trait.

As with the majority of pebble-based flint assemblages, the relatively small size of the material dictates both the size and potentially the form of the final worked pieces. It also resulted in the not unusual use of anvils. Knight (1991, 57-80) has looked at the use of anvils during preliminary reduction of pebbles and found it to be a particularly good way of using smaller-sized flint. At least one piece in this assemblage was clearly produced using an anvil (Table 7.1, context (100)), which left tell-tale damage in the form of a crushed distal flake removal.

There are no primary sources of nodular flint in Cornwall, although nodular flint does occur periodically on beaches in western Cornwall, washed up from submerged chalk deposits. As a result, the appearance of nodular flint in an inland location is of significance in Cornwall, since it may indicate introduction to the site from significantly further east (Healy 1985, 18-20; 1989, 189; Saville 1981, 101-152). Beer Head on the south-east Devon coast is the best known and nearest *in situ* mainland (quarried) source of nodular flint (Tingle 1998), although recent work carried out by Newberry (2002, 1-36) highlights other good but much smaller Devon deposits. The movement of flint (including Portland chert), or other material such as greenstone gradually became a more frequent component within lithic assemblages. Whether the movement of nodular flint into Cornwall through trade or exchange was the direct result of increasing sedentism (Edmonds 1987, 155-79) or not is uncertain. But, it is clear that the desire (if not the need) to obtain supplies from specific sources was important.

Comments by context

Tree-throw feature (108) produced a single fresh-looking piece of probable pebble debitage or tool manufacture waste. Its inclusion within this context should almost certainly be seen as residual.

Shallow bowl-shaped pit [102]/(100) produced three pieces of worked flint – a piece of pebble waste (not modified or used), a finely-worked triangular arrowhead **L1** in Portland chert from Dorset (Figure 7.1), and part of a broken, but used miscellaneous tool **L2**, plus several sherds of Neolithic pottery; all were included within a dark reddish-brown, stony, charcoal-rich soil.

The basal fill (103) of pit [105] produced three pieces of flint – a tiny, sharp piece of waste, a very sharp, very fresh, very dark multi-platform core tool, and the butt end of a broken but beautifully worked probable leaf-shaped arrowhead **L3** – plus a sherd of Neolithic pottery, contained within a dark black or grey charcoal-rich soil with burnt stone.

Despite slight differences in pit shape and uniformity, and marked differences in the quantity of pottery found in each, the two pits share certain similarities. The main one (from the point of view of this report) is the presence of unburnt flint within an otherwise burnt fill containing charcoal and a notable quantity of heat-fractured and discoloured granite, killas and quartz. This would suggest that the flint was intentionally added to, or mixed with the main fill after burning, but prior to its inclusion within the pits: the pit fill appears to have been 'prepared' prior to deposition. Each pit contained a very small but potentially orchestrated flint assemblage, which included both locally collected and potentially imported material. Both contained a broken, possibly deliberately snapped piece of worked flint and both contained an arrowhead (or part of), including the butt end of a well-made, classic leaf-shaped arrowhead of Early to Middle Neolithic date (Green 1984, 32).

The frequent inclusion of lithic artefacts within Neolithic pits of this character has been noted elsewhere (for example, Thomas 1991, 60), while a high proportion of tools to waste in similarly orchestrated Neolithic pit fills has been recorded by Cleal (1984, 148). The Tremough pits thus slot into a recognised category of pit types found across much of the country during the Neolithic period. Within the lithic material, unbroken, broken and finely-worked pieces have been noted, again a recognised trait, as has the inclusion of arrowheads (among other forms).

It is possible that the flint, pottery and burnt material recorded in pits [102] and [105] represent the residue or remains left over from a short-term event. Whether their inclusion within a specific pit merely represent 'tidying-up' or the ritualised 'closure' of a site is open to interpretation.

The remaining 11 pieces of the assemblage were unstratified. Like the flint from the pits some of this material was finely worked and diagnostically Early to Middle Neolithic in date; for example, the cutting flake, the ovate knife **L4** and the small, polished flint axe fragment **L6**. The remaining assemblage is similarly characteristic of the Neolithic and includes an engraver, a piercer, a possible piercer on a rejuvenation piece, a miscellaneous tool, a small (hand-held) chopper / cutting tool **L5** and three pieces of waste. The skill displayed in the production of some of these pieces indicates complete control over the raw material, but also a level of workmanship and expenditure of time that would seem superfluous from a solely utilitarian point of view, with particular reference to the polished axe fragment.

Axes, associated with the cutting down of trees / land clearance and the working of wood into a range of objects, have been found in association with many contexts, including as stray finds, deliberate deposits in rivers and bogs, associated with funerary activity and in structured pit deposits. They can be made from flint, Cornish greenstone or other hard stone, and can be found broken or battered through use, complete and pristine, re-worked or re-sharpened, polished, partially polished or unpolished. They are a relatively large and distinctive tool type, which were almost invariably hafted for use. Axes have undergone study in terms of their raw material source or 'Group' (Clough and Cummins 1979; and see Quinnell (2007, 80-81) regarding the Group 1 greenstone axe found at Tremough in 2000), and in terms of typology or classification based on size, shape and profile. The profile (cross-section) of the polished flint axe fragment listed above (Table 7.1) shows it as belonging to the thin-butted (Type B) form (Butler 2005, 144). Polished (or ground) flint axes when damaged or rendered blunt though use, were frequently re-sharpened by the removal of controlled flakes from along the

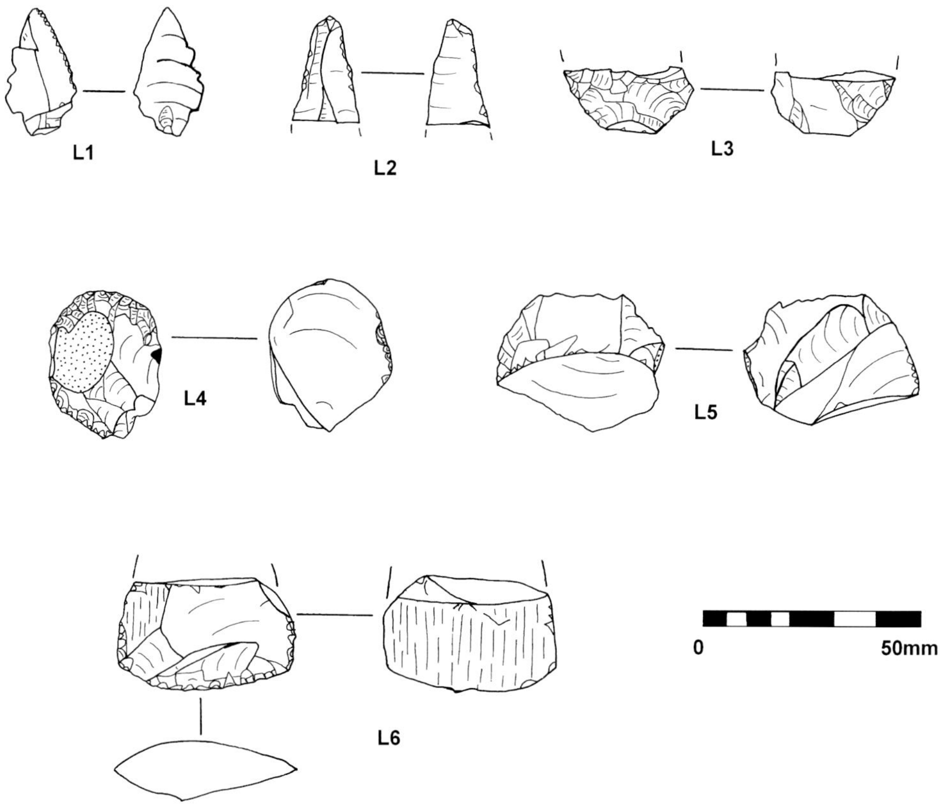

Figure 7.1 Selected flints from the PAC pits [102] and [105] (L1-6).

working edge, followed by retouch to form a new cutting edge, as can be seen on the illustration of **L6** (Figure 7.1). The main break may or may not be accidental and as a result of use. Like the broken leaf-shaped arrowhead, the other half was not found during the excavation. Unlike the arrowhead, the axe fragment was not located within a specific pit deposit, but rather within a localised, associated scatter of material found within the immediate vicinity of the pits.

Lithics from Roundhouses 1 and 2 and Enclosure 1

This small assemblage of 18 flint and cherty flint pieces consists of four retouched tools, five pebbles, eight cortical flakes and one secondary waste flake recovered during the excavations of a Middle Bronze Age roundhouse and the Late Bronze Age Enclosure 1 in 2011.

Raw material sources

All corticated pieces are made on pebble flint, probably derived from the local estuarine beach (Rodgers 1923, 45-50). There is nothing to suggest that the non-corticated pieces have a different source, or that any imported nodular material is represented. Some reference is made to strikingly coloured flint. It is likely that the two scrapers at least were made on deliberately selected, colourful flint, possibly enhanced by the use of heat (*cf* Lee 2001, 39-44; Pannett 2011, 235-47).

Comments by type

Pebbles

The five pebbles recovered are varied. All came from deposits associated with the roundhouses. The largest pebble, 60mm long, has been heavily burnt, heat-reddened and fractured. It came from gully fill (278). The two complete (and smallest pebbles - 28mm and 24mm maximum dimension) are both notably smooth and distinctively coloured: the larger piece, from layer (280), is near spherical and deep orange; the smaller unstratified bean-shaped piece has a green, swirling, marbled appearance. It is possible that both of these pieces were used as tokens or game counters. Other non-flint pebbles found on site and noted in the archive may also have fallen into this category.

Of the two remaining pebbles, one is almost complete except for a very small abrasion at one end, suggestive of percussive damage. It came from gully fill (278) and is an oval, very smooth, pale, speckled and marbled piece 40mm long. The final very smooth, oval piece, from infill deposit (273) over Roundhouse 1, is a striking pale brownish-orange. It has a flake removed from the more tapered end. The scar is suggestive of testing for use as a core, despite the small size of the original pebble. However, since both these final pieces are notably smooth and distinctive in appearance, it is possible that they too were counters (perhaps playing pieces) or otherwise utilised, perhaps, for example, in the polishing or smoothing of wood or leather.

Cortical flakes

The nine cortical flakes recovered (displaying a near 100 per cent corticated dorsal surface) attest to on-site testing and knapping of flint (Butler 2005, 20). All were found in or close to the Middle Bronze Age roundhouses. Four are notably flat and thin (less than 9mm thick), composed of a complete side of a pebble with the naturally rounded edges of the original pebble extending all around the flake. At least four of the flakes have been removed from notably smooth flint pebbles, one of which, from posthole [725] within Roundhouse 1, appears to have been polished, with dorsal damage at both ends; this suggests use rather than pre-knapping surface damage. The largest and thickest flake is more typical of a Bronze Age split or tested pebble. It measures 50mm by 31mm by 11mm and was found in gully fill (278), together with two other pieces, one of which is a narrow chunky secondary waste flake.

Five of the pieces came from a single context (788) in small stakehole or shallow cut [789], located to the south west of Roundhouse 1. Of these, one of the smoothest and palest flat cortical flakes has been snapped in half lengthways (34mm long by 13mm wide by 5mm thick). There is no evidence for it having been snapped for use as a tool (Anderson-Whymark 2011, 16-21), despite the fact that it was almost certainly deliberately and not accidentally snapped. Several of the most carefully made and most colourful, smooth cortical flakes could have made good game pieces. Their fresh looking edges with a complete lack of wear and their very smooth colourful surfaces all suggest non-utilitarian use, but rather imply deliberate pebble selection, splitting and snapping.

The majority of the cortical flakes have been made with notable care. There is little evidence for the less controlled splitting of pebbles using hard hammers, followed by selective use only of suitable pieces which is normally seen in Middle and Late Bronze Age pebble knapping assemblages (Butler 2005, 179). The combined use of an anvil – indicated by distal flaking or crushing (Knight 1991, 57-80) - with a soft (wood or bone?) hammer – recorded as near non-existent bulbs of percussion and minimal rippling (Andrefsky 1998, 116) - suggest a Late Neolithic or Early to Middle Bronze Age date.

Only four pieces show specific retouch or modification through use: a large thumbnail-like scraper (**L8**), an unstratified find near to the roundhouses; a side- and end-scraper (**L7**), found within upper fill (165) in the ditch [160] of Late Bronze Age Enclosure 1; a probable broken point found in the fill (117) of recut [263] in the terminal of ditch [160]; and a small, thin, knife-like flake from infill deposit (275) in Roundhouse 1.

Scraper L8

The large, thumbnail-like scraper was made on a distinctive, fault-free and uniformly coloured near-black flint (Figure 7.2, **L8**). It has a diameter of 26mm, fitting well within Butler's (2005, 168) thumbnail size-ratio, and retains some original cortex. It has a typical central dorsal scar depression, allowing for comfortable hand-held use between the thumb and forefinger; the presence of cortex will have facilitated hand-held use by reducing thumb slippage. Semi-invasive, approximately 45-degree retouch extends around two-thirds of the circumference. There is no clear evidence for use on the ventral underside or of abrasive wear overlying the retouched dorsal edges. If it was used, it is likely that it only saw light, short-term use, perhaps during a single event. Large thumbnail scrapers are associated with the Late Neolithic to Early Bronze Age period, with many of the finest examples belonging to Beaker-associated activity (Edmonds 1995, 140). Scrapers of all types are the most common tool form found in Late Neolithic and Early Bronze Age contexts.

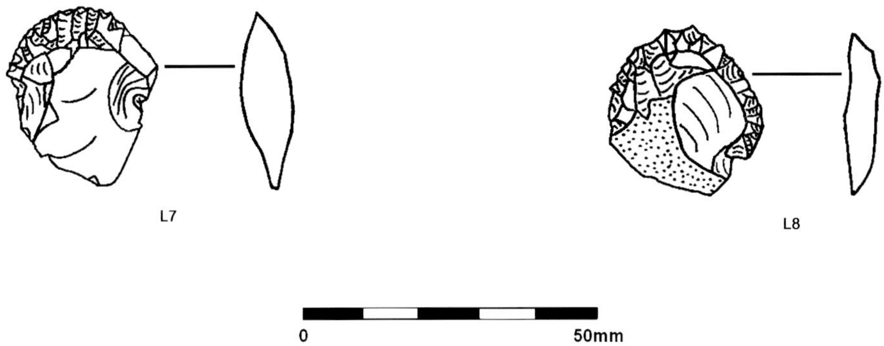

Figure 7.2 Flints from the 2011 excavations: L7 a side- and end-scraper and L8, a thumbnail-like scraper.

Scraper L7

This side- and end-scraper from fill (165) of the Enclosure 1 ditch is made on a notable honey – grey-brown coloured flint and measures 25mm by 26mm across (Figure 7.2, **L7**). Retouch extends half way around the flint on the thickest edge. The retouch terminates at each side with opposing notches, while the non-retouched side tapers to an angle and thins. The opposing notches do appear to show some associated edge softening and suggest that this tool was hafted or bound in some way for use. The piece does not retain any cortex and has only seen minimal use, which is visible as tiny ventral removals extending along the working edge only. Like the thumbnail scraper **L8**, this piece typifies Late Neolithic to Early Bronze Age scraper forms. It should be noted that the two are remarkably similar in size.

Knife

The small knife-like flake (24mm by 20mm by 4mm) from infill deposit (275) is, in contrast to the scrapers, a less heavily worked tool, more suggestive of an opportunistic or spontaneously made piece. It shows delicate shallow retouch along one short, thin, convex working edge, but is small and fiddly for hand-held use. The partly corticated opposing edge has a couple of crushed-looking removals indicative of backing, plus a single notched ventral removal. This damage and scarring, although limited suggests hafting damage associated with it being slotted into a wood or bone handle, or perhaps leather binding (*cf* experimental work carried out by Rots and Vermeersch 2004, 156-168). If so, its small size would suggest optimal use as part of a composite knife composed of a number of mounted but small retouched pieces to form a longer cutting edge. Use of this tool appears to have been minimal given the lack of macroscopically visible wear.

Point

Points are also a frequent Late Neolithic – Bronze Age tool type. The use of softened hinged edges and abrupt retouch made the piece from this assemblage a small but comfortable to hold tool which probably supported a short but sturdy point suitable for many tasks, including wood and leather working. Unlike the two scrapers, which have a more considered and deliberate or planned design and appearance, typical of a specific function, occasion or association, this piece appears strongly utilitarian and domestic in character. Unfortunately the point has been largely lost, probably through use rather than post-depositional breakage. Only the base of it remains, although the likely angle or width of the point can be discerned.

Discussion

To summarise, this assemblage is predominantly Bronze Age in date, with the potential for a residual Late Neolithic element. Although small, the assemblage adds to an already known focus of lithic activity found around the Tremough campus (Lawson-Jones 2007, 88-96; Gossip and Jones 2009-10, 6-7). The majority of the assemblage is of Early to Middle Bronze Age date in character with three of the 18 pieces being found in or around the ditch of the Late Bronze Age Enclosure 1, and the remaining 15 pieces within or close to two Middle Bronze Age structures, Roundhouse 1 and Roundhouse 2. No significant difference in date between the two assemblages has been identified, suggesting that those pieces from the enclosure ditch are residual and perhaps contemporary or associated with the use and occupation of the roundhouses. None of the flints have come from an obviously deliberately created deposit, despite many of them having broad associations with pottery. The only possible exceptions to this are the five cortical flakes from feature [789]/(788), although these probably reflect a single period of activity, rather than a deliberately constructed deposit.

Chapter 8

The charred plant remains

Julie Jones

Environmental sampling at Tremough was associated with four phases of activity. These comprised two Early Neolithic pits, Structure I, a small post-built construction of earlier Bronze Age date, the Middle Bronze Age Roundhouse 1, and the Late Bronze Age Enclosure 1, the latter associated with numerous pits and postholes.

Bulk soil samples were taken from a range of features including pits, postholes, gullies and ditch fills. At the PAC site samples were recovered from two Early Neolithic features, pit [102] and pit [105]. Twelve samples were collected from deposits at the AIR building and 55 from Roundhouse 1 and Enclosure 1 in Car Park 4. Sample size varied between 10 and 40 litres, with many of the posthole and hearth features 100 per cent sampled. The residues were collected on a 500-micron mesh and floats on a 250-micron mesh.

The samples were examined under illuminated low-powered magnification with a stereo-binocular microscope with magnifications between x10 and x45. The charred cereal remains were identified with reference to Jacomet (2006), with seeds and fruits identified with the aid of the author's reference collection and consultation with Cappers *et al* (2006) and Bertsch (1941). As there was no assessment stage all of the samples were carefully examined and two tables produced. Table 8.1 contains the results from the analysis of the two Neolithic pits and Table 8.2 (see end of chapter) shows the results from all 67 samples taken from the 2011 excavations, including the 35 samples which included charred plant remains.

All remains refer to fruits and seeds unless otherwise stated and plant nomenclature and habitat information follows Stace (1991). Many of the floats, especially those from posthole fills, were very small, despite some having an initial sample size of over 20 litres. Surprisingly, however, it was often these small floats which produced most charred weeds and smaller chaff items; the larger floats were often composed almost entirely of charcoal fragments.

Charred plant remains

Preservation of all plant material was by charring. Many of the cereal remains in particular were in a poor condition, with a fine coating of sediment on many of the grain and weed seeds, and it is likely that the acidic clay soils at Tremough have affected preservation; however, many grains showed characteristic pitting reflecting exposure to high temperatures during processing.

Some of the weed taxa were the same species as modern contaminants in the sample floats, particularly *Persicaria maculosa* (redshank), although it was very clear which were the modern intrusions. This was also commented on by Carruthers (2007), who examined samples from earlier excavations at Tremough; she also found an abundance of *Persicaria* and discussed the problems of shallow profiles and features on archaeological sites with the possibility of modern weed seeds moving through the soil profile.

Results

Early Neolithic pits

The plant macrofossils from two features, pit [102], fill (100), and pit [105], fill (103), were examined (Table 8.1). Samples of approximately 10 litres from each of the pits also produced sherds of Early Neolithic pottery, flint and hazelnut shell fragments.

The sample floats were primarily charcoal fragments, with pit [105] dominated by hazel charcoal, while pit [102] produced a more mixed assemblage of oak, hazel and hawthorn group (chapter 9). The only macrofossils preserved were charred hazelnut (*Corylus avellana*) fragments, with 1 fragment from [102] and 17 from [105]. Previous excavations of Early Neolithic pits at Tremough produced very little in the way of charred plant remains; however, a Late Neolithic pit group was dominated by hazelnut fragments (Carruthers 2007, 100-102).

Fragmented remains of hazelnut frequently occur in early prehistoric features, where evidence for arable agriculture is scarce. At Tremough these are likely to be linked to hazel wood gathered as firewood, as well as collection for food.

Structure 1 (Earlier Bronze Age)

Nine postholes were sampled from the perimeter of Structure 1. Radiocarbon dating from posthole [49] placed this feature in the earlier Bronze Age (chapter 10). Only one of the postholes, [19], included plant remains with just a single hulled wheat (*Triticum* sp.) grain and other poorly preserved cereal grain with two bulbils of onion couch (*Arrhenatherum elatius*).

Pit [23] was located close to the structure. As well as occasional charcoal there were seven hulled wheat grains. The pit was not radiocarbon dated but Bronze Age pottery was recovered from it.

Context	Feature (No)	Float size (ml)	Sample composition	Charcoal >2mm	Charred plant remains
(100)	Pit [102]	21	70% charcoal;30% mineral, modern roots	80	*Corylus avellana* 1 frag (Hazelnut)
(103)	Pit [105]	800	100% charcoal	2000+	*Corylus avellana* 17 frags (Hazelnut)

Table 8.1: Taxonomic composition of plant macrofossils from Early Neolithic pits [102] and [105].

Pit [37] (Romano-British)

Five metres to the west of Structure 1 was a shallow concave pit [37]. As its relationship with Structure 1 was uncertain radiocarbon dating was undertaken on oat (*Avena*) grains (253-419 cal AD) and wild radish (*Raphanus raphanistrum* ssp. *Raphanistrum*) capsules (254-425 cal AD), showing that the pit was of Romano-British date and considerably post-dated Structure 1.

The 20-litre sample from its fill (106) produced a rich charred cereal assemblage with 1450 grains. Many of these were hulled wheat grains, including smaller tail grains and many more fragmented but still recognisably wheat grains, although there was no chaff to further these identifications. Barley grains were much less common, with six of the more angular forms identified as hulled barley. There were several tiny fragments of barley rachis internode base, plus sections of rachis with several internode bases. Oat (*Avena* sp.) grains were also abundant, including three grains still enclosed in their floret, with two well-preserved floret bases showing the characteristic horseshoe-shaped base of wild oat (*Avena fatua*). Many other poorly preserved unidentified grains are thought likely to be mostly wheat or barley.

The weed assemblage was dominated by redshank, pale persicaria (*Persicaria lapathifolia*) and dock (*Rumex*). These were all also present as modern contaminants in the sample float, although the fossil seeds were easily distinguishable as they were completely charred. These are weeds typically associated with arable habitats along with black-bindweed (*Fallopia convolvulus*), scentless mayweed (*Tripleurospermum inodorum*) and nipplewort (*Lapsana communis*). There were also four fragments of hazelnut shell (*Corylus avellana*) and a single hawthorn (*Crataegus monogyna*) fruit. These may reflect collection of wood for fuel as both *Corylus* and Maloidae (Rose family) charcoal were identified from this sample.

Roundhouse 1 (Middle Bronze Age)

Few plant remains were recovered from the fill of the roundhouse hollow in quadrant 1. Samples from two postholes, [705] and [701], in the post-ring inside the roundhouse hollow similarly contained little evidence, producing only a single barley grain and nipplewort (*Lapsana communis*) achene.

Located Fill (161) of posthole [162], located centrally within the roundhouse included, wheat and barley grain, two charred Celtic beans (*Vicia faba*) and a small weed assemblage.

A long gully [292] that cut across several quadrants of the roundhouse was filled with a homogenous dark brown clayey silt (291) which contained a small arable weed assemblage. However, this feature is undated and post-dates the roundhouse.

Enclosure 1: ditch and internal features (Late Bronze Age)

Enclosure ditch [160/[170]

The basal fill (267)/(798) of a curvilinear enclosure ditch was sampled in several sections. The basal fill included charcoal fragments with occasional hulled wheat grain, a single spelt (*Triticum spelta*) glume base and poorly preserved spikelet fork, with a single barley grain and two heath grass (*Danthonia decumbens*) caryopses.

Pit / Posthole Group 1

Plant remains from two postholes [158] and [144] were limited to small weed seeds, including fat-hen (*Chenopodium album*), pale persicaria, ribwort plantain (*Plantago lanceolata)* and heath-grass. Close to these features were pits [164] and [249], which contained burnt stones and frequent charcoal with a single barley grain, hulled wheat glume base and spikelet fork, oak (*Quercus*) bud and a few weeds.

Four nearby features, [132], [154], [177] and [193], also incorporated charred remains. Some like posthole [154] contained burnt stone, with posthole [132] in particular filled with a dark and charcoal-rich deposit (131). Traces of charred cereals were limited to a hulled wheat glume base and spikelet fork, with an onion couch bulbil from posthole [177]. Barley and wheat / barley grains, plus five wheat glume bases were among hazel and oak charcoal in pit [193].

Pit Alignment 2

Pits [202], [126] and [123] formed part of an alignment of pits and postholes in the central area of the enclosure. These were fairly shallow, mostly less than 0.3m deep, with the fills mostly single deposits, often charcoal-rich with burnt stones. Charred cereal remains were again mostly limited to occasional wheat grains and glume bases, an oat/grass (*Avena/Poaceae*) grain and occasional weeds, with a charred hazelnut fragment and oak bud. Two further pits [134] and [128] to the north of this alignment again contained charcoal and burnt granite stones. The upper fill (133) of pit [134] had only a few wheat grains, chaff and weed seeds, but fill (127) of pit [128] incorporated a slightly larger assemblage including 22 hulled wheat grains and 21 smaller tail grains.

Structure 205

Structure (205), built within a shallow circular, concave hollow [116], was composed of a pile of fire-cracked stones, on top of which lay a large flat sub-rectangular stone. The core (115)/(103) of the structure was dated to the Late Bronze Age (chapter 10) and included single examples of wheat and barley grains, a hazelnut fragment and a small arable weed assemblage. Context (271) described as a 'greasy' deposit below (205) had a single-hulled wheat grain and onion couch bulbil.

Post Structure 4

To the south of the pit alignment was a rectangular post structure 4.5m long and 3.5m wide. Five of these postholes, which all contained single fills with charcoal flecks, were also found to contain charred plant material. Two of the three postholes on the north-west long axis, [181] and [187], contained single examples of barley and wheat grain, with a small arable weed assemblage, while posthole [179], on the south-east corner of the structure, had no grain but several wheat glume bases and a spikelet fork with a similar weed assemblage. Further small assemblages were found in postholes [175] and [198]/[121].

Inside the structure was a shallow elongated pit [167] with a fill (166) of burnt granite stones with a few hulled wheat grains and chaff, a single oat awn and weed seeds.

Pit [124]

The single fill (112) of pit [124], which lay to the south west of the southern rectangular structure, again included only single examples of a wheat glume base and spikelet fork with a ribwort plantain and grass caryopsis amongst a matrix of charcoal, burnt bone fragments and heat-affected granite stones. *Corylus* charcoal provided a Late Bronze Age determination (chapter 10).

Crop plants and weed assemblages

Triticum sp (wheat)

In terms of grain recovered from the Bronze Age features, the occurrence of wheat was fairly limited, with mostly fewer than ten items in any one feature and the grains appeared more fragmented than for other types. The better preserved grains were a hulled variety and are likely to be either emmer (*Triticum dicoccum*) or spelt (*Triticum spelta*). Campbell and Straker (2003, 15) note that emmer wheat was probably the most frequently grown cereal from the Neolithic and Early Bronze Age periods, although distinction between these two varieties is difficult, largely because their morphology is affected by the charring process but also due to an overlap in their forms. Wheat chaff, necessary to confirm identification of emmer from spelt was very limited here. In most cases only the very basal areas of the glumes or spikelet forks were preserved, none displaying any of the diagnostic features needed. Only one glume base was well enough preserved to identify as spelt wheat; this came from the Late Bronze Age curvilinear ditch [160]/[170]. Wheat grains were more abundant in the Romano-British hearth, with over 400 of the better preserved grains of the hulled variety, although no chaff was preserved.

Hordeum sp. (Barley)

As with wheat, barley grain was only present in very low concentrations. The grain was generally poorly preserved with the grain surface lost, making it impossible to determine whether the naked or hulled form was present; however, the more angular shape of the better preserved examples suggests that hulled barley was present.

Avena sp. (Oats)

Many of the better preserved grains were identified as oat, but where there was significant fragmentation and / or distortion, especially where the surfaces were eroded these were classified as *Avena* / Poaceae (oat / grass). A large proportion of the grain was much less well preserved with degrees of fragmentation and / or pitting and these have been classified as *Avena* / Poaceae (oat / grass).

In contrast to wheat and barley, oat has its spikelets in panicles with three grains in each spikelet enclosed in a floret. Oat grains are slender with the widest point in the middle. In general terms, in cultivated oats (*Avena sativa*) the first grains are large, with the second grains smaller, while wild oat (*Avena fatua*) is similar, if possibly more slender (Jacomet 2006). There are only occasional traces of oat from the Middle Bronze Age features, although they become more frequent in the Romano-British hearth. Measurements were made of 135 of the better preserved grains from here. These showed little erosion of the grain surface or 'puffing' from charring. The 121 kernels varied in length between 5 and 6mm, and 14 kernels between 3.5 and 4mm with a fairly consistent width of 1.5-2mm, this smaller size perhaps more indicative of wild oat.

Cultivated oats are difficult to distinguish from other non-crop grass species unless the diagnostic features of the floret base are preserved. Wild oats are aggressive weeds so it is always possible that these are present as crop contaminants, together with other weed species. The lemma bases of wild oats have a horseshoe-shaped 'sucker mouth' scar where the base has disarticulated from the rachis (Moffett 1988), but only two floret bases of wild oats were present from hearth [37], further suggesting these occurred as field weeds.

Oats, wild or cultivated are occasionally present in small numbers in Middle Bronze Age and later samples, although they are generally only thought to become common on sites from the later Iron Age onwards although rarely present in quantity until the Roman period. However, there are now several records from Cornwall including earlier investigations at Tremough (Carruthers 2007), Trethellan (Straker 1991) and features associated with a Middle to Late Bronze Age post-ring monument found on the Maudlin to Liskeard pipeline (J Jones 1999; Cole 1999). If some of these oats were cultivated they could have been grown as fodder for horses or cattle but may also have been important for human nutrition in the form of porridge and gruel.

Vicia faba (Celtic Bean)

One cotyledon of Celtic Bean was recovered from a Middle Bronze Age posthole in Roundhouse 1. Remains of beans and peas are less likely to survive as they don't require exposure to heat prior to cooking, although a cache of charred beans was found in a Middle Bronze Age roundhouse at Trevilson (J Jones 2004). These are likely to have been grown as an additional crop to provide a useful source of protein and carbohydrate to add to soups and stews.

Wild plants

There is limited evidence for hedgerow plants which may have been collected as fuel or as food plants. These include hazel, hawthorn, bramble (*Rubus* sect *Glandulosus*) and elder (*Sambucus nigra*). However, the presence of several charred oak (*Quercus*) buds raises the possibility that these taxa were collected as fuel. Hazel and oak charcoal were dominant in many features examined, reflecting the oak-hazel woodland of the local landscape.

Arable weeds

A small suite of weed seeds occurs throughout all phases of activity at Tremough, suggesting little change in practises or land use. The most commonly occurring are redshank, pale persicaria and docks. These are among a small and rather unspecialised weed flora that seems to occur from the Bronze Age (Greig 1991) and it is generally assumed that these would have been growing with the crops and formed part of crop-processing residues.

Also included are black bindweed (*Fallopia convolvulus*) and cleavers (*Galium aparine*). Both have a twining nature and may have used cereal stems as support, indicating that the straw was gathered with the crop, which may have been uprooted or cut near the base rather than by harvesting of individual ears by plucking. Black bindweed, scentless mayweed and wild radish are annual weeds of autumn-sown crops such as wheat that germinate in the autumn and grow rapidly with the crop and are then harvested with the cereals.

Grassland taxa

Through the Middle and later Bronze Age phases there is also a constant, although small, presence of several grassland taxa. These include ribwort plantain (*Plantago lanceolata*), grasses (Poaceae) and selfheal (*Prunella vulgaris*). These may have been growing as arable weeds in recently ploughed fields or plots or as invaders from adjacent grassland.

Many of the samples also include caryopses of heath-grass (*Danthonia decumbens*) and tubers from onion couch (*Arrhenatherum elatius*), which have been variously interpreted as originating from turves burnt as fuel on hearths or possibly used in the construction of kilns (Hall 2003) and have often been recorded on Bronze Age sites (Greig 1991, 304).

There are two forms of onion couch, one of which produces swollen basal internodes (tubers). This is *Arrhenatherum elatius* var. *bulbosum* that can be a pernicious weed of arable land spread by breaking up of tubers by ploughing. In non-arable situations such as rough grassland far fewer tubers are produced (Robinson 1988). In this situation onion couch can form part of a community of coarse-leaved tussock grasses with other grasses and dicotyledons including those taxa recovered here - *Plantago lanceolata, Prunella vulgaris* and several *Rumex* species (Rodwell 1998, 32) – in a habitat of ungrazed grassland or neglected agricultural land. The presence of some grassland taxa such as these may be a result of ploughing-up grassland followed by cultivation, as taxa such as ribwort plantain can survive in arable conditions, but it is difficult to be sure from such small assemblages as those from Tremough.

Discussion

The Early Neolithic pits at the PAC building site produced only a few fragments of charred hazelnut shell and this is consistent with other Neolithic features recorded at Tremough in the past.

Likewise, the earlier Bronze Age post-built Structure 1 produced very little material: only one of the postholes from the perimeter of the circular structure and a shallow pit from the interior produced evidence of wheat grain.

The evidence from the Middle Bronze Age Roundhouse 1 was recovered from postholes situated within the perimeter roundhouse hollow, postholes within the interior and a later gully. Most of the features examined contained characteristically poor assemblages with individual occurrences of charred grain and weed seeds, although one of the posthole fills (761) included several more hulled wheat and barley grains and two charred Celtic beans. Other evidence from here including copper-alloy objects and stone moulds suggest that this was an area for metal-working activities, so the scarcity of plant remains is perhaps not surprising.

There is a similar pattern from the later Bronze Age features associated with Enclosure 1. Many of these features contained large quantities of granite stone, many heat-cracked from burning (chapter 2), within charcoal-rich fills, although charred grain and chaff occurred mostly as individual records or with fewer than five specimens, with small weed assemblages.

Within this enclosure some features may have been used for specific activities (chapter 11), although there were no certain domestic structures. In the centre of the enclosure the fill of pit [128] contained a slightly larger assemblage, including 22 hulled wheat grains plus 21 smaller tail grains; other pits within this central area included mostly low concentrations of cereal waste. In his discussion of traditional communities of wet regions of modern Turkey, Hillman (1981; 1984) relates that cereals were stored as spikelets. Small quantities would have been taken and processed as required on a daily basis within the settlement, possibly around a hearth, with any waste products discarded onto the fire. In many of the Tremough samples, weed seeds outnumber both grain and chaff remains, with several fills containing only seeds, both large and small, a characteristic that could be suggestive of the storage of crops as uncleaned spikelets. Clapham and Stevens (1999) have interpreted this type of assemblage as being indicative of low levels of social organisation.

The stone structure (205), may represent carefully piled up material derived from a burnt mound, with an adjacent pit [119] used as a cooking pit. The function of burnt mounds remains uncertain although the presence of shattered rock fragments are thought to be the remains of stones heated in fires to heat water. It has been suggested that they were used for dyeing, leather treatment, metalworking or more usually for cooking, and especially for cooking joints of meat (chapter 11). In the past, however, there has been a lack of direct supporting evidence from archaeological sites for interpretation of burnt mounds as cooking pits, as animal bone is largely absent; although in the South West peninsula and other parts of western Britain and Ireland this lack of evidence can perhaps be explained by poor bone preservation in acidic soil conditions, although a tiny amount of fragmented burnt bone was found in a second pit [124] amongst a matrix of heat-affected stones and charcoal (chapter 2). Charred plant remains are again limited, although in both features are perhaps indications of fuel from hazel charcoal and burnt turf signified by grassland taxa, including *Arrhenatherum* bulbils (J Jones, above).

It is difficult; however, with such small assemblages as those recovered from the Bronze Age features at Tremough to make any definite interpretations, especially as it seems likely that the structures within the enclosure may have had several functions, including perhaps domestic, storage and/or other economic activities.

Evidence of Romano-British activity is limited to a shallow concave pit [37], probably a hearth. A much richer cereal assemblage recovered from here included grains of hulled wheat, forming 41 per cent of the assemblage, with barley 4 per cent, oats 9 per cent, oats / grass 31 per cent and unidentified cereals 15 per cent. Measurements of the oat grains and two wild oat floret bases may indicate that the oats were present as crop weeds.

Comparison with other earlier and Middle Bronze Age sites in Cornwall

A comparable assemblage of charred cereal remains was recovered during previous work at Tremough, where a complex multi-period site included evidence for a Neolithic and Bronze Age ceremonial landscape, as well as evidence for Iron Age and Romano-British settlement and medieval farming (Gossip and Jones 2007; 2009-10). Carruthers (2007, 100-6) similarly found that plant remains from excavated features were fairly scarce.

An Early Bronze Age pit group produced mostly hazelnut shell, with naked and hulled barley the principal cereals and smaller amounts of emmer / spelt wheat. She suggested that these all originated from a burning event close to a particular pit [57], with numbers falling off further away. Pignut-type (*Conopodium majus*) tubers may have been burnt in cut turves used for fuel or have been gathered as a valuable food source.

In Middle Bronze Age structure [102] the highest concentration of cereal grains and arable / disturbed ground weeds occurred in a hearth pit. The assemblage included hulled barley and several emmer / spelt wheat grains; these were interpreted as spilt or over-parched grain that had fallen or been thrown into a fire, with some of the larger weed contaminants, including *Persicaria* and *Fallopia,* having been picked out during preparations for cooking. Included in this assemblage were four possible oat (cf. *Avena*) grains, although preservation was poor and no chaff was recovered.

Most evidence came from a later Middle Bronze Age structure [392], with the main component cereal grains, mostly emmer/spelt from a hearth pit, with a spread of material in posthole samples around the structure. Emmer would have been the principal grain for human consumption. Hulled barley was dominant in two entrance postholes and Carruthers (2007, 103-4) suggested that as a crop normally used as animal fodder or bedding, barley was more likely to be widely scattered around outside the structure, subsequently being swept up and thrown onto the hearth where it also formed a major component in two features close to the hearth pit area.

Campbell and Straker's (2003) paper on prehistoric crop husbandry and plant use in southern England argued that plant macrofossil evidence was still scarce from early prehistoric sites in the South West, and it remains the case that Late Bronze Age sites are still exceptionally rare in the region. Nonetheless, there are an increasing number of sites in Cornwall that have produced important assemblages of plant remains from contexts associated with Middle Bronze Age roundhouses. Postholes from these sites are often surprisingly informative, in contrast to the earlier charcoal-filled pits where cereal remains seem to be consistently lacking. Although individual site records are often from small assemblages, taken as a whole these analyses are gradually increasing our knowledge of crop cultivation and local economies. The scarcity of charred crop remains should not perhaps be regarded as unusual, particularly from the earlier Bronze Age, as populations are likely to have been small, with arable agriculture also small-scale; processing of cereals within settlement enclosures is likely to have been carried out by individual households on a daily basis.

Evidence for Early Bronze Age ploughing comes from the study of a Bronze Age farming landscape at the coastal site of Gwithian on St Ives Bay, where three phases of settlement occupation from *circa* 1800 to 900 cal BC were exposed, including evidence of stone-walled fields with ard plough and spade marks (Fowler 1983). The settlement was probably associated with agricultural activity, with a series of Bronze Age fields apparently under fairly continuous cultivation by cross ploughing. We can therefore posit an increase in agricultural activity from the Early Bronze Age that is likely to have involved clearance of grassland for cultivation of crops, with emmer / spelt wheat, barley, possibly oats, and Celtic Bean recorded at Tremough and other Cornish sites. A cache of Celtic Beans and a record for garden pea are known at Scarcewater, with the addition of flax from Trethellan Farm.

Middle Bronze Age (*circa* 1500-1000 cal BC) features from three hollow-set roundhouses at Scarcewater (J Jones 2010, 142-9) presented low concentrations of hulled wheat and occasional barley, but no cereal chaff from pits and postholes. Seed assemblages similar to Tremough included arable weeds, with more typical grassland taxa, including onion couch; here, too, the charred remains were interpreted as stray items from activities such as food preparation that were swept from floor surfaces onto household fires, there becoming mixed with the other fuel identified from charcoal remains.

Low concentrations of cultivated crops, including hulled wheat, barley, possibly oat, Celtic bean and garden pea (*Pisum sativum*), from a range of features were also recorded from a Middle Bronze Age roundhouse at Trevilson, located in central Cornwall (J Jones 2004). As with the roundhouses at Scarcewater, the evidence largely relates to phases of construction and abandonment, with little direct evidence for domestic activities within the house itself, apart from a shallow scoop [532] that produced a cache of over 150 whole and 100 half cotyledons of Celtic beans, thought to have been accidentally charred as part of food preparation, all subsequently incorporated in post and stake-hole fills with fuel debris.

At Boden Vean, St Anthony-in-Meneage, samples from the floor of a hollow identified as part of a Middle Bronze Age structure included a small assemblage of hulled and free-threshing wheat and barley (J Jones 2005). Geophysical survey identified a field system around this roundhouse; however, excavation revealed that it was of later, Iron Age date (Gossip 2008c; 2013). A Bronze Age roundhouse at Trethellan Farm, near Newquay, revealed evidence for the cultivation of predominantly naked barley, with emmer and a small number of oats (either cultivated or wild), with occasional Celtic bean (Straker 1991). The settlement at Trethellan was adjacent to a contemporary field system, so it is likely that the crops were locally cultivated. By contrast, Middle to Late Bronze Age features associated with the Maudlin to Liskeard pipeline (J Jones 1999; Cole 1999) revealed pits and postholes associated with a timber post-ring monument. Here again, postholes seem to have acted as grain traps; one feature in particular was found to contain a rich assemblage including over 400 oats, although there was only one *Avena fatua* floret base to suggest this may have been a deposit of wild oats.

Key to charred plant remains

Plant remains	**Common name**
Hordeum sp.	Barley
Triticum spelta	Spelt wheat
Triticum sp.	Wheat
Cereal indet.	Cereals
Avena sp.	Oat
Avena / Poaceae	Oat / grass
Arrhenatherum elatius (L.)P. Beauv.ex J.S. & C.Presl	Onion couch / False Oat-grass
Carex sp	Sedge
Chenopodium album L.	Fat-hen
Corylus avellana L.	Hazel
Crataegus monogyna JacQ	Hawthorn
Danthonia decumbens (L.) DC	Heath-grass
Fallopia convolvulus (L.)A.Love	Black-bindweed
Galium aparine L.	Cleavers
Lapsana communis L.	Nipplewort
Persicaria lapathifolia (l.)Gray	Pale Persicaria
Persicaria maculosa Gray	Redshank
Persicaria lapathifolia/maculosa	Pale Persicaria / Redshank
Poa/Phleum spp.	Meadow-grass/Cat's-tail
Plantago lanceolata L.	Ribwort Plantain
Prunella vulgaris L.	Selfheal
Quercus sp.	Oak
Poaceae	Grass
Raphanus raphanistrum ssp. *raphanistrum*	Wild Radish
Rubus sect. Glandulosus Wimmer & Grab	Bramble
Rumex spp.	Dock
Sambucus nigra L.	Elder
Silene dioica	Red Campion
Spergula arvensis L.	Corn Spurrey
Trifolium/Medicago spp.	Clover/Medick
Tripleurospermum inodorum (L.) Schultz-Bip	Scentless Mayweed
Vicia faba L.	Celtic/Horse Bean

Sample	Context	Feature	Sample size (litres)	Float size (ml)	Charred plant remains
Structure 1 (Early Bronze Age)					
100	(18)	posthole [19]	10	3	*Triticum* sp. (hulled wheat grain) 1 Cereal indet. (grain) 1 *Arrhenatherum elatius* (bulbil) 2
102	(11)	pit [23]	10	13	*Triticum* sp. (hulled grain) 7
Roundhouse 1 (Middle Bronze Age)					
353	(280)	gully fill	20	60	*Avena* sp. (grain) 2 Poaceae indet. 1
351	(704)	posthole [705],	10	17	*Hordeum* sp. (grain) 1
347	(700)	posthole [701]	/	30	*Lapsana communis* 1
357	(761)	posthole [762]	7	85	*Hordeum* sp. (tail grain) 2 *Triticum* sp. (hulled wheat) 6 c.f. *Triticum* sp. (hulled wheat) 5 *Triticum* sp. (hulled wheat tail grain) 1 *Arrhenatherum elatius* (bulbil) 1 *Avena* sp. 1 *Fallopia convolvulus* 1 *Galium aparine* 1 *Plantago lanceolata* 1 Poaceae indet. 1 *Vicia faba* 2
356	(794)	posthole [795]	2	33	Poaceae indet. 1
348	(291)	ditch [292] Post-dates Roundhouse 1	40	32	*Fallopia convolvulus* 2 *Lapsana communis* 1 *Persicaria lapathifolia* 1 *Plantago lanceolata* 1 *Poa/Phleum* spp. 8 Poaceae indet. 2 *Trifolium/Medicago* sp. 1
Enclosure 1 ditch and internal features (Late Bronze Age)					
Curvilinear ditch [160]					
337	(267)	ditch [160]	10	16	*Triticum spelta* (glume base) 1 *Triticum* sp. (spikelet fork) 1 *Danthonia decumbens* 2
359	(798)	ditch [160]	30	110	*Hordeum* sp. (grain) 1 *Triticum* sp (hulled grain) 3
Pit / Posthole Group 1					
324	(157)	posthole [158]	30	9	*Chenopodium album* 1 *Persicaria lapathifolia* 1 *Plantago lanceolata* 1
317	(143)	posthole [144]	20	14	*Danthonia decumbens* 1 Poaceae indet. 1
323	(163)	pit [164]	20	15	*Danthonia decumbens* 1
336	(248)	charcoal scoop [249]	10	29	*Hordeum* sp. (grain) 2 *Triticum* sp. (glume base) 3 *Triticum* sp. (spikelet fork) 1 *Plantago lanceolata* 1 *Quercus* sp. (bud) 1
316	(131)	posthole [132]	10	6	*Poaceae* indet. 2

Table 8.2 (this page and following pages): Charred plant remains from all Bronze Age features and Romano-British pit [37].

Sample	Context	Feature	Sample size (litres)	Float size (ml)	Charred plant remains
325	(176)	posthole [177]	10	39	*Arrhenatherum elatius* (bulbil) fragment
321	(153)	posthole [154]	10	12	*Triticum* sp. (glume base) 1 *Triticum* sp. (spikelet fork) 1
334	(206)	pit [193]	2	100	*Hordeum* sp. (grain) 1 *Hordeum/Triticum* sp. (grain) 1 *Triticum* sp. (glume base) 5
Pit Alignment 2					
333	(201)	pit [202]	3	14	*Triticum* sp. (hulled grain) 1 *Triticum* sp. (glume base) 1
312	(125)	pit [126]	10	170	*Triticum* sp. (hulled wheat) 3 *Triticum* sp. (glume base) 1 *Corylus avellana* 1 frag *Danthonia decumbens* 2 *Galium aparine* 1 *Plantago lanceolata* 4
305	(122)	pit [123]	10	14	*Triticum* sp. (hulled grain) 3 c.f. *Triticum* sp. (hulled grain) 1 *Avena*/Poaceae indet. (grain) 1 *Plantago lanceolata* 1 *Quercus* sp. (bud) 1
313	(133)	pit [134]	25	160	*Triticum* sp. (grain) 2 *Triticum* sp. (glume base) 2 *Triticum* sp. (spikelet fork) 1 *Avena*/Poaceae 1 *Danthonia decumbens* 2 *Persicaria maculosa* 3 *Rubus* sect. *Glandulosus* 1
309	(127)	pit [128]	20	20	*Triticum* sp. (hulled grain) 22 c.f. *Triticum* sp. (hulled grain) 8 *Triticum* sp. (tail grain) 21 *Triticum* sp. (glume base) 1 *Avena*/Poaceae indet. (grain) 2
Structure 205					
338	(115)	hollow [116]	20	32	*Hordeum* sp. (grain) 1 *Triticum* sp. (hulled grain) 1
306	(115)	hollow [116]	10	37	*Corylus avellana* 1 fragment
355	(743)	pit [744]	10	300	*Chenopodium album* 1 *Fallopia convolvulus* 2 *Persicaria maculosa* 4 *Plantago lanceolata* 1 *Prunella vulgaris* 1
340	(271)	below (205)	/	4	*Triticum* sp. (hulled grain) 1 *Arrhenatherum elatius* (bulbil) 1

Sample	Context	Feature	Sample size (litres)	Float size (ml)	Charred plant remains
Post Structure 4					
328	(180)	posthole [181]	10	48	c.f. *Hordeum* sp. (grain) 1 *Triticum* sp. (hulled grain) 1 *Chenopodium album* 1 *Fallopia convolvulus* 1 *Galium aparine* 1 fragment *Persicaria lapathifolia* 2 *Spergula arvensis* 1
332	(186)	posthole [187]	11	12	*Hordeum* sp. (grain) 1 *Carex* sp 1
326	(178)	posthole [179]	20	64	*Triticum* sp. (glume base) 2 *Triticum* sp. (spikelet fork) 1 *Corylus avellana* 1 frag *Fallopia convolvulus* 1 *Galium aparine* 2 *Persicaria lapathifolia* 1 *Persicaria maculosa* 10 *Plantago lanceolata* 1 Poaceae 1
331	(174)	posthole [175]	10	56	*Triticum* sp. (hulled grain) 1 *Galium aparine* 1 *Persicaria maculosa* 3
307	(120)	posthole [121]	10	44	*Triticum* sp. (hulled grain) 5 *Triticum* sp. (glume base) 2 *Avena/Bromus* sp. 1 *Arrhenatherum elatius* (bulbil) 1 *Galium aparine* 2 *Persicaria maculosa* 1
329	(166)	pit [167]	40	50	*Triticum* sp. (hulled grain) 3 *Triticum* sp. (glume base) 1 *Triticum* sp. (spikelet fork) 1 *Avena* sp. (awn) 1 *Galium aparine* 1+ 1 frag *Persicaria lapathifolia* 2 *Sambucus nigra* 1
Pit [124]					
308	(112)	pit [124]	10	21	*Triticum* sp. (glume base) 1 *Triticum* sp. (spikelet fork) 1 *Plantago lanceolata* 1 Poaceae indet. 1

Sample	Context	Feature	Sample size (litres)	Float size (ml)	Charred plant remains
Hearth Pit [37] (Romano-British)					
106	(36)	hearth [37]	20	385	*Hordeum* sp. (hulled grain) 6 *Hordeum* sp. (hulled/straight grain) 13 *Hordeum* sp. (rachis internode base) 4 *Hordeum* sp. (rachis section with 2 internode bases) 4 *Hordeum* sp. (grain) 25 *Hordeum* sp. (tail grain) 7 *Triticum* sp. (hulled grain) 402 c.f. *Triticum* sp. (grain) 124 *Triticum* sp. (tail grain) 75 Cereal indet. 220 *Arrhenatherum elatius* (bulbil) 1 *Avena* sp. (grain) 135 *Avena*/Poaceae (grain) 440 *Avena* sp. (grain enclosed in floret) 3 *Avena fatua* (floret base) 2 *Avena* sp. (floret base) 2 *Avena* sp. (awn) 1 *Corylus avellana* (nut) 4 fragments *Crataegus monogyna* 1 *Danthonia decumbens* 1 *Fallopia convolvulus* 4 *Lapsana communis* 2 + 1 fragment *Persicaria lapathifolia* 41 *Persicaria maculosa* 16 *Persicaria lapathifolia/maculosa* 20 Poaceae 10 *Raphanus raphanistrum* (pods) 12 + 5 fragments *Rumex* spp. 87 *Silene dioica* 3 *Tripleurospermum inodorum* 16

Chapter 9

The charcoal

Dana Challinor

In 2009 two Early Neolithic pits were excavated and a small number of samples taken which produced charcoal. During the 2011 excavations a range of environmental samples were taken at the AIR building and Car Park 4 in order to examine charred remains associated with various Bronze Age structures.

Methodology

All of the samples were examined under low magnification, with a selection of the richer and / or more diverse assemblages studied in greater detail: 20-50 fragments per sample (depending upon diversity) were identified. This approach provides a reliable indication of the most commonly used taxa and individual predominance within a sample, without providing a complete species list.

The charcoal was fractured and sorted into groups based on the anatomical features observed in transverse section at x7 to x45 magnifications. Representative fragments from each group were then selected for further examination in longitudinal sections using a Meiji incident-light microscope at up to x400 magnification. Identifications were made with reference to Schweingruber (1990), Hather (2000) and modern reference material. The maturity of the wood and relevant ring characteristics were noted where possible. Classification and nomenclature follow Stace (1997). For the purposes of the analysis, a combined approach of ubiquity analysis (encompassing all the samples with identified charcoal) and fragment count (comprising the quantified samples) was used.

Early Neolithic pits [102] and [105]

The charcoal was examined from samples of approximately 10 litres of soil excavated from two pits which produced Early Neolithic pottery, deposits (100) and (103).

Results

The preservation of the material was variable; (100) produced a fairly sparse assemblage of small, friable fragments, while (103) contained abundant, firm charcoal, including large fragments (>20mm in transverse section). Table 9.1 presents a summary of the results, including estimates of abundance based upon the scanning of the whole flot, and the full results are recorded in the archive.

Feature	[102]	[105]
Context	(100)	(103)
Quercus sp. (oak)	X hr	X
Corylus avellana (hazel)	xr	Xr
Maloideae (hawthorn group)	xr	

Table 9.1: Taxonomic composition of charcoal from Early Neolithic pits [102] and [105] (x = present; X = dominant; h = heartwood; r = roundwood).

The curvature of the rings indicated that several of the fragments came from small diameter roundwood. There were no complete stems, but some of the larger hazel pieces in sample 401 were reasonably slow grown and included at least 16 rings. Two pieces of *Corylus avellana* (hazel) were selected from each sample for dating.

Discussion

The assemblage from pit [105], fill (103) was overwhelmingly dominated by hazel charcoal, while pit [102], fill (100), produced a more mixed assemblage of oak, hazel and hawthorn group. The assemblages are comparable to those recorded by Gale (2007) from earlier excavations at Tremough, where one Early Neolithic pit was dominated by hazel, and another prehistoric pit contained oak and hazel. Gale also suggests that the fast growth rate of the hazel stems is indicative of woodland management. There was nothing in the character of the wood from the current site, which tended to be slow grown, to suggest woodland management, although this cannot be entirely discounted.

It is apparent that the assemblages at both sites reflect the surrounding vegetation, which was predominantly oak-hazel woodland in this period (Wilkinson and Straker 2008). Other Neolithic sites in the region have also indicated that oak and hazel wood were most commonly utilised for fuel (Cartwright 1988; Challinor, forthcoming; Gale 2006). The presence of hazelnut shell in both pits also suggests a link between the gathering practices of fuelwood and food.

Bronze Age

Twelve samples from the AIR site were from postholes or pits / hearths associated with the Early Bronze Age Structure 1. Fifty-one samples were available from Car Park 4, with the majority producing identifiable fragments of charcoal, albeit of varying quantities. For the purposes of this report, the samples are discussed in groups, according to their association with major features such as Roundhouse 1 and the rectangular Post Structure 4 in Enclosure 1. The results are presented in Tables 9.2 and 9.3 below by area and feature group.

Results

The condition and preservation of the charcoal was variable, with some samples containing small, friable or sediment-infused material and others with relatively large fragments with a clean and clear anatomical structure. This is likely to be due to the depositional environment and taphonomic process as well as the nature of the charcoal-production events.

Ten taxa were positively identified, all consistent with native taxa.

Fagaceae:

Quercus spp., oak, large tree, two native species, not distinguishable anatomically.

Betulaceae:

Betula spp. (birch), trees or shrubs, two native species, not distinguishable anatomically.

Alnus glutinosa, Gaertn., alder, tree, sole native species. *Corylus* has a very similar anatomical structure to *Alnus* and can be difficult to separate.

Corylus avellana L., hazel, shrub or small tree, only native species.

Salicaceae:

The genera *Salix* spp. (willow) and *Populus* spp. (poplar) are rarely possible to separate. Both are trees although there is variation within the genera.

Rosaceae:

Prunus spp., trees or shrubs, including *P. spinosa* L. (blackthorn), *P. avium* L. (wild cherry) and *P. padus* L. (bird cherry), all native, which can sometimes be separated on the basis of ray width. Only *P. spinosa* was positively identified, but the key distinguishing characteristics were often ambiguous due to poor condition.

Maloideae, subfamily of various shrubs / small trees including several genera, *Pyrus* (pear), *Malus* (apple), *Sorbus* (rowan / service / whitebeam) and *Crataegus* (hawthorn), which are rarely distinguishable by anatomical characteristics.

Fabaceae:

Cytisus / Ulex, broom / gorse, shrubs, several native species, not distinguishable anatomically.

Aquifoliaceae:

Ilex aquifolium L., (holly), evergreen tree or shrub, native.

Araliaceae:

Hedera helix L., ivy, climber, sole native species.

Structure 1

This earlier Bronze Age post-built structure was located in isolation from other investigated features. Three samples, from the 12 examined, produced abundant assemblages of charcoal and were analysed in some detail (Table 9.2). Pit [27] was composed entirely of *Quercus* sp. (oak), which also dominated the assemblage of posthole [66], although with some *Corylus avellana* (hazel) and *Cytisus / Ulex* (broom / gorse). Hearth [37] provided the most diverse charcoal assemblage with oak, hazel, *Populus / Salix* (poplar / willow), Maloideae (hawthorn group) and *Ilex aquifolium* (holly).

	Feature type	Pit	Hearth	Posthole
	Feature number	[27]	[37]	[66]
	Context number	(26)	(36)	(65)
Quercus sp.	oak	30 (4h)	16 (5r, 2h)	19 (5r, 3h)
Corylus avellana L.	hazel		16 (8r)	4
Alnus / Corylus	Alder / hazel		3	2
Populus / Salix	Poplar / willow		1	
Maloideae	hawthorn group		10 (4r)	
Cytisus / Ulex	Broom / gorse			5
Ilex aquifolium L.	holly		4	

Table 9.2: Quantified charcoal from Earlier Bronze Age Structure 1 (h = heartwood; s = sapwood; r = roundwood).

The remaining samples from postholes [15], [17], [19], [25], [49], [51] and [58] produced small quantities (five to ten fragments) of oak and hazel, with a single fragment of *Betula* sp. (birch) from [51]. Pits [23] and [56] were slightly richer in quantity of charcoal, but the taxonomic composition was comparable to the other samples, with some holly and broom / gorse from [23].

Roundhouse 1

Fifteen samples were examined from the Middle Bronze Age Roundhouse 1 (see Table 9.3 at the end of the chapter). Seven of these, from postholes [701], [705], [740], [762], [795], a ditch [292] and the infill deposit containing the stone moulds (280), produced abundant assemblages and merited further work. The remaining eight samples produced either very small quantities of charcoal or were limited by poor preservation, but all contained *Quercus* (oak) and some positive identifications were also made of *Corylus avellana* (hazel), Maloideae (hawthorn group) and *Ilex aquifolium* (holly). In addition to these four taxa, the richer samples provided evidence for *Betula* sp. (birch), *Alnus glutinosa* (alder), *Prunus* sp. (cherry / blackthorn) and *Cytisus / Ulex* (broom / gorse).

Late Bronze Age Enclosure 1

Enclosure ditch [160]/[170]

There were two samples from enclosure ditch [160]/[170], with the richer one (798) from [170] examined in greater detail (see Table 9.4 at the end of the chapter). *Quercus* sp. (oak) dominated the assemblages, with *Corylus avellana* (hazel) and traces of *Prunus* sp. (cherry/blackthorn), *Betula* sp. (birch) and *Alnus glutinosa* (alder).

Posthole / Pit Group 1

Twelve samples from cut features in Posthole / Pit Group 1 produced variable quantities of charcoal, with abundant assemblages from pits [177], [193] and [249]. Five taxa were positively identified from the richer samples: *Quercus* sp. (oak), *Corylus avellana* (hazel), *Prunus spinosa* (blackthorn), Maloideae (hawthorn group) and *Cytisus / Ulex* (broom / gorse). To this list may be added probable *Betula* sp. (birch) from posthole [152]. Analysis of the richer samples (Table 9.4) indicated that fragments of taxa which were not oak or hazel tended to be rare and this pattern appeared to be the same in all of the other samples; all, with the exception of pit [114], which contained little and small material, produced oak and nine included hazel. There were also abundant roundwood fragments, indicating small diameter branch or stem wood.

Pit Alignment 2

Six samples from pits were examined, with the assemblages from pits [126], [134] and [136] composed entirely of *Quercus* sp. (oak) and [128] with additional traces of *Corylus avellana* (hazel). The remaining two samples produced slightly more diverse assemblages, albeit still oak-dominated, with the additional taxa of *Betula* sp. (birch) and *Cytisus / Ulex* (broom / gorse). Much of the oak had split, characteristically, down the rays leaving thin slivers from which it was difficult to determine maturity. However, some was clearly heartwood, with evidence of tyloses, and the majority of larger fragments did not show any curvature to the growth rings, indicating that trunkwood was represented. One fragment from pit [134] showed evidence of round insect tunnels with frass (faecal material).

Structure 205

The stone structure uncovered within hollow [116] showed evidence of burning and the materials were interpreted as possibly deriving from a burnt mound (see chapter 2, above). Three samples from context (115) (and 743) which filled hollow [116] were mostly dominated by *Quercus* sp. (oak), with small components of other taxa including *Betula* sp. (birch), *Prunus* sp. (blackthorn / cherry) and *Cytisus / Ulex* (broom / gorse). The condition of the charcoal was quite poor, the oak largely limited to thin slivers and the diffuse porous taxa infused with sediment. Two samples from deposits (270) and (271), situated below the stone structure, produced very little charcoal, with the exception of a couple of small oak fragments.

Post Structure 3

The two postholes, [146] and [148], sampled from this structure produced only small flecks of unidentifiable charcoal.

Post Structure 4

With the exception of posthole [187], all of the charcoal assemblages from postholes [121], [175], [179], [181] and pit [167] contained large quantities of *Quercus* sp. (oak). There was, however, some diversity in the taxonomic composition, with *Betula* sp. (birch), *Alnus glutinosa* (alder), *Corylus avellana* (hazel), *Prunus spinosa* (blackthorn), Maloideae (hawthorn), *Cytisus / Ulex* (broom / gorse), *Ilex aquifolium* (holly) and *Hedera helix* (ivy). The ivy was probably an accidental inclusion, entering the assemblage attached to another branch. There were some roundwood fragments, especially notable in context (174). Posthole [187] was unusual in the presence of only a few fragments of oak, and a larger quantity of hazel. Strong ring curvature and a few whole stems indicated that the hazel came from small diameter branchwood or young stems.

Pit [124]

This large Late Bronze Age pit contained heat fractured stones, possibly derived from an adjacent burnt mound, and included numerous pottery fragments and other finds. The charcoal assemblage comprised 70 per cent *Quercus*, with 23 per cent *Corylus avellana* and small amounts of Maloideae (hawthorn group) and *Cytisus / Ulex* (broom / gorse). Some of the hazel fragments exhibited insect tunnels, which were small and round in shape.

Discussion

Woodland resources

It is immediately apparent from the charcoal assemblage at Tremough that oak was the most important of the woody resources utilised at the site throughout the Bronze Age. It is clearly the most frequently encountered taxon (Figure 9.1), as well as the most dominant in fragment count (Figure 9.2). The ubiquity analysis (Figure 9. 1) shows that the most common four taxa in all phases are oak, hazel, birch and hawthorn group, but it does not demonstrate the dominance of oak within individual assemblages which is revealed by the quantified samples (Figure 9.2). Additionally, it becomes apparent from this combined approach that the 'other' taxa (which comprise cherry / blackthorn, holly, alder, poplar / willow and ivy) are found both sporadically and in significantly lower quantities than the four major taxa.

Without claiming that the charcoal provides an exact representation of the environment, it is nonetheless reasonable to infer that oak-hazel woodland would have been both easily accessible and readily available for exploitation. The pollen record for South West Britain indicates that oak-hazel woodland broadly dominated the area in prehistory, and was slowly eroded by clearances from the Early Bronze Age onwards (Wilkinson and Straker 2007). Birch is known as a pioneer species (especially *Betula pendula* which is a likely contender in this region), as it rapidly colonises open areas. It is tempting to speculate, therefore, that the apparent dip in oak and hazel usage in the Middle Bronze Age (Figures 9.1 and 9.2), together with the rise in birch in this phase, reflect some changes in the landscape. However, the picture may not be so clear-cut, as the Middle Bronze Age phase is effectively limited to the samples associated with Roundhouse 1, from which the charcoal may have had a very specific function associated with metalworking (above). The origin of the charcoal assemblages, that is to say, whether as a selected fuelwood related to a specific activity or burnt structural remains, obviously has a bearing on any interpretation of the landscape and is discussed in detail below.

Nonetheless, even taking into account some bias for selection processes, the charcoal demonstrates that mixed oak-hazel woodland was exploited and probably managed throughout the Bronze Age, with a range of supplementary taxa drawn from marginal or scrub / hedgerow type environments (hawthorn group, blackthorn) and heathland. The heathland was probably gorse-dominated, especially on the acidic granite of Carnmenellis. It is also possible that the birch may be indicative of colonisation in emergent heathland. The onset of heathland

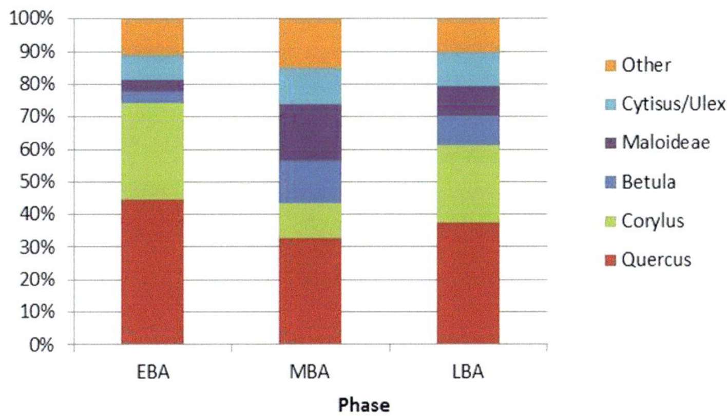

Figure 9.1 Percentage frequency of taxa by phase: Ubiquity analysis (based upon 57 samples).

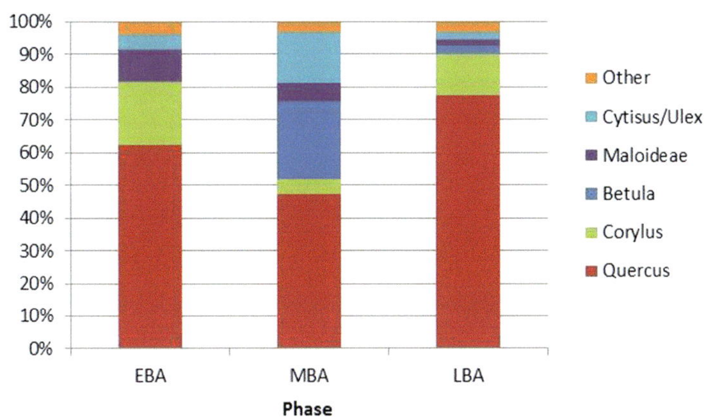

Figure 9.2 Percentage frequency of taxa by phase: Fragment count (based upon 31 samples, 813 fragments).

in the region is still being investigated (Straker *et al* 2007, 112), but it may be of significance that two Early Neolithic sites in the Tremough area did not provide evidence for the use of gorse (Gale 2007; Challinor above). The paucity of riparian taxa in the charcoal assemblage suggests that there was a plentiful supply of preferred woodland resources (that is to say oak and hazel), since the habitat around the River Fal (and tributaries) to the north of the site would have readily supported wet ground taxa such as willow and alder.

Origin of the charcoal assemblages

As seen above, the derivation of the charcoal is the key to understanding the selection processes involved in the formation of the assemblages. The majority of the features from Tremough were postholes and almost all were associated with buildings of some kind. Since there was no on-site evidence for the burning down of any of the structures, the charcoal does not represent burnt structural remains from a catastrophic event. However, there are several other processes which might have led to the assemblage formation:

Charcoal accumulated from spent fuelwood which naturally found its way in small quantities into these features during the construction and use of the building.

Dumps of waste fuel material were deliberately deposited in pits / ditches during the use of the building or in postholes post-abandonment.

Fragments of charred post-ends – charring may have been thought to reduce potential decay on posts set in the ground – remained *in situ* after the post was removed or decayed away.

Consequently, there may be some evidence for structural timbers represented in the charcoal record. Taxonomic identifications alone do not particularly illuminate the issue: oak and hazel (and birch) all make suitable construction woods and it is highly probable that the main posts used in these Bronze Age buildings would have been of oak. The sheer quantity of these taxa recovered throughout the Tremough features indicates, however, that they must also have been utilised as fuelwood. The association of artefacts with the charcoal may provide some aid for interpretation: some of the postholes and pits in Pit / Posthole Group 1 and Pit Alignment 2 contained burnt stones; others contained fragments of pottery and burnt bone indicative of domestic waste. Analysis was undertaken to determine if there were any patterns within the taxonomic composition of the charcoal relating to the presence or absence of burnt stones, with Structure [205] included for comparison (Figure 9.3). Figure 9.3 shows that oak and hazel are dominant in both categories (with and without burnt stone), and there is some higher diversity (represented by the 'other' group) in the pits / postholes with burnt stone. However, the actual values were very small and a similar analysis based upon fragment count also showed that any contrast was negligible.

Perhaps of greater significance is the absence of hazel from Structure 205 which might indicate deliberate avoidance. However, hazel is commonly used for fuel at other sites, including, for instance, in a Beaker burnt mound at Lower Boscaswell (Gale 2006), so it seems unlikely to have been a significant omission. Ultimately, the charcoal record is inconclusive and this probably reflects the mixed nature of the assemblages.

The evidence for copper-alloy working in Roundhouse 1, represented by several stone moulds and copper-alloy objects, suggests a more specific activity was taking place in this structure. The charcoal assemblages, however, do not offer any supporting evidence for context-related variation between the mould contexts (internal fill), possible associated deposits (internal features) and probably unrelated assemblages (outer post ring) (Figure 9.4). It is interesting, in a general sense, to note the paucity of hazel and quantity of birch in these assemblages, but it is not possible to determine if this relates to activity or to phase, bearing in mind that Roundhouse 1 was dated to the Middle Bronze Age compared to the dominance of oak-hazel in the Late Bronze Age structures located within Enclosure 1.

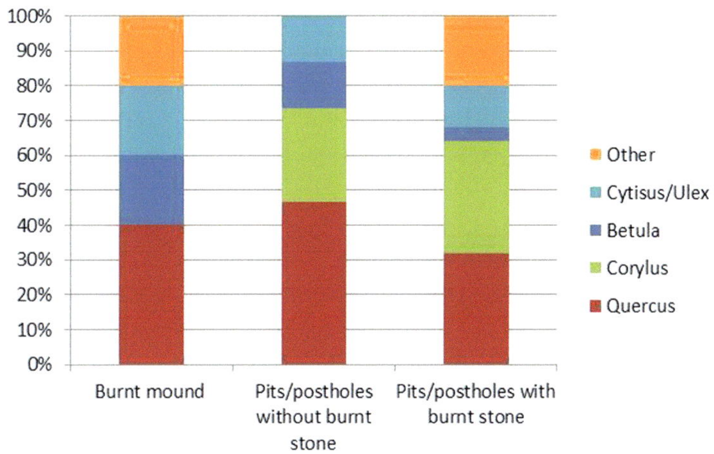

Figure 9.3 Ubiquity analysis of charcoal from pits / postholes with and without burnt stone from the Pit / Posthole Group 1 and Pit Alignment 2, and Structure 205 (based upon 18 samples).

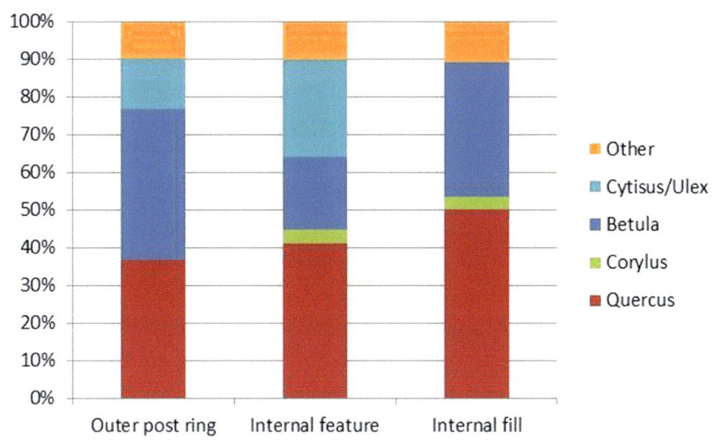

Figure 9.4 Taxonomic composition of features found in Roundhouse 1, based upon fragment count (6 samples; 227 fragments).

Conclusions

Examination of the charcoal assemblages from Tremough did not reveal any significant context-related variations; however, it is clear that the charcoal record reflects the oak-hazel woodland that dominated the Cornish landscape in prehistory (Wilkinson and Straker 2007). In general, oak was well-utilised in all phases, for a variety of wood uses, from construction timbers to wood fuel, and possibly even charcoal fuel, for which oak is eminently suitable (Gale and Cutler 2000). Some differences in the quantities of birch and hazel charcoal in the Middle Bronze Age are noted but it is uncertain whether this relates to activity types or localised changes in the landscape, which are evident in other areas.

At Tremough, by the Late Bronze Age, hazel consumption had recovered which suggests that any variations were due to either short-lived landscape change or preferential selection. The data from Tremough are consistent with other Bronze Age sites in Cornwall (for example, Challinor, forthcoming; Gale 2006) which testify to the dominance of oak and hazel, and there is some suggestion of the exploitation of heathland resources by the Early Bronze Age.

	Group	Roundhouse 1						
	Feature	Ditch	Posthole	Posthole	Posthole	Posthole	Posthole	Infill layer
	Feature number	[292]	[701]	[705]	[286]	[762]	[795]	-
	Context	(291)	(700)	(704)	(284)	(761)	(794)	(280)
Quercus sp.	oak	17 (4r, 1h)	9 (2h, 1s, 6r)	13 (1h, 1r)	9 (1h, 2s, 1r)	28 (10r)	8 (7r)	14 (7h, 3r)
Betula sp.	birch	4	14 (1r)	10	12	9		10
Alnus glutinosa Gaertn.	alder			1				
Corylus avellana L.	hazel	5 (1r)				4		1r
Betulaceae	birch family							2
Prunus spinosa L.	blackthorn	1						
Prunus sp.	cherry type		1		1	1		
Maloideae	hawthorn group	1	1	3	4	2r		3 (1r)
cf. Maloideae								
Cytisus / Ulex	broom / gorse	2r	5r	3r		6 (4r)	22r	
Ilex aquifolium L.	holly				3			
Bark					1			

Table 9.3: Charcoal assemblage from Middle Bronze Age Roundhouse 1 (fragment count; quantified samples only) (h = heartwood; s = sapwood; r = roundwood; b =bark).

Group	**Enclosure 1 ditch**	**Pit / Posthole Group 1**			**Pit Alignment 2**				**Structure 205**		**Post Structure 4**					**Pit [124]**
Feature type	Ditch	Pits / Postholes			Pits				Pit		Posthole	Pit	Postholes			Pit
Feature number	[160]	[177]	[193]	[249]	[123]	[128]	[134]	[201]	[116]	[116]	[121]	[167]	[175]	[179]	[187]	[124]
Context number	(798)	(176)	(206)	(248)	(122)	(127)	133	(201)	(115)	(115)	(120)	(166)	(174)	(178)	(186)	(112)
Quercus sp. oak	18 (2s, 1h, 6r)	23 (12r, 1h, 2s)	21 (7h, 4r)	12 (1h, 2r)	10 (2r)	19 (3r)	30 (3h)	13 (1h)	18 (2s)	14 (4r)	18 (2r)	21 (1h,4r)	19 (6r)	19 (2h, 3s, 2r)	4	21 (1h,11r)
Betula sp. birch	1				5			cf.1	1			1	2			
Alnus glutinosa Gaertn. alder	1															
Corylus avellana L. hazel	7	5 (2r)	9r	2	2	1		4				2	2r		16r	7
Alnus / Corylus alder / hazel										1						
Betulaceae birch family	1															
Prunus spinosa L. blackthorn		1												1		
Prunus sp. cherry type	2									1						
Maloideae hawthorn group				4							cf.1	4				1
Cytisus / Ulex broom / gorse		1r		1r	1r			2r	1r	1r			2r			1
Ilex aquifolium L. holly												2				
Hedera helix L. ivy													5r			
Indeterminate				1b	2b					3	1b					

Table 9.4 (following page): Charcoal from Enclosure 1: Late Bronze Age features (fragment count; quantified samples only) (h = heartwood; s = sapwood; r = roundwood; b = bark.

Chapter 10

Radiocarbon dating

Andy M Jones

The primary aim of the dating strategy was to obtain a series of determinations from a representative range of archaeological features, relating to Structure 1 in the AIR building area and Roundhouse 1 and Enclosure 1 and associated features in Car Park 4. All of these features were excavated in 2011 and on ceramic grounds were thought to date to the Bronze Age, with Structure 1 potentially dating to the earlier part of the period and Enclosure 1 being rather later (chapter 3). Both of the sites also had the potential to shed light on metalworking in Bronze Age Cornwall. Roundhouse 1, for example was associated with a series of moulds, metalworking residues and copper-alloy objects. Given that these finds are usually found in unstratified contexts, the dating of a 'metalworker's house' had the potential to provide very close dating for these artefacts. As such, the results from the dating were of national importance.

Finally it was also hoped that the radiocarbon determinations would help to further develop an understanding of the Bronze Age chronology of the site and complement the twelve dates for this period obtained from the 2002 excavations (Gossip and Jones 2007, chapter 6). For example, did the metalworking activity in Roundhouse 1 overlap with the use of the ceremonial timber circles in the field to the north? How long after the other features had gone out of use was the Late Bronze Age Enclosure 1 in Car Park 4 constructed?

In addition, this chapter also includes the results of the radiocarbon dating of samples taken from two pits with Early Neolithic pottery found within the PAC area in 2009. Again, it was hoped that the dating would build upon two determinations which were obtained from earlier excavations and would help to improve the chronological resolution for activities taking place across the site. For example, other areas across the site had been associated with flint knapping or with pits containing burnt material, whereas the area of the PAC building contained evidence for pits associated with pottery. In other words, it was hoped that the new radiocarbon determinations would shed light on whether these activities were contemporary with one another.

Dating strategy

Given the general absence of stratigraphical relationships between features found across the site, the development of any finer-grained understanding of the site's chronology would be largely dependent upon obtaining a reliable series of radiocarbon determinations, taken from sealed contexts.

All of the samples selected for dating were either derived from charcoal from grains, charred hazelnut shells, short-lived species or were on ceramic residues. All were submitted for accelerator mass spectrometry dating (AMS). This method of dating can be carried out on very small amounts of material and gives a high precision date.

The radiocarbon dating was undertaken by the Scottish Universities Environmental Research Centre (SUERC) at Glasgow. All the determinations have been calibrated using Oxcal 4.1 and, unless otherwise stated, are quoted at the 95 per cent level of confidence. Older dates cited from Tremough and other sites have been recalibrated to the same curve. This means that they may differ slightly from previous publications (for example, Gossip and Jones 2007, 112-17).

Results from dating programme

Two samples were submitted on charred hazelnut shells obtained from pits in the PAC building area. Fourteen samples were originally submitted for radiocarbon dating on material from archaeological features in the AIR building and Car Park 4 areas. In addition, two further samples were submitted from pit [37] which was adjacent to Structure 1. Samples were submitted from this feature because a large assemblage of oats was identified (J Jones, above). The radiocarbon dating of oat grains and wild radish returned near identical determinations 1690±35 BP, cal AD 253-419 (SUERC-53786) and 1680±35 BP, cal AD 254-425 (SUERC-53783), which places it in the Romano-British period. As such, it will not be discussed below.

The resulting dating has been ordered by broad chronology (that is to say, Early Neolithic, Early Bronze Age, Middle Bronze Age and Late Bronze Age). Coincidentally, these period divisions were also reflected in the different sites excavated (PAC building, AIR building and Car Park 4). Consequently, the determinations relate to both chronological and changing spatial uses of the area over time.

Earlier Neolithic period (circa 3900-3350 cal BC)

Two securely sealed pits found in the PAC area were selected for radiocarbon dating. Both features were found to date to the middle centuries of the fourth millennium cal BC (Table 10.1, below). The submitted samples were on charred hazelnut shells (SUERC 29383 and SUERC-29387) and they produced identical radiocarbon determinations of 4750±40 BP, calibrated to 3640-3370 cal BC, which lies at the end of the Early Neolithic and extends into the Middle Neolithic period. These provide *terminus ante quem* dates which relate to the final use of the

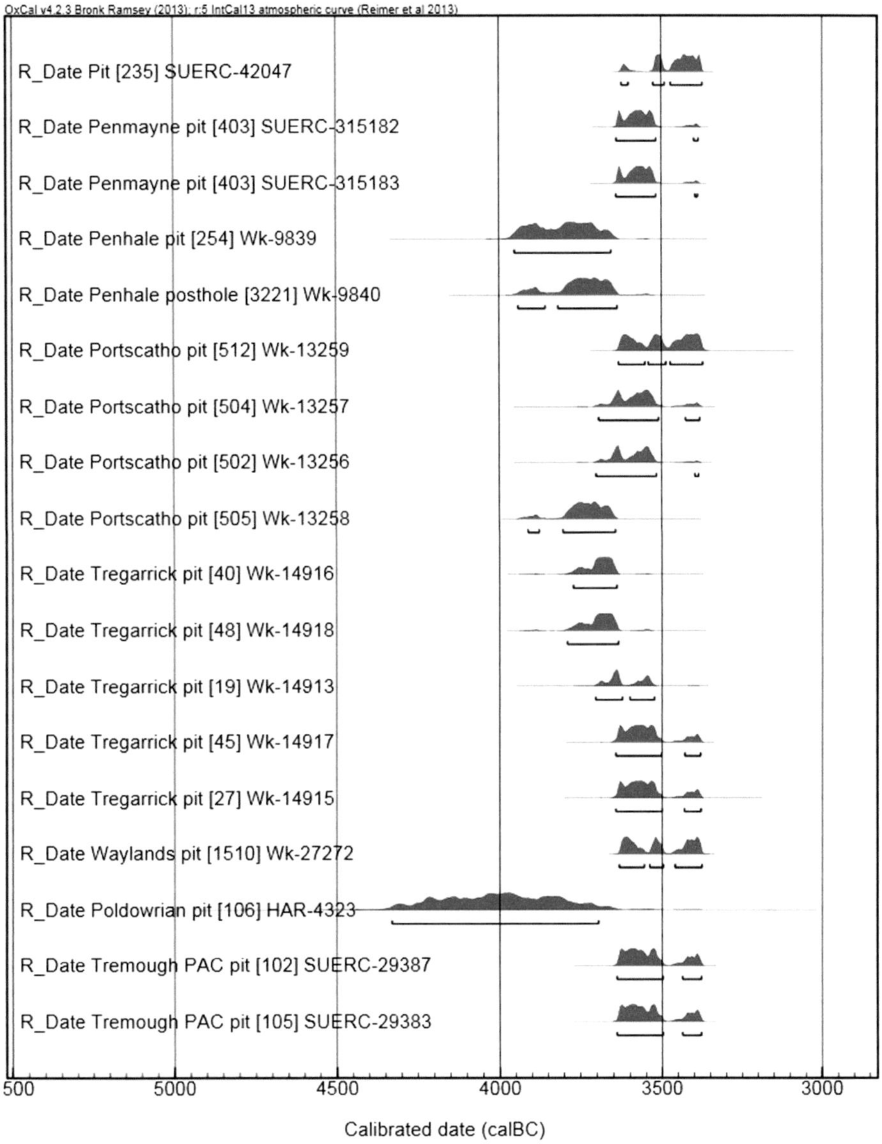

Figure 10.1 Date ranges from Early Neolithic pits containing pottery in Cornwall.

Feature	Material	Lab. no	Age BP years	Calendrical years 95%
Pit [102], fill (100)	Charred hazelnut. *Corylus Avellana*	SUERC 29383	4750±40	3640-3378 cal BC
Pit [105], fill (103).	Charred hazelnut. *Corylus Avellana*	SUERC-29387	4750±40	3640-3378 cal BC

Table 10.1: Results from the radiocarbon dating of pits [102] and [105].

Feature	Material	Lab. no	Age BP years	Calendrical years BC 95%
Ditch [76], fill (77)	Charcoal. *Corylus*	AA-44604	4995±50 BP	3944-3662 BC
Pit [21], fill (22)	Charcoal. *Corylus*	AA-44601	4850±55 BP	3765-3520 BC

Table 10.2: Results from the radiocarbon dating of Early Neolithic features excavated in 2000.

pits. Since these are not thought to have been open for long and the samples were from a fast-growing species (*Corylus Avellana*, hazelnut), the dates probably relate closely to the creation and infilling of the pits.

The determinations are significant because they provide secure dating for the Neolithic pottery assemblage (chapter 3) with which they were associated, and this will be discussed below (chapter 11). They add to a growing number of radiocarbon determinations associated with Early Neolithic pottery in Cornwall (Figure 10.1).

However, they are also important because they relate to two other fourth millennium cal BC radiocarbon determinations (Table 10.2, above) which were obtained following archaeological recording at Tremough in 2000 (Gossip and Jones 2007, 7). They are the first pits at Tremough to be associated with Early Neolithic pottery. This contrasts with the earlier excavations to the north, which was largely devoid of ceramics and Neolithic flintwork was found in a scatter (Gossip and Jones 2007, 28-9). The contrasting use of the plateau will be discussed below (chapter 11).

Interestingly, pits [102] and [105] appear to be a century or so later than the two features dated to the Early Neolithic period excavated in 2000 (Gossip and Jones 2007, 8). Ditch [76] in Field 7 produced a determination of 4995±50 BP, 3944-3662 cal BC (AA-44604) and pit [21] in Field 4, 4850±55 BP, 3765-3520 cal BC (AA-44601) (Table 10.2, above). These determinations are similar to one another and could be taken to represent roughly contemporary activity on the site, although it is also possible that that from pit [21] could be a little later.

It appears that the determinations from the 2000 excavations are earlier than those from the 2009 investigations. Nonetheless, the deposition of pottery into pits which are located in a different part of the site to the pits without pottery and the flint scatter supports the hypothesis made in the previous excavation report which suggested that there was a significant spatial separation of tasks in the Early Neolithic period (Gossip and Jones 2007, 29; chapter 11, this volume). This will be explored further below.

Earlier Bronze Age period (circa 2400-1400 cal BC)

Four samples for radiocarbon determinations were taken from features associated with the simple post-built Structure 1, located in the AIR building area (Table 10.3).

One of the samples failed to produce a date. In part the difficulty with dating the structure was due to the relatively limited amount of material which was available for dating. However, the results are also unsatisfactory because, the other three determinations produced results which are not consistent with one another. There is, therefore, the problem of deciding which (if any) of the dates is likely to represent the actual date of the structure. The latest determination,

Feature	Material	Lab. no	Age BP years	Calendrical years BC 95%
Pit [23] fill (11)	Charcoal. *Cytisus / Ulex*	GU30878	Failed	-
Posthole [49], fill (48)	Charcoal. *Corylus*	SUERC-47281	3623±27 BP	2116-2098 BC (3.4%) 2039-1900 BC (92%)
Pit [56], fill (55)	*Quercus sp. rw*	SUERC-47282	2989±29 BP	1371-1346 BC (3.4%) 1316-1126 BC (92%)
Posthole [25], fill (24)	Charcoal. Cereal grain.	SUERC-48150	3237±30 BP	1608-1570 BC (11.4%) 1561-1546 BC (3.1%) 1541-1435 BC (81%)

Table 10.3: Results from the radiocarbon dating of the earlier Bronze Age, Structure 1.

2989±29 BP, 1371-1126 cal BC (SUERC-47282), obtained on *Quercus* charcoal can almost certainly be ruled out on the grounds that pit [56] was in an area which had been disturbed by later activity; on balance it seems probable that this date is associated with later contamination and it has therefore been discounted. The middle determination, from posthole [25], 3237±30 BP, 1608-1435 cal BC (SUERC-48150), dates to the middle of the Bronze Age. It was on a small grain of cereal which could have been intrusive, as it post-dates the ceramics, which are probably of an earlier Bronze Age date (chapter 3). The earliest determination, 3623±27 BP, 2116-1900 cal BC (SUERC-47281), on *Corylus* charcoal from posthole [49], falls at the start of the second millennium cal BC, which would be more consistent with the limited ceramic dating. The relatively flimsy nature of the building and lack of evidence for replacement of posts makes it unlikely that it was used for any length of time. However, given the uncertainty over the dates we would broadly assign the structure to the first half of the second millennium cal BC.

Although the determinations from Structure 1 did not precisely date its construction, the dating does to some extent build upon the earlier dating carried out at Tremough in 2002 (Gossip and Jones 2007, 11-13). Four of the determinations from this work spanned the Early Bronze Age (Table 10.4, below). Three of these produced almost identical date ranges. The earliest, from posthole [75], 3704±38 BP, 2204-1977 cal BC (Wk-14995), was associated with structure 66, the southernmost of a series of post-rings, which have been interpreted ashaving a ceremonial function. Pits [64] – 3677±45 BP, 2199-1941 cal BC

Feature	Material	Lab. no	Age BP years	Calendrical years BC 95%
Structure 66 posthole [75], fill (76)	Charcoal, *Corylus*	Wk-14995	3704±38 BP	2204-1977 BC
Early Bronze Age pit [64], fill (65)	Charcoal, *Corylus*	Wk-14993	3677±45 BP	2199-1941 BC
Early Bronze Age pit [59], fill (60)	Charcoal, *Corylus*	Wk-14992	3668±45 BP	2196-1926 BC
Structure 66 posthole [69], fill (70)	Charcoal, *Quercus sw*	Wk-14994	3380±38 BP	1756-1534 BC

Table 10.4: Results from the radiocarbon dating of Early Bronze Age features excavated in 2002.

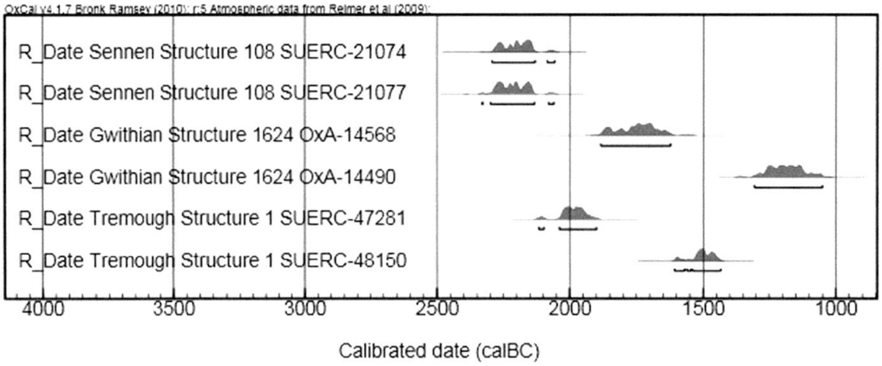

Figure 10.2 Date ranges from earlier Bronze Age structures in Cornwall.

(Wk-14993) - and [59] - 3668±45 BP, 2196-1926 cal BC (Wk-14992) - were part of a circular arrangement of pits located in the southern part of the 2002 excavation area (TRM 02). However, a second determination obtained from Structure 66, from posthole [69], gave a determination of 3380±38 BP, 1756-1534 cal BC (Wk-14994), which is late in the Early Bronze Age. This might imply that the post-ring had been renewed. The dating from Structure 1 suggests that there is likely to have been a degree of chronological overlap with use of the ceremonial post-ring and activity associated with the pits. Structure 1 is the first hint of occupation-related activity that we have from the Early Bronze Age at Tremough, and the dating therefore contributes to the discussion of the earlier second millennium landscape below.

The dating is also of interest as it gives further evidence for the character of buildings in use in Cornwall prior to *circa* 1500 cal BC, after which roundhouses were constructed on a much larger-scale. To date only three occupation-related structures in Cornwall have been radiocarbon dated to the period before 1500 cal BC. The other two are structure 1624 at Gwithian site GMXV and the Beaker-associated structure 108 found near to Sennen in West Penwith during the recording of a pipeline (Nowakowski *et al* 2007; Jones *et al* 2012) (Figure 10.2). These buildings will be discussed in chapter 11.

Middle Bronze Age period (circa 1500-1100 cal BC)

Four radiocarbon determinations were obtained from material associated with a Middle Bronze Age hollow-set roundhouse which was located in the wider Car Park 4 area (Table 10.5, below).

The radiocarbon dating from Roundhouse 1 was altogether more successful than that from Structure 1. Three of the determinations were on charcoal from postholes and all are broadly similar in date: 3169±29 BP, 1501-1400 BC cal BC (SUERC-47292); 3109±29 BP, 1441-1407 BC (SUERC-47293); 3065±31 BP, 1415-1252 BC (SUERC-47297). Interestingly, the fourth determination, 3091±27 BP, 1429-1297 BC (SUERC-47298), which came from the infill layer (280), did not differ from the others which were obtained from postholes. This might be

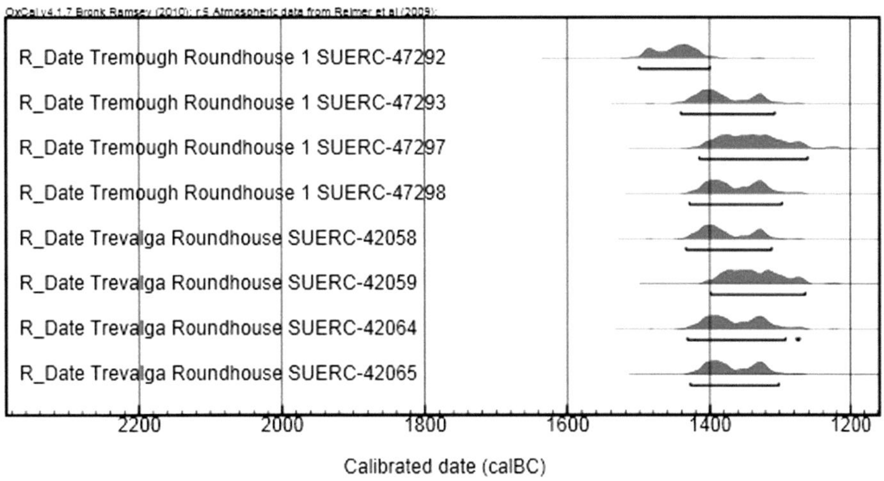

Figure 10.3 Date ranges from Middle Bronze Age hollow-set roundhouses associated with metalworking in Cornwall.

due to material associated with the occupation of the house being backfilled into it, material from the infilling seeping into the postholes, or to the structure being relatively short-lived.

The four determinations suggest that the roundhouse dated to the centuries between *circa* 1500 and 1300 cal BC, with the weight of the dating suggesting the mid fifteenth fourteenth centuries cal BC for the use of the building. This building therefore sits within the well-established chronology established for Middle Bronze Age hollow-set roundhouses in Cornwall (Jones and Taylor 2010, 160).

In addition to securely dating the building itself, the results are important because together they closely date a nationally important collection of moulds that were used for the manufacture of copper-alloy objects. Interestingly, the dating from Roundhouse 1 is almost indistinguishable from that of a recently dated Middle Bronze Age roundhouse at Trevalga (Figure 10.3), which was also associated with a mould, in that case one for a *racloir* (Jones and Quinnell 2014). Finds of metalwork and moulds from Cornish roundhouses are discussed in the synthesis below (chapter 11).

Feature	**Material**	**Lab. no**	**Age BP years**	**Calendrical years BC 95%**
Posthole [286], fill (285)	Charcoal. *Ilex aquifolium*	SUERC-47292	3169±29 BP	1501-1400 BC
Posthole [701], fill (700)	Charcoal. *Betula*	SUERC-47293	3109±29 BP	1441-1407 BC
Posthole [705], fill (704)	Charcoal. *Ulex/Cytisus*	SUERC-47297	3065±31 BP	1415-1252 BC
Layer (280)	Charcoal. *Betula* sp. x 1	SUERC-47298	3091±27 BP	1429-1297 BC

Table 10.5: Results from the radiocarbon dating of Middle Bronze Age Roundhouse 1.

Feature	Material	Lab. no	Age BP years	Calendrical years BC 95%
Structure 102 Posthole [109], fill (110)	Charcoal. *Corylus*	Wk-14996	3180±39 BP	1526-1390 BC
Structure 102 Posthole [112], fill (111)	Charcoal. *Corylus*	Wk-14997	3111±37 BP	1490-1271 BC
Structure 102 Hearth- pit [157], fill (158)	Charcoal. *Corylus*	Wk-14998	3009±40 BP	1386-1129 BC
Posthole Group 37, posthole [29], fill (30)	Charcoal. *Corylus*	Wk-14991	3060±51 BP	1435-1132 BC
Structure 392 Posthole [623], (622)	Charcoal. *Betula*	Wk-15003	2964±40 BP	1370-1047 BC
Structure 392 Hearth-pit [320], fill 319)	Charcoal. *Corylus*	Wk-15002	2947±43 BP	1301-1016 BC
Pit [25], fill (26)	(26) Charcoal. *Corylus*	AA-44602	3080±55 BP	1492-1134 BC
Ditch [30], fill (31). Date is residual as it was obtained where ditch cut land surface (17).	(31) Charcoal. Corylus	AA-44603	3055±55 BP	1434-1130 BC

Table 10.6: Results from the radiocarbon dating of Middle Bronze Age features excavated in 2002.

The dates from Roundhouse 1 are also significant because they can be compared with others obtained from the earlier excavations in 2002 (Gossip and Jones 2007, 114-116). Eight radiocarbon determinations were obtained which related to a Middle Bronze Age phase of activity (Table 10.6). These spanned the period *circa* 1500-1100 cal BC. Six were obtained from circular post-rings, interpreted as ceremonial timber structures, and two were from other contexts. Post-ring structure 102 produced the earliest of the Middle Bronze Age determinations. They were obtained from posthole [109] – 3180±39 BP, 1526-1390 cal BC (Wk-14996) – and posthole [112]: 3111±37 BP, 1490-1271 cal BC (Wk-14997). These dates slightly overlap with one another but could also be taken to suggest that a post had been renewed. Contemporary activity on the site is also indicated by a third date from a hearth-pit [157]: 3009±40 BP, 1386-1129 cal BC (Wk-14998).

A date was obtained from posthole [29], 3060±51 BP, 1435-1132 cal BC (Wk-14991), which was located at the southern end of linear Posthole Group 37 on the western side of the Tremough site. Two further broadly contemporary determinations came from post-ring structure 392: posthole [623] dated to 2964±40 BP, 1370-1047 cal BC (Wk-15003), and hearth-pit [320] to 2947±43 BP, 1301-1016 cal BC (Wk-15002).

The final pair of determinations were obtained from two features to the east of the post-ring structures. Pit [25] and ditch [30] produced very similar determinations of 3080±55 BP, 1492-1134 cal BC (AA-44602), and 3055±55 BP, 1434-1130 cal BC (AA-44603). Pit [25] contained a structured deposit of Trevisker Ware pottery. The last determination from ditch [30] was not regarded as providing a date for the ditch which contained Iron Age ceramics and is instead likely to relate to the adjacent land surface (17), which produced Bronze Age artefacts.

When all the radiocarbon dates are taken together, the dates from Roundhouse 1 overlap significantly with those for the ceremonial post-rings and with others from features on the western part of the Tremough site, suggesting a clear spatial division of contemporary activities across the area. This will be discussed in the concluding section below.

Late Bronze Age Period (circa 1100-800 cal BC)

Six radiocarbon determinations were obtained from material associated with features associated with an enclosure which was located in the Car Park 4 area (Table 10.7, below). A seventh was obtained on residue from an unstratified sherd of Late Bronze Age pottery found during hoeing over Roundhouse 2.

The radiocarbon determinations from Tremough provide only the third significant set of Late Bronze Age dates from Cornwall, the others coming from a settlement at Higher Besore, Truro (Gossip, forthcoming), and a palisade enclosure and roundhouse at Scarcewater, St Stephen in Brannel (Jones and Taylor 2010, 159). However, given their association with Enclosure 1, metalworking, a mound of burnt stone and other structures, the new determinations from Tremough arguably represent the most important set of Late Bronze Age dates to be recovered from Cornwall so far. It might have been expected that the determination from the base of enclosure ditch [160], fill (798), 2782±29 BP, 1006-843 cal BC (SUERC-47283) would have been distinctly earlier than those from features inside the enclosure; however, it was derived from *Corylus* charcoal, which had entered the open ditch cut, and it is therefore uncertain how long the ditch had been kept open before the charcoal entered it. In other words, the ditch cut could have been older, and given that no Late Bronze Age features were uncovered outside the ditch, it seems likely that all the other features were probably associated with activity inside the enclosure.

Feature	Material	Lab. no	Age BP years	Calendrical years BC 95%
Enclosure 1 ditch [160], fill (798)	Charcoal. Corylus	SUERC-47283	2782±29 BP	1006-843 BC
Pit [124], fill (112)	Residue	SUERC-47287	2747±26 BP	972-959 BC (3.5%) 937-827 BC (91.9%)
Pit / Posthole Group 1, pit [114], fill (102)	Residue	SUERC-47288	2822±30 BP	1071-1065 BC (0.4%) 1056-899 BC (95%)
Structure 205, fill (103)	Residue	SUERC-47289	2808±29 BP	1048-896 BC
Post Structure 4, pit [167], fill (166)	Residue	SUERC-47290	2791±27 BP	1011-892 BC (89.1%) 880-846 BC (6.3%)
Pit / Posthole Group 1, posthole [156], (155)	Residue	SUERC-47291	2766±29 BP	997-987 BC (2.3%) 980-835 BC (93.1%)
Roundhouse 2, layer (110) cleaning over Roundhouse 2	Residue	SUERC-47299	2820±29 BP	1053-901 BC

Table 10.7: Results from the radiocarbon dating of Late Bronze Age features within Enclosure 1 and residue on a sherd from over Roundhouse 2.

Within the enclosure itself there were a range of features. The earliest date from these was from pit [114]: 2822±30 BP, 1071-899 cal BC (SUERC-47288). The next earliest determination was associated with Structure 205 2808±29 BP, 1048-896 cal BC (SUERC-47289). This date is of interest as the feature was a carefully constructed cairn of burnt stone and the determination is the first to be associated with a Late Bronze Age site of this type in Cornwall.

The three remaining determinations (SUERC-47287, SUERC-47290 and SUERC-47291) are all associated with pits and postholes within the enclosure and all are quite close together, dating from *circa* 1000 cal BC to 850 cal BC (Table 10.7). Although it is not possible to say whether features were entirely contemporary with one another these dates do imply a focused period of activity. Indeed, taken together, all six determinations from Enclosure 1 form a coherent group associated with activity within the two centuries following 1000 cal BC. The determination 2747±26 BP, 972-827 cal BC (SUERC-47287) associated with pit [124] is of interest as the feature contained burnt stone, pottery and fragments of moulds, including the tip from a sword mould.

In addition to the determinations associated with the enclosure, a seventh Late Bronze Age date was obtained from residue on an unstratified sherd of pottery recovered during initial clearance over the unexcavated Roundhouse 2: 2820±29 BP, 1053-901 cal BC (SUERC-47299). This sherd was dated in order to further ceramic studies (chapter 3), as no pottery of this type had been dated in Cornwall before. The date is broadly contemporary with that from Pit [114] in Pit / Posthole Group 1 (SUERC-47288), and it may therefore represent the dumping of midden material outside the enclosure.

By contrast with the excavated Early Neolithic, Early Bronze Age and Middle Bronze Age sites, no Late Bronze Age features had previously been identified at Tremough. This means that it not possible to compare them with previous datasets. It is, however, of interest that the dating reveals that after a gap of around two centuries, the Late Bronze Age enclosure was sited in the space between both the hollow-set Middle Bronze Age roundhouses to the south and the ceremonial post-rings to the north. This might imply that there was a continuing memory of place, which had influenced where the Late Bronze Age features could be situated, and this will be explored in chapter 11.

Chapter 11

Discussion: pits, deposition metalworking and circularity

Andy M Jones

This chapter presents a synthesis of the results from the recent excavations. The findings from relevant earlier work at Tremough will be drawn upon to provide an overview of the chronology of the immediate area. In doing so, the following section not only discusses the excavated sites themselves but will also place them within their regional and national contexts. Where appropriate, comparanda from a wider area will also be drawn in.

Although the discussion will be organised chronologically, we will try to avoid falling into the trap of considering the features as discrete chronological units and instead will have cross-cutting themes which run across periods. This will include consideration of the changing use of space across the plateau. Indeed, one of the clearest patterns to emerge from more than a decade of work at Tremough is the lack of overlap between features of different periods and in fact of different types of activity during the same period. Discussion will be given to identifying differing types of inhabitation and occupation both spatially across the investigated areas and chronologically over the millennia. The intention is not to demonstrate that values or associations were singular, remained constant or were so ingrained that they fixed the use of an area (for example, see papers in Bender (ed) 1993), but rather to explore the ways that certain practices or social memory may have affected use of space over time (for example, Connerton 1989; Gosden and Lock 1998).

The second major strand for consideration is the character of the deposits which were found within the investigated features. As will be discussed below, certain terms such as 'structured deposition' and 'special deposits' have been readily and, according to a number of commentators (see below), perhaps sometimes overly used in relation to the archaeological record. In light of this, we consider the formation of particular deposits closely to determine the level of intentionality behind them, as well as, where possible, exploring the links between deposits found in different types of contemporary feature across the site.

Lastly, throughout the discussion we will draw the evidence for metalworking from all three phases of the Bronze Age to the fore, and consider its character. In doing so, we will consider the significance of Tremough in relation to other sites which have been recorded in the South West region and beyond.

Early Neolithic pits

The PAC building pits

Archaeological recording at the Tremough PAC building produced the only new evidence for Neolithic activity. This revealed a single phase dated to 3640-3370 cal BC or the earlier Neolithic period, and comprised two pits, both containing fragments of pottery and flint in charcoal-rich deposits. These were possibly the remains of adjacent fires mixed with the excavated soil and artefacts which might have been associated with activities or events on the site. Significantly, pit [102] appeared to have been marked by a pile of stones while pit [105] had a possible posthole at its northern end, perhaps supporting a marker post. Nearby were two tree-throw pits, the hollows left from the disturbed ground beneath fallen trees. These contained similar deposits to the pits recorded at Tremough and may have been deliberately backfilled as part of a comparable process.

The digging of pits and the burial of artefacts belongs to a widespread Neolithic tradition and is a phenomenon that has been recognised at numerous sites throughout southern Britain and along the Atlantic facade. In Cornwall, as elsewhere, the artefactual and environmental assemblages associated with these pits typically includes pottery, stone, flint, charcoal and hazelnut shells and their occurrence spans the period from at least the earliest to the latest Neolithic (Cole and Jones 2002-3, 134; Gossip and Jones 2007, 28-9). Settlement evidence in southern Britain from this period is generally scarce; however, it seems that these pit sites are not associated with permanent settlement, but were instead linked with intermittent or seasonal occupations.

The pit-digging tradition in Cornwall therefore forms a regional variation of wider practices characteristic of the British Neolithic, and it is apparent that pits dug during the Early Neolithic belong to a much broader continuum and were linked with a wider set of ritualized practices which were prevalent in Britain from the onset of the Neolithic (Thomas 1999, 64-74; Garrow 2007; Pannett 2012). Indeed, as a recent review of Neolithic pits recorded across Britain has revealed, in Cornwall they constitute the most widely occurring evidence for the Neolithic period (Garrow 2012a).

Regional context

However, by contrast with some other parts of Britain, including East Anglia (Healy 1988, 5-18; Garrow 2007), where pits are located in large groups, those in Cornwall and the wider South West region (with the exception of a larger group of 25 pits which has recently been found at Ottery St Mary in eastern Devon (Quinnell 2014)), tend to be found as isolated features, in pairs as at the Tremough site, or in small groups of less than a dozen pits.

Cornish Neolithic pits are typically bowl-shaped, small and shallow, although less regular examples are known. In fact one of the examples described here, pit [105], was of an irregular oval shape and is perhaps the largest recorded in Cornwall at 2.5m long by 1.6m wide. Elsewhere in Britain, pits tend to be larger than the Cornish examples and can contain notably exotic items, as at Cadbury Castle in Somerset, where a series of Early Neolithic pits contained leaf-shaped arrowheads, plain bowl pottery, antler and both animal and human bone (Griffith *et al* 2008, 82), or at Reading Business Park, where a pit was found to contain a complete bovine skeleton (Moore and Jennings 1992, 6). Nonetheless, pottery, flint, charcoal and worked or unusual stones remain the most consistently and frequently found deposits.

In Cornwall, the earliest Neolithic pit group with a more sophisticated finds assemblage was recorded at Tregarrick, Roche. Here ten pits ranged in date over four centuries, from *circa* 3790 cal BC to 3370 cal BC (Cole and Jones 2002-3, 134). There was evidence for the careful selection of artefacts for burial and for the careful placing of sherds of pottery within some of the pits, a practice also recorded in Grooved Ware assemblages from Late Neolithic pits elsewhere on the Tremough campus (Gossip and Jones 2007, 8).

Other Early Neolithic pit sites in Cornwall have also been found to contain similar suites of artefacts (Figure 11.1). These include pits at Portscatho, on the Roseland (Jones and Reed 2006), Trenowah, near St Austell (Johns 2008), several along the route of the Tintagel to Boscastle pipeline in north Cornwall (Jones and Quinnell 2014), and at Penmayne, Rock, near the Camel estuary

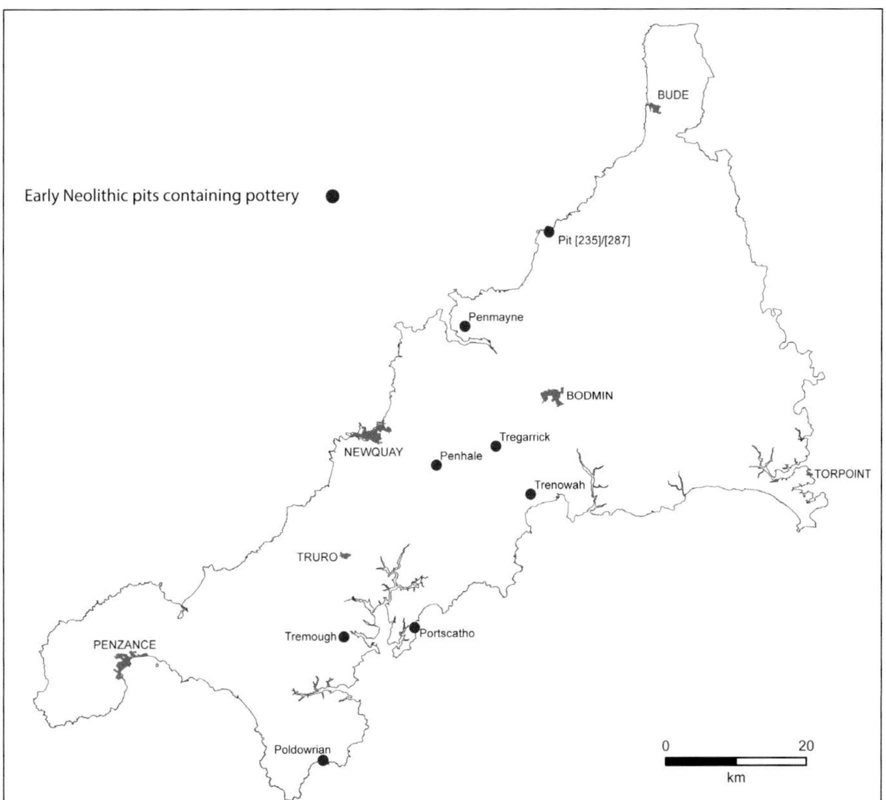

Figure 11.1 The distribution of pits with Early Neolithic pottery in Cornwall.

(Gossip *et al* 2012). All these sites had one to four pits containing earlier Neolithic pottery and the PAC building pits fit the same pattern.

Over the last decade, Early Neolithic pits in Cornwall have become much better dated; radiocarbon determinations for Early Neolithic pits with pottery in Cornwall are presented in Table 11.1 below (and see Figure 10.1). The PAC building pits can therefore be discussed in the context of other Cornish pits which have produced Neolithic pottery.

At Poldowrian, on the Lizard, a group of small pits were identified, one of which, pit [106], contained pottery and a leaf-shaped arrowhead, and another, pit [139], had been backfilled with large quantities of stones and charcoal (Smith and Harris 1982). The value of the dating from this site, is however, lessened by the fact that the radiocarbon determination was undertaken on bulked charcoal and may appear earlier than it actually was. Early Neolithic dates were, however, obtained from one of four pits excavated at Porthscatho, where four pits contained pottery, charcoal, hazelnuts and charcoal; one also produced a few cereal grains (Jones and Read 2006).

At Penmayne one of the pits was associated with carinated bowl pottery and hazelnut shells and had radiocarbon determinations spanning the thirty-seventh and thirty-sixth centuries cal BC. The contents and association with charred hazelnut shells are similar to Tremough. Likewise, several pits which were excavated along the north Cornwall pipeline were of Early Neolithic date (Jones and Quinnell 2014, 128-30). One of these, pit [235], contained pottery, hazelnut shell fragments and, unusually, a small quantity of cereal grains. Again the dating is very close to that from the PAC building pits at Tremough (Table 11.1).

At Trenowah three of the pits contained finds, including one, pit [300], with a sherd of pottery, a flint blade, charred crab apple pips and white quartz fragments in a charcoal-rich fill (Johns 2008, 6). This pit was not radiocarbon dated but an adjacent one produced a Middle Neolithic determination (Table 11.1).

However, although the Tremough PAC building pits share characteristics with other Cornish Neolithic pits, in containing deposits of pottery and broken flint (including finely-worked tools), charred macrofossils, especially hazelnut, and abundant charcoal, it is with those at Portscatho and Penmayne that they have the most similarities. They are broadly contemporary with one another. The formation of pit deposits is also comparable: at Portscatho, as at Tremough PAC, there is no evidence for the curation of vessels as sherds were fresh (Jones and Reed 2006, 22) and they appear to have been deposited very soon after breakage. This lack of formality in infilling was echoed in another pit at Tremough (pit [21]), to the north of the PAC site, which gave the date 4850±55 BP, 3770 – 3510 BC (AA-44601) (Gossip and Jones 2007, 28); that feature, however, was not associated with pottery.

Table 11.1 (following page): Pits with Early Neolithic pottery with closely associated radiocarbon determinations from Cornwall and Devon.

Site	Context/association	Lab. no	Age BP years	Calendrical years 95%
Cornwall				
North Cornwall pipeline, pit.	Pit [235], hazel charcoal, found with open bowl pottery a quarzitic pebble and a leaf-shaped arrowhead (Jones and Quinnell 2014).	SUERC-42047	4690±23	3625-3372
Penmayne, pit.	Pit [403], hazelnut found in pit with carinated bowl sherds (Gossip *et al* 2012).	SUERC-315182	4770±30	3641-3384
Penmayne, pit.	Pit [403], hazelnut found in pit with carinated bowl sherds (Gossip *et al* 2012).	SUERC-315183	4775±30	3641-3386
Penhale, pit.	Pit [254], within structure 3299, charred cereal grains associated with pottery (Whittle *et al* 2011, 514)	Wk-9839	5001±75	3953-3657
Penhale, posthole.	Posthole [3221], within structure 3299, hazel charcoal associated with pottery (Whittle *et al* 2011, 514).	Wk-9840	4951±61	3942-3639
Poldowrian, pit.	Pit [106], oak and Pomoideae charcoal found with pottery (Smith and Harris 1982)	HAR-4323	5180±150	4331-3696
Portscatho, pit.	Pit [512], hazel charcoal found in pit with carinated bowl P1 (Jones and Read 2006).	Wk-13259	4713±45	3635-3372
Portscatho, pit.	Pit [504], hazel charcoal found in pit with sherds of Neolithic pottery (Jones and Read 2006).	Wk-13257	4805±51	3696-3382
Portscatho, pit.	Pit [502], hazel charcoal found in pit with sherds of Neolithic pottery (Jones and Read 2006).	Wk-13256	4818±48	3704-3385
Portscatho, pit.	Pit [505], hazel charcoal found in pit with sherds of Neolithic pottery (Jones and Read 2006).	Wk-13258	4952±45	3912-3644
Tregarrick, pit.	Pit [40], hazel charcoal found with carinated bowl P6 (Cole and Jones 2002-3).	Wk-14916	4914±40BP	3773-3641
Tregarrick, pit.	Pit [48], hawthorn charcoal found with sherds of Neolithic pottery (Cole and Jones 2002-3).	Wk-14918	4908±47	3791-3636
Tregarrick, pit.	Pit [19], hazelnut shell found with sherds of Neolithic pottery (Cole and Jones 2002-3).	Wk-14913	4839±42	3705-3524
Tregarrick, pit.	Pit [45], hazelnut shell found with sherds of Neolithic pottery (Cole and Jones 2002-3).	Wk-14917	4768±43	3643-3380
Tregarrick, pit.	Pit [27], hazelnut shell found with sherds of Neolithic pottery (Cole and Jones 2002-3).	Wk-14915	4776±44	3644-3379
Tremough PAC, pit.	Pit [102], Charcoal, Hazel dated. Sherds of Neolithic pottery (this volume).	SUERC-29387	4750±40	3640-3377
Tremough PAC, pit.	Pit [105], Charcoal, Hazel dated. Sherds of Neolithic pottery (This volume).	SUERC-29383	4750±40	3640-3377
Devon				
Waylands, Tiverton, pit.	Pit [1510], Oak charcoal found in association with sherds of Neolithic pottery (Leverett and Quinnell 2010).	Wk-27272	4722±30	3634-3376

Interpreting pit contents

Interpretation of the way pits were infilled has formed the basis for much discussion and debate. Since the 1980s (for example, Richards and Thomas 1984; Thomas 1991; 1999, 64-74) it has been argued that many Neolithic pits were deliberately infilled and that residues from occupation may have been meaningful and carefully buried. The term 'structured deposition' has been widely used since the 1990s as a convenient short-hand for this process (Garrow 2012b).

However, it has also been pointed out that not all material which enters pits need have symbolically placed with great care or been undertaken as a ritual event in itself. Joanna Brück (1999b), in discussing the problems of interpreting 'ritual' at prehistoric sites, has suggested that many archaeologists have fallen into the trap of accepting a false dichotomy in explaining their site data as either associated with 'practical' or with a distinct 'non-functional' category of behaviour. The latter category is then often identified as of a 'ritual' nature. This is problematic because such divisions are unlikely to have been meaningful to prehistoric communities. As noted above, material found within pits has often been interpreted in this way and has sometimes been singled out by archaeologists as 'special'. However, Brück (*ibid*) has suggested that 'special' or 'odd' deposits need not have been viewed as such at all by prehistoric communities, who may have seen them as being routine, rational and effective actions, which led to desired outcomes.

Duncan Garrow (2012b) has also pointed out that there has been a tendency to concentrate on interpretations which favour 'special activity' of an overtly ritual character and as such to underplay the formation of deposits through routine day-to-day life. Instead, he has proposed that deposits found in Neolithic pits and other contexts formed part of a continuum which ranged from 'odd deposits' (for example, articulated human remains or complete pots) through to 'material cultural patterning' produced by routine quotidian activity (for example, the burial of refuse from a meal). Indeed, in most prehistoric societies it is likely that divisions between the sacred and the profane were far less distinct than they are today and that even the burial of selected items of domestic refuse in selected ways may have held significance (Bradley 2005, 169).

Given recent debates over structured deposition and the potential over-use of this term, it is worth noting that, as we have seen above, there does in Cornwall appear to be a continuum in practices associated with pits ranging from casual discard to more formal deposition. There are some instances where pottery was clearly placed very carefully, as at Tregarrick (Cole and Jones 2002-3, 135). By contrast, rather less care would appear to have taken place with the infilling of pits at Tremough. Nonetheless, the Tremough PAC site pits are of interest as they do provide evidence for the way certain items were treated after use.

The PAC pits contained sherds of freshly broken pottery, which do not appear to have been placed in any order, a broken projectile-point **L3** and a finely-worked Portland chert arrowhead **L1**, mixed with a charcoal-rich soil. The presence of both gabbroic clays from the Lizard and glassy Meneage basalts in the fabrics of the vessels is an indicator that the pots were manufactured away from their clay source and could be a pointer to their significance. Also of interest is the inclusion in both pits of both local and possibly imported lithic material, including the Portland chert arrowhead, the raw material for which came from approximately 250 kilometres to the east on the Dorset coast. Both pits also contained worked flint that had been broken, perhaps deliberately, and both contained arrowheads, including a beautifully worked probable leaf-shaped arrowhead of Early Neolithic date **L3**. The inclusion of these items indicates that their burial was not entirely down to random loss or carelessness (Lawson-Jones, chapter 7). Both the distance of the clay source, the flint and the chert from the Tremough plateau, could have made them redolent of those places and of the people who made the artefacts (*cf*, for example, Harris 2009; Smythe 2014, 130), and their deposition could have made reference to those connections.

The PAC building pits at Tremough contained charcoal-rich fills, as did the tree-throw holes (below), and stones (killas, granite and quartz) showing signs of having been subjected to high temperatures (heat fracture and scorching). The subsoil adjacent to pit [105] also showed some signs of having been heated. While not hearth pits in themselves, it is possible that material from adjacent fires was mixed with the artefacts as part of a process surrounding the infilling of the pit, perhaps marking the end of an occupation or an event such as a gathering involving the consumption of food. This included hazelnut shells, the only surviving remnant of a meal consumed immediately before the burial of the artefacts. The abundant charcoal deposits recorded in the majority of contemporaneous pits in Cornwall indicates that fires may have been closely linked to the pit digging and reburial process, with significance attached to the inclusion of some of the charred remains. The presence of hazelnuts and wild food species, such as apple or pear at Trenowah and Tregarrick (Johns 2008, 33, 36; Cole and Jones 2002-3), and occasionally of small amounts of cereal grain (Jones and Quinnell 2014, 128), may be an indicator that the preparation and consumption of a food were followed by the ritualized burial of its traces.

Some items found within the PAC building pits, including the pottery, may have had a short biography of use, being deposited not long after breakage, but it is difficult to imagine that their deposition was not deeply embedded cultural practice, perhaps part of an 'ingrained disposition' of 'clearing away' away at the end of an event or an occupation (Jones 2013). This process would not, as Brück (1999b) has argued, have necessarily been seen as being 'special' but would probably have been considered (if it were consciously thought through at all) to have conformed with the 'right' way of acting or dwelling in the landscape. It has been argued previously that the burial of domestic rubbish in prehistoric features at Tremough is likely to have been part of deeply embedded cultural traditions and that everyday and ritual activities may have been 'inextricably entwined' (Gossip and Jones 2007, 29).

Marking space

Significantly, the results from Tremough have shed light on how pits might have been marked after they had been infilled. The lack of intercutting relationships between Neolithic pits has been noted elsewhere in Cornwall and it has been suggested that this was either because pits were contemporary with one another or because they were marked in some way which has not survived in the archaeological record (for example, Jones and Quinnell 2014). There is evidence to suggest that the PAC pits may have been marked on the surface after being infilled. The large pile of stones adjacent to pit [102] indicates that it had been marked on the surface, perhaps to avoid accidental disturbance to its contents at some point in the future or to leave a more permanent marker of the place of a past event. The posthole [111] at the end of pit [105] may have supported a post which marked the site of the pit after it had been backfilled. It has been argued that pit digging (and the burial of the objects within them) was a way of fixing a community to the land on which they were dug (Pollard 2001; Thomas 1999, 72, 87; Cole and Jones 2003, 134; Harding 2006), and the marking of the pit sites with stones or posts would have made the sites of the pits more visible to subsequent visitors to the plateau.

Tree-throws as shelters and 'pits'

The presence of the two tree-throw hollows may relate to the selection of this land for woodland clearance or possibly their *ad hoc* use as temporary shelters. Similar features are being recognised more frequently in the Cornish archaeological record. For example, an amorphous pit identified at the Travel Inn site, Helston, is thought to be a possible tree-throw. This feature had been deliberately backfilled with Middle Neolithic Fengate Ware, the first instance of its kind in Cornwall (Quinnell 2009), in addition to flints. In the wider region, other recently identified potential tree-throw holes with anthropogenic deposits have been recorded at Willand Road, Cullompton, Devon, where flint was found in association with amorphous pits filled with otherwise natural deposits (Hood 2009b), and at Waylands, near Tiverton, where sherds of earlier Neolithic pottery were found (Leverett and Quinnell 2010).

Beyond the South West region, tree-throws have been widely found to have been associated with Neolithic activity around Britain and Ireland (Brown 2000; Cuttler *et al* 2012, 144; Smythe 2014 115-6). They have been recorded in particularly large numbers along the Thames Valley, in the south of England, and this has led to discussions regarding the intentional deposition of material culture in tree hollows created either by natural processes (storm damage or diseased trees) or as part of woodland clearance (Evans *et al* 1999; Butterworth 1999, 138; Macphail and Linderholm 2004, 34-36).

One interpretation of the evidence from the Thames Valley has been that tree-throw holes were used as shelters and that these later became deliberate middens for significant groups of artefacts. It is also suggested that tree-throws are a feature of episodes of tree clearing during the Mesolithic-Neolithic transition, but that the use of them disappears after the Early Neolithic (Allen *et al* 2004, 91-92). It has, however, also been pointed out that the discovery of Neolithic artefacts in tree-throws may in some instances have related to symbolic beliefs connected with trees (for example, Hills and Lucy 2013). In a world which was covered by large areas of woodland, it is possible that the long life-cycles of trees could have become associated with generational conceptions of human time (Evans *et al* 1999), with trees becoming seen as animate in their own right. Anthropological research has revealed that trees can be conceived as being 'alive', or inhabited by spirits, and as having metaphorical analogies with the human body (Bonnemere 1998), and ethnological studies (for example, Busia 1954; Hackett 1996, 40) have shown that tree felling is often accompanied by placatory rituals to woodland spirits or other supernatural beings. For example, before cutting down trees for use in settlements, the people of Ara, South Sulawesi, in Indonesia, engage ritual specialists to talk to the spirits of the tree to make sure the tree is willing to be cut down (Gibson 1995). Given some broadly similar cultural context in the Early Neolithic of southern Britain, it is possible that the sites of 'well-known' fallen trees with long biographies may also have been marked with deposits, out of respect.

Returning to Tremough, the piece of debitage or tool manufacture waste found with burnt stones and charcoal in tree-throw infilling deposit (108) may be an indicator that the hollow was used a temporary shelter or perhaps more probably as a receptacle for occupation-related refuse. Although there is a near absence of artefacts and no radiocarbon determinations from either of the Tremough tree-throw holes, the composition of their deposits is comparable with Early Neolithic pits found at Tremough and across Cornwall (for example, Gossip and Jones 2007, 7-8; Jones and Quinnell 2014), which often contain charcoal-rich fills and abundant stone and flint. It is possible therefore that these natural hollows were in some ways seen as being similar to and were in use at the same time as the deliberately dug pits.

As such, they may have fulfilled a similar role to dug pits, and been the foci for comparable activities. It is possible, therefore, that the tree-throws were the foci for deposits following the acquisition of new land for agriculture and settlement, with the marking of a 'special' fallen tree or were associated with other activities which took place within clearings in the woodland (Leverett and Quinnell 2010).

The pits and experiencing space

The locations chosen for pits may have been significant to Neolithic communities; for example, the selection of coastal locations for pit sites at Portscatho and Poldowrian, and for those near to the north Cornish coast, may have been an important consideration, occupying liminal zones between sea and land (Jones and Reed 2006, 139-40; Jones and Quinnell 2014, 130; Gossip *et al* 2012). Others such as those near Roche Rock may have been associated with larger gatherings at topographically distinctive focal points in the landscape (Cole and Jones 2002-3). By contrast, those in lowland environments, as at Tremough, may have been created by small groups passing through a partially-cleared wooded landscape. The occurrence of pits in the Early Neolithic without associated occupation-related evidence, such as large flint scatters or permanent structures, suggests these activities were being carried out by sections of the community, possibly during seasonal gatherings (Cole and Jones 2002-3) or as part of regular movement around the landscape.

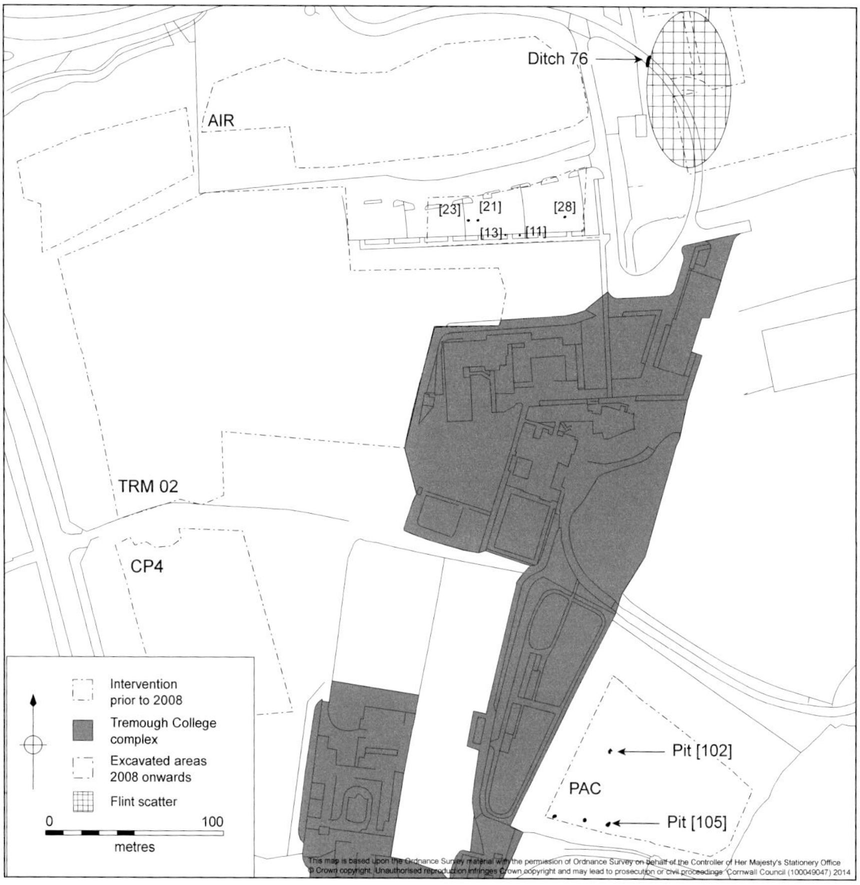

Figure 11.2 Early Neolithic features.

At the level of the Tremough plateau, the PAC building pits are among a small number of archaeological features dating to the first half of the fourth millennium cal BC (Figure 11.2) and are of interest because, with the exception of a single small abraded sherd of pottery from ditch [76] (Gossip and Jones 2007, 7), they are the first Early Neolithic features at Tremough to be associated with ceramics. By contrast, the pits excavated in 2002 in Field 4 were associated with burnt stones and charcoal but were entirely devoid of artefacts (Gossip and Jones 2007, 6-7). They are also broadly of the same date as the ditch [76] which appeared to delineate an area that was associated with primary flint knapping (Lawson-Jones 2007) but devoid of pits. The two pits at the PAC building therefore offer some further support for the suggestion raised by the earlier investigations, which proposed that different types of activity were occurring across the plateau area during the Early Neolithic period, with perhaps more sustained activity taking place at the eastern end of the plateau, to the east of ditch [76], and shorter visits elsewhere.

Early Bronze Age activity

Structure 1 was associated with the second major phase of activity to be identified by the recent excavations at Tremough. This dated to the earlier second millennium cal BC. Unlike the previous large-scale investigations, no evidence was found for Late Neolithic Grooved Ware-associated pits. In common with the earlier excavations there was also a paucity of evidence for occupation at the end of the third millennium too, when Beaker pottery was current in southern Britain. There is, therefore, a gap in our knowledge about how the Tremough plateau was inhabited for much of the third millennium cal BC. Structure 1 was, however, broadly contemporary with other activity identified on the plateau and the relationships between the features will be discussed below.

Earlier Bronze Age Structure 1

Structure 1 represents an important discovery because, in common with the Neolithic, much of what could be broadly termed 'domestic' or 'non-funerary' Early Bronze Age activity in the South West (for example, Jones *et al* 2012), and elsewhere in Britain, is typically characterised by small pits and stray finds of pottery which may be residual or in contexts which might not necessarily be 'domestic' (Halsted 2007; Garwood 2011; 123; Morigi *et al* 2011, 311-330). Currently, only one other circular earlier Bronze Age 'domestic' structure has been found in Cornwall which has been dated to the first half of the second millennium cal BC, with the majority of roundhouses firmly belonging to the period after *circa* 1500 cal BC (for example, Jones and Taylor 2010, 158-9).

Tremough Structure 1 was a sub-circular construction which was defined by a ring of postholes with a diameter of approximately 7m. There was no trace of any surviving wall material; however, judging by the size of the postholes which formed the circuit of the ring it is likely to have been covered by a relatively light superstructure. The entrance was difficult to establish, although the postholes were fairly evenly spaced, around 1m apart, with a far wider gap of 3m on the eastern side between postholes [19] and [62]. The presence of shallow pit [56], a possible hearth or burnt area, central within this gap suggests it was set within the area of the entranceway (chapter 2). There was little evidence for recutting of features and from this we can surmise that the building was probably rather short-lived.

There were further features outside the structure. One which was thought to be possibly related to it was pit [37]; this was situated a few metres to the west, displayed evidence for burning and contained a charred plant macrofossil assemblage which included cultivated oats. Two radiocarbon determination, on the oats and a wild radish capsule, were both radiocarbon dated to the Romano-British period (chapters 8 and 10). Other nearby features mostly could not be dated and their relationship with Structure 1 could not be ascertained, so they will not be discussed here (for details, Gossip 2011).

Comparanda for Structure 1 in the South West as a whole are scarce. Two earlier late third to early second millennium cal BC structures have been identified in Cornwall. The first, an ephemeral, oval-shaped, post-built Beaker-associated structure dating to *circa* 2000-1730 cal BC was excavated at Higher Besore, west of Truro (Gossip, forthcoming). The second, structure 108 at Sennen, was also associated with Beaker pottery and was a flimsy stake-built structure set over a hollow measuring approximately 4m by 3m (Jones *et al* 2012). It has been radiocarbon dated to *circa* 2300-2100 cal BC, which was much earlier than Structure 1. Neither of these structures appears to have been associated with permanent occupation, and little is known about use of the contemporary surrounding landscape, although a saddle quern fragment from Higher Besore might have been associated with the Beaker structure and mullers which may have been used for the processing of cereals were found in the structure at Sennen.

Chronologically, the closest known structure to Structure 1 is Gwithian structure 1642 (formerly often referred to as the Beaker house), which has two radiocarbon determinations; one of these dated to 1890-1610 cal BC but the second of 1310-1040 cal BC fell in the Middle Bronze Age (Nowakowski *et al* 2007). This structure was more complex, being 7.5m in diameter and comprised of stake-rings associated with gullies containing posts and earth banks which are likely to have formed a double-skinned wall. The building also possessed a porch and a central hearth. It seems to have been more permanent than either of the

Figure 11.3 The principal earlier Bronze Age structures referred to in the text.

Beaker-associated structures discussed above, or Tremough Structure 1, and was associated with an agricultural settlement comprised of small fields (*ibid).*

Beyond Cornwall, Early Bronze Age settlement activity of the later third and earlier second millennium cal BC is fairly widely distributed across southern Britain (Figure 11.3) As noted above, however, this normally takes the form of pits containing sherds of pottery and occasionally charred cereal remains (Brück 2000; Garwood 2011, 123), or clusters of posts and stakeholes which are difficult to assemble into well-defined structures, as for example at Belle Tout in Sussex and Snail Down in Wiltshire (Bradley 1970; Thomas 2005, 74-5).

Circular or oval settings of posts and stakeholes are commonly found under Early Bronze Age round barrows (for example, Fox 1959; Lynch 1993). Many of these structures are likely to be closely associated with primary phases of barrow construction or activity linked with funerary rites and did not exist as independent settlement-related structures. Other structures sealed by barrows, however, are more difficult to be sure of, and may well represent earlier episodes of settlement activity, as, for example, at Upper Ninepence in the Walton Basin in Wales, where stakeholes forming a structure with a diameter of 12m was found beneath a barrow mound (Gibson 1999, 163).

However, some identifiable structures have been recorded in southern England. At Yarnton, Oxfordshire, a small dwelling with a diameter of 4m with an entrance porch has been found to date to the first two centuries of the second millennium cal BC (Morigi *et al* 2011, 321) and five other structures found there may have belonged to the same phase, although these were not securely dated. More permanent roundhouses have been suggested for the settlement at Bishops Canning Down, Wiltshire. Chris Gingell (1992, 153) argued that the post-built structures might date to the latest part of the Early Bronze Age, although the radiocarbon dating places them in the Middle Bronze Age (*ibid*, 159). To the west of Wessex, at Brean Down in Somerset, an oval, stone-lined building, structure 57, measuring 4.5m by 3m was excavated. This structure is not, however, closely dated and could belong to either a Beaker-using phase, or may instead be of a date later in the Bronze Age (Bell 1990, 34).

In Wales very few Early Bronze Age settlements have been identified (Lynch *et al* 2000, 87). However, the largest and best recorded example was found at Stackpole Warren in Pembrokeshire, where sherds of Collared Urn, flint and cremated human bone were recovered from a small hollow-set roundhouse, structure 146. This structure had a diameter of *circa* 5m and was defined by a post-ring with a porch (Benson *et al* 1990). Two radiocarbon determinations falling in the periods 2134-1700 cal BC and 1876-1467 cal BC were obtained from destruction deposits within the structure. These dates overlap with those from Structure 1 at Tremough, and the size of the buildings is similar.

Because of the lack of evidence for substantial architecture, it is necessary to consider alternative modes of settlement activity. Joanna Brück (1999c) has argued, for example, that the relatively insubstantial structures found across southern England during the Early Bronze Age may have been associated with short-term periods of occupation involving residential mobility; in essence, dwellings of the

Early Bronze Age were less permanent than those of the Middle Bronze Age. The evidence from Structure 1, which does not indicate that it was occupied for a long period of time, would certainly be consistent with this interpretation.

Leaving the structure behind

Ritualized abandonment will be discussed more fully below in relation to Middle Bronze Roundhouse 1. However, it seems probable that Structure 1 was abandoned with some degree of deliberation. Although there was little evidence for patterning in the distribution of artefacts, some formality in deposition practices is indicated by the fact that some of the postholes and adjacent features were filled with deposits which contained a large assemblage of artefacts. As has been argued above for the Neolithic pits, there may have been a routinely ritualized process of clearing away and returning of objects to the ground which cut across many aspects of life, from the 'domestic' through to the overtly ceremonial, throughout the third and second millennia cal BC.

Some light can be shed on this process by considering the condition of the artefacts which were found within the structure. The majority of the assemblage comprised sherds of more or less fresh or lightly abraded sherds of Trevisker pottery (chapter 3, above), which had not been crushed by *in situ* standing posts. This suggests that broken ceramics were not left lying around on the surface but were instead rapidly placed soon after breakage into the posthole cuts, and given that they were not crushed, the posts must already have been removed from their sockets. It is therefore reasonable to suggest that the ceramics were associated with the latest use of the structure and that they were deliberately, if not necessarily carefully placed into the empty post sockets during the abandonment of the site.

In addition to the finds of ceramics, the postholes were also found to contain worked stones, which included a saddle quern fragment, a whetstone, and other stones which had been used as pestles for grinding; another posthole was found to contain a cassiterite pebble. There must be significance in the fact that all the stone artefacts, and the cassiterite pebble, had been broken before deposition. Although the assemblage is small, such uniformity in non-completeness has not been observed in Cornish Bronze Age structures elsewhere. The cassiterite pebble was also of interest as such pebbles would not have occurred naturally on the site and must have been obtained from a stream or river and brought to the structure. It could, of course, have been crushed and ground down to produce ore, and much of the stonework assemblage would have been suitable for such a purpose. The whetstone could also have been used for the sharpening of finished copper-alloy objects. The inclusion of these finds might suggest that they were not chance losses and, as will be discussed below in relation to Roundhouse 1, the items chosen for inclusion in abandonment contexts could reflect the use or biography of the building or perhaps the activities which the person who occupied it might have been engaged in. Either way the selected artefacts might have been associated with conveying a biography of the place.

As will be discussed below, the abandonment of structures, especially roundhouses, with deposition of occupation-related material and more finely-worked objects, reached its peak after about 1500 cal BC and continued to around 1200 cal BC with the ritualized abandonment of the Middle Bronze Age hollow-set roundhouses that are found across the lowlands of Cornwall (for example, Nowakowski 2001; Jones, forthcoming a). The infilling of postholes associated with Structure 1, however, indicates that the planned abandonment of 'domestic' structures was already taking place before *circa* 1500 cal BC.

The setting of Structure 1

The local context of Structure 1 is uncertain. The rather limited evidence from plant macrofossils and charcoal from the current and previous environmental analysis has suggested that during the Early Bronze Age woodland resources were still available, with oak and hazel being common in the archaeological record (Gossip and Jones 2007, 22; chapter 9, above). At the same time, hazelnuts are still found in occupation contexts, and it is not until the Middle Bronze Age that cereals become more common in the archaeological record. However, there are some indications that cultivation may have taken place in the surrounding landscape rather earlier. In Structure 1, posthole [19] produced a single hulled wheat grain and just outside the post-ring, pit [23] produced a small quantity of hulled wheat grains (chapter 8). Several of the Early Bronze Age pits excavated in 2002 were also found to contain small amounts of charred grain (Gossip and Jones 2007, 22) and the saddle quern fragment from Structure 1 may have been used to grind cereals (chapter 4). Limited evidence for earlier Bronze Age cultivation has been found elsewhere in Cornwall. At Gwithian, sherds of Beaker pottery may have been incorporated into the manuring of fields, and as noted above structure 1642 appeared to be associated with a field system (Nowakowski *et al* 2007). The remaining evidence is much more scanty. A large pit [44] at Portreath on the north Cornish coast, for example, which is likely to have held a standing stone, produced a small quantity of cultivated cereal grains (Reynolds 2006). In the De Lank valley on Bodmin Moor traces of later Early Bronze Age cultivation were identified in the pollen record (Jones and Tinsley 2000-1). Across the broader South West region (Devon and Somerset) the environmental record indicates an increase in cultivation from the middle centuries of the second millennium cal BC (for example, Wilkinson and Straker 2008).

In fact, indications of cultivation in southern Britain before *circa* 1500 cal BC are generally still quite scarce (Yates 2007, 111-12). Prior to 2000 cal BC, there is evidence for cultivation during the Beaker-using period in some parts of southern Britain, including areas of the Wessex chalk and the Upper Thames Valley (Gingell 1992, 155; Evans 1990; Evans *et al* 1993, 188-9; Whittle 1997, 7; Whittle *et al* 1993, 232). Nonetheless, although settlements in some parts of southern Britain may have been surrounded by relatively extensive cultivated areas (Allen 2005), it is also possible that agriculture during this period was of an episodic or short-term character, as there is little evidence for formal field systems with well-defined boundaries around them (Thomas 1999, 200; Brück 2000). Indeed, Andrew

Lawson (2007, 172-3) has argued that on the Wessex chalk shifting episodes of pastoralism rather than cultivation may have been the principal mode of subsistence during the latter part of the third millennium cal BC, and this may have persisted into the second millennium cal BC.

However, as with the identification of domestic structures, there are few securely dated indicators of cultivation during the earlier part of the second millennium cal BC in southern Britain, with evidence taking the form of small amounts of grain recovered from pits and postholes and cereal impressions on pottery (Case and Whittle 1982; Halsted 2005, 23; Morigi *et al* 2011, 317-20). As discussed above, this paucity is partly attributable to the paucity of well-defined settlement sites and also because of the lack of securely dated field systems belonging to the first half of the second millennium cal BC.

The limited data from Tremough are, therefore, broadly similar to what has been found elsewhere both in Cornwall and across much of southern Britain. On current evidence we might envisage significant tree coverage in the wider vicinity of Structure 1, with some cultivation, perhaps on shifting plots, and this would be consistent with the probable short duration of Structure 1 itself.

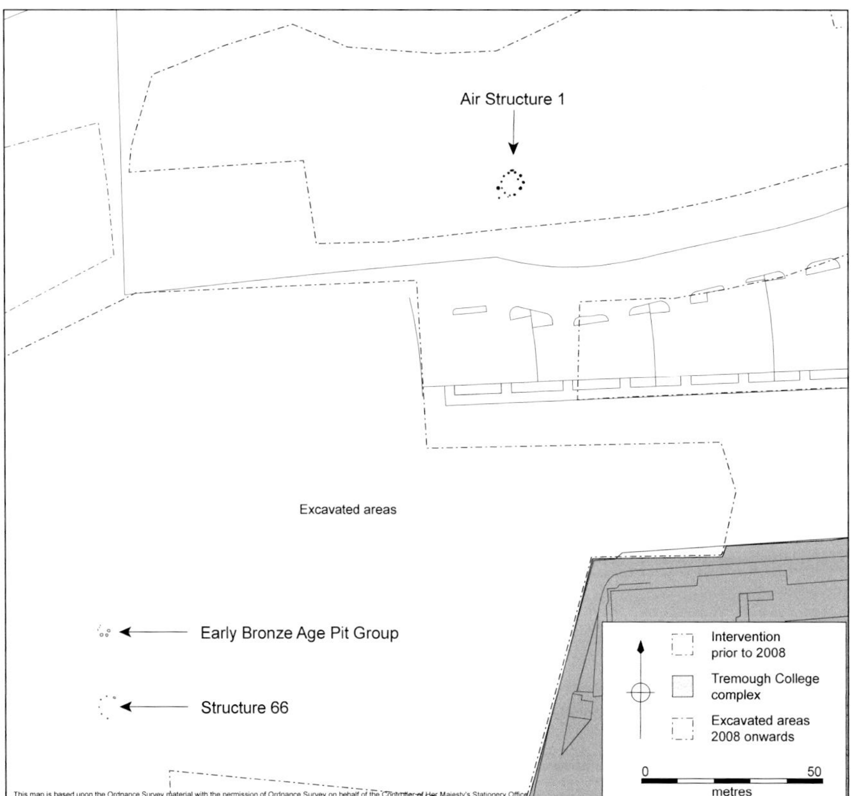

Figure 11.4 Early Bronze Age features.

In addition to cultivation, however, the relationship between Structure 1 and other forms of Early Bronze Age activity on the site also needs to be considered. There was evidence from the 2002 investigations that other activities, including the digging of pits and the construction of a free-standing post-ring, were also taking place in a different part of the Tremough plateau during the Early Bronze Age (Figure 11.4). This raises questions about the organization of space and the relationship between Structure 1 and other practices which were of broadly contemporary date.

Formal ceremonial activity was identified at the western end of the plateau, approximately 170m to the south west of Structure 1 (Gossip and Jones 2007, 11). In this area was located Structure 66 (Figure 11.5), the earliest of a series of five timber circles that spanned most of the second millennium cal BC. It was erected around 2200-1950 cal BC and the posts were probably renewed around 1750-1550 cal BC. The post-ring was 6m in diameter and was made up of six surviving posts, the eastern side having been removed by a later field division. Some evidence for formalized deposition was indicated by an unweathered fired-clay block, possibly part of a mould associated with metalworking, which had been placed into a posthole on the western side of the ring.

The earliest phase of this post-ring appears to have been associated with a group of six nearby pits which had been backfilled with charcoal, burnt stone, hazelnut shells and a small quantity of charred grain. Other than these pits, there was no evidence for any occupation-related activity. It is possible that the pits, which date to *circa* 2200-1900 cal BC were contemporary with the construction of Structure 66, or activities associated with its earliest usage. However, the subsequent renewal of the posts within Structure 66 means that it is likely to have

Figure 11.5 Photograph of structure 66 taken from the south-west.

been standing for a long period of time, and was possibly for some period at least contemporary with Structure 1.

It is therefore of interest that Structure 1, a domestic building, was built at a respectful distance from the ceremonial post-ring, and appears to have set a precedent for the distancing of formal ceremonial activity from settlement areas which continued into the Middle Bronze Age (below). The two structures were, however, at no great distance from one another and there were clearly some conceptual links between them. As has already been discussed, this is unsurprising because it is unlikely that communities in the Early Bronze Age would have made rigid distinctions between ritual and secular activity (for example, Bradley 2005) and we might therefore expect there to be overlaps between formal ceremonial activity and ritualized activity occurring in inhabited structures.

The first area of overlap lies with the architecture of both structures. Both comprised a setting of posts with a similar diameter. This marks a departure from previous Early and Late Neolithic activity on the site which was associated with amorphous groups of pits (Gossip and Jones 2007, 7-10). As circular structures of similar size, they may have embodied shared symbolism and aside from the differences in use – one as a short-term residence and the other for less frequent but much longer-term ceremonial activity, there are likely to have been connections between the sites.

These connections would have included the materiality of the timber used for the posts and any symbolic properties that the wood they were made from was perceived to have had (Townend 2007; Aldhouse-Green 2000; Coles 1998). The selection of suitable timber, the felling of trees, the cutting of the posts and the digging of postholes to hold the timbers would also have involved shared techniques. Anthropological study reveals that the construction process is frequently one which is punctuated by ritualized actions and events and that the timbers themselves may have been chosen for their symbolic properties (for example, Kis-Jovak *et al* 1988, 46-9; Turton 1978; Waterson 1997, chapter 6); this might also have been true for the construction of Structure 1 and structure 66.

There may also have been shared underlying symbolic associations which were associated with their circularity. The post-rings represent the imposition of standing architecture onto the plateau and the adoption of the circular archetype, which became the prevalent form for both ceremonial monuments and domestic structures across the British Isles from the later Neolithic to the end of the Iron Age (for example, Bradley 2012, 189-203). In the end, the major difference between Structure 1 and structure 66 was their final wrapping (Richards 2014a). At Structure 1, the post-ring was sheathed by a roof and walling, which would have covered the posts forming the superstructure of the building. At structure 66 the posts were left open and the boundary remained permeable, but the symbolic importance of the posts and their circular arrangement may have been significant in both structures.

In addition to these architectural links, both structures also produced evidence of formalized deposition. As we have seen, in Structure 1 this included the inclusion of pottery, hammerstones, a whetstone and a pebble of cassiterite. As noted above, much of the stonework assemblage would not be out of place in association with the working of metal ores. It may therefore be of significance that, the only deliberately deposited find from structure 66 was also likely to have been a mould associated with metalworking. Both structures may therefore have made links to a magical transformative process that turned stones into metal objects. In the case of Structure 1, it is possible that the actual process of transformation took place there or nearby, or that the inhabitant was associated with those practices. In the case of structure 66, the symbolism of transformation may have been referred to.

It is also worth noting at this juncture, that just as structure 66 seems to have been the first in a series of timber ceremonial monuments which spanned much of the second millennium cal BC, so Structure 1 represents the first of a series of structures with associations with metalworking, including Roundhouse 1 and to a lesser degree, the Late Bronze Age Enclosure 1 (below). Although this could be argued to be coincidental, Bronze Age metalworking sites have seldom been identified in Cornwall or elsewhere in the South West peninsula (see below), and to have three successive Bronze Age sites with metalworking associations seems a little fortuitous. Is it perhaps, therefore, possible that, just as some areas became associated with burial monuments, that a landscape biography or oral tradition had accrued, which associated Tremough with a place of metalworkers? If correct, this would be significant because it would mean that not only did ritual traditions continue, albeit in a transformed context, from the Early Bronze Age into the Middle Bronze Age (Jones 2008; and below), but also that specialized practices associated with place may have done so as well.

Structure 1, a summary

In summary, Structure 1 was almost certainly a short-lived building which belongs within a wider tradition of ephemeral buildings, including the example from Gwithian in Cornwall and those at Stackpole Warren and Yarnton. These date to before the middle second millennium cal BC, at which time domestic architecture in the form of roundhouses became more visible in the landscape. It is not certain whether it was linked with a wider occupation involving activities, such as pastoralism, or if it was sited in an area which had been cultivated. It is, however, possible that it was linked with seasonal episodes of occupation. The finds recovered from abandonment contexts suggest that it could have associated with the working of metal ores, or at least have been used by someone who had undertaken such tasks.

It is also probable that Structure 1 was erected in an area which was the focus for activity over a longer period than the life of the building. It is likely to have been contemporary with ceremonial activities associated with structure 66 and both structures in their own ways may have contributed to the way that the plateau was used by subsequent generations.

Middle Bronze Age settlement

Two Middle Bronze Age roundhouses were uncovered during the 2011 excavations. Although Middle Bronze Age post-rings had been identified in 2002 (Gossip and Jones 2007, 14-22), they were the first houses of this period to be discovered on the plateau. Both were of the hollow-set type, around 20 of which are found across the lowlands of Cornwall, including sites at Trevisker and Trethellan, Callestick and Trevilson (ApSimon and Greenfield 1972; Nowakowski 1991; Jones 1998-9a; Jones and Taylor 2004). They have been found across the lowlands from Boden on the Lizard (Gossip 2008c) to Scarcewater, located on the edge of the St Austell granite (Jones and Taylor 2010, 6-26) and the Carnon Gate roundhouse, situated near to the Carnon River (Gossip and Jones 2008), which is the closest to Tremough, lying approximately 6 kilometres to the north west higher up the river system, or around 5 kilometres as the crow flies across land (Figure 11.6).

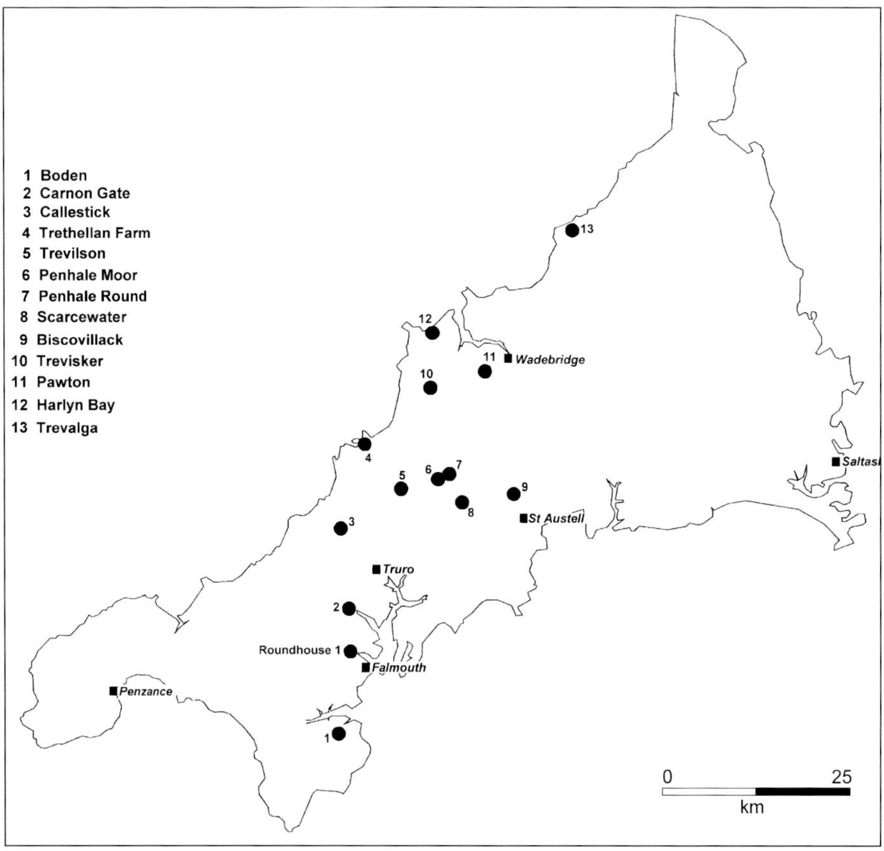

Figure 11.6 The distribution of hollow-set roundhouses in Cornwall.

Roundhouse 1: A 'life' history

Many anthropological and archaeological writers have stressed the central importance of roundhouses for the reproduction of later prehistoric communities, arguing that these could act as places of socialization, embody cosmologies in their designs and can even be considered as being animate in their own right (Tringham 1991; Parker Pearson 1996; Waterson 1997, chapter 6; Brück 1999a; Bender *et al* 2007). These and other works have been highly influential in the interpretation of prehistoric roundhouses. The idea that houses had life-cycles has also been an important concept, and Ruth Tringham (1995) has highlighted the fact that buildings have life histories involving interactions with people which go beyond mere 'use-lives'. These interactions can begin with the selection of the building materials and the rituals undertaken during their construction, to their use in daily life over time and through to the way that they are left (Turton 1977; Brück 2001; Townend 2007; Smythe 2013, 12-20; Jones, forthcoming a). In other words, houses can have biographies which are as rich as those of their inhabitants, and the two can become interwoven with one another. The following section therefore considers Roundhouse 1 in relation to other excavated houses in the South West peninsula, but also in regard to it having had its own biography, especially in relation to its abandonment.

Form and use

Roundhouse 1 is similar in size to other excavated examples The 9m diameter of the house hollow, is for example comparable to both roundhouse 1250 at Scarcewater and the Trevalga roundhouse on the north Cornish coast (Jones and Taylor 2010, 11; Jones and Quinnell 2014). The architecture is also consistent with other excavated lowland roundhouses, like those at Trethellan or Scarcewater (Nowakowski 1991; Jones and Taylor 2010, 16-26). It was a hollow-set structure, within which a ring of posts were set to support the roof. The surviving house hollow was not as deep as in some other structures, but the site is likely to have seen a degree of truncation as a result of post-prehistoric ploughing and this may have reduced the depth. There was no surviving evidence of walling. This would have been located within the inside edge of the hollow cut, but it may again have been removed, either through subsequent ploughing or as part of the demolition process. The cut for the hollow was, however, deeper along part of the north-western side of the roundhouse and some stones were present here, which may have represented displaced walling material. Elsewhere there is evidence that house walling was removed as part of the abandonment process, as at Callestick, for example, where the wall had been pushed into the house interior (Jones 1998-9a).

Internal features, in the form of stakeholes and postholes, were frequent but difficult to disentangle in terms of their functions and relationships. There were, however, two hearths north of the centre of the roundhouse and these had been heated to such an extent that the natural had been scorched and a layer of tamped clay (799) had been partially burnt by the temperature of the fire. It is extremely rare for floor layers to survive, and where they do it is often because of the proximity of the hearth, as at Trevalga and Boden (Jones and Quinnell 2014; Gossip 2008c). Presumably this floor originally extended across the remainder of the structure but had not survived due to wear and tear and erosion by feet.

Despite having sunken interior floors, typically there are relatively few occupation-related layers and comparatively little is known about daily life. As we shall see below, much of what has been written about Middle Bronze Age roundhouses has in fact concerned their abandonment. Fortunately, we know rather more about the function of Roundhouse 1 than is the case with almost any other excavated roundhouse in the south west of Britain. The artefacts from the roundhouse were all in abandonment contexts and this will be discussed below; nonetheless, the strands from the artefactual assemblage combine to give an indication of activities which took place inside the building. The most obvious indicators of possible use were the nine bivalve stone moulds which had been used to make pins and socketed tools (for example, axes, palstaves and chisels) (chapter 5). The stonework assemblage also included other items of worked stone including pestles / hammerstones which could have been used for metalworking. However, there was no slag, which implies that they were being used on finished metals, which leave far less debris. By themselves these artefacts need not have been linked to the roundhouse. However, droplets of copper-alloy were recovered from soil samples taken from inside the roundhouse and geochemical analysis also revealed raised levels of copper and tin within the house and around hearth [748]/[774] (chapter 6). Taken together, these results provide convincing evidence for Roundhouse 1 having been used for metalworking. The significance of this will be discussed below.

The entrance was not clearly defined, although it seems likely that it was on the south eastern side. A roughly southern facing entrance is common to many of the Middle Bronze Age roundhouses found across the South West peninsula (Mercer 1970; Jones and Taylor 2010, 70; Jones and Quinnell 2011; Butler 1997, 126) and beyond (Barrett *et al* 1991, 183-95; Drewett 1982; Ladle and Woodward 2009, 365). There has been much debate over the reasons for this orientation of doorways, which range from an embodiment of cosmological ideas towards the rising sun on one hand (Parker Pearson 1996; Parker Pearson and Sharples 1999, 16-21), to the maximization of daylight on the other (Drewett 1982), with other scholars arguing that there is more in the way of regional variation than some commentators have allowed for (Webley 2007; Pope 2007).

In Cornwall, it is certainly the case that any part of the southern horizon seems to have been preferred. At Callestick, for example, the doorway faced south west, at Scarcewater the doors of all three roundhouses opened to the south and at the Trevalga roundhouse, on the north Cornish coast, the entrance opened to the south east. There are also rare examples where the orientation was entirely reversed: the entrance of Bosiliack house 8 (Jones and Quinnell 2011) in West Penwith faced north to Carn Galva, a prominent landscape feature.

Nonetheless, it is evident that in most instances cosmological factors appear to have been paramount. At Trevalga the south east-facing doorway of the roundhouse opened directly against the side of the hill. As a consequence, the interior of the roundhouse would have been gloomy, dependent for light on the dull glow from the hearth; in this case the orientation led to the house becoming flooded (Jones and Quinnell 2014, 139). Likewise, at Bosiliack, most of the 13 roundhouses in the settlement, which were arranged in two arcs around a central space, did not open into this but instead faced south (Jones and Quinnell 2011). Taken together, these examples imply that a roughly south-facing entrance was preferred in the Middle Bronze Age. There are likely to have been long-standing cosmological traditions affecting the orientation of doorways, although high-precision alignments do not seem to have been important and at times other factors such as the referencing of landscape features could override accepted practice.

A lengthy period of occupation is also potentially indicated by the radiocarbon determinations, which place Roundhouse 1 between 1500 cal BC and 1300 cal BC, with the weight of the dating falling in the period 1430-1350 cal BC. This could imply that it was used for a century, although it is uncertain how much of that span it actually stood for. Although the opportunity has not arisen to apply Bayesian techniques to dates from hollow-set structures, potentially lengthy 'life-spans' are indicated by the radiocarbon determinations which have been obtained from other excavated lowland roundhouses in Cornwall. For example, roundhouse 1500 at Scarcewater seems to have stood for up to three centuries (Jones and Taylor 2010, 70). In other instances the duration was far shorter, as at Scarcewater roundhouse 1100, which appears to have been a single-phased building (*ibid*). In the case of Roundhouse 1, there are indications that repairs had been made to it, as several of the posts seem to have been replaced. Again, this is something which has been found elsewhere in Cornwall, with, for example, roundhouses at Trethellan, Boden and Scarcewater being renewed (Nowakowski 1991; Jones and Taylor 2010; Gossip 2008c).

In Cornwall lowland house renewals seem to have taken place in two contrasting ways. The first, as at Scarcewater roundhouse 1500, involved the wholesale removal of the superstructure followed by the laying of a new floor in the hollow, and then the construction of a new superstructure. The second method was less drastic and involved the replacement of posts, as at Scarcewater house 1250. This later technique seems closer to what occurred at Roundhouse 1.

The contrasts in the ways buildings were treated and renewed (or not) are of interest because they may reflect the individual biographies of the structures, especially if they were in some way considered to be living entities in their own right (Waterson 1997), and / or tied into the biographies of their occupants (Jones and Taylor 2010, 72-6; Jones, forthcoming a). Given that moulds and the copper-alloy artefacts were recovered from the roundhouse it is very possible that this was reflecting the biography of the occupants or of the house itself. This point will be returned to below.

Longevity of settlement is not confined to the lowlands; extended use of structures has also been identified in the uplands of Cornwall (Jones and Quinnell 2011), where stone-walled roundhouses appear to have been used seasonally or episodically over several centuries. Taken together with the radiocarbon determinations from lowland roundhouses it implies that during the Middle

Bronze Age, in Cornwall at least, there was a developing process of communities marking attachment to place through domestic architecture.

It is also of interest that Cornish roundhouses appear to have been occupied for far longer than their counterparts in central southern England, which seem to have been lived in for far shorter periods of time, with little evidence for renewal (Brück 2001). Longevity of settlement has, however, also been indicated by radiocarbon dating of settlements elsewhere in Britain and Ireland, including at Corrstown, Co Derry, in Northern Ireland, where many of the houses had been rebuilt on repeated occasions, and at Ronaldsway on the Isle of Man, which appears to have been occupied over several centuries (Ginn and Rathbone 2012, 233; Rathbone 2013). This implies that different temporal traditions of roundhouse occupation existed across Britain.

In common with many of the hollow-set roundhouses which have been excavated across Cornwall over the last 40 years, the Tremough roundhouses were part of a small settlement, which in Cornwall typically ranges from two to six structures (ApSimon and Greenfield 1972; Nowakowski 1991; Jones 1998-9a; Jones and Taylor 2010, 69-70). Paired examples are quite common as at Penhale Moor and Trevisker (Nowakowski and Johns 2015; ApSimon and Greenfield 1972). This arrangement is comparable with other Middle Bronze Age settlements across Britain and Ireland, where the majority of settlements are made up of small numbers of roundhouses, scattered pits and four-post structures (Ellison 1981; Brück 2000).

The lack of diversity in the settlement record and similarity of the material assemblages across roundhouses has been argued to suggest that there was not much in way of social stratification during the Middle Bronze Age (Brück 2000; Davis 2012; Ginn 2012, 352). Overall there is little to separate any of the excavated roundhouse settlements found across Cornwall in terms of wealth. The only real difference is a contrast between lowland settlements, which tend to produce larger artefactual assemblages, and upland settlements which have relatively fewer finds. This difference may, however, represent differences in settlement occupation, with moorland houses perhaps only being used intermittently at certain times of the year or intentionally abandoned for short periods, and then re-used, so that their biographies are very different to lowland roundhouses (for example, Jones and Quinnell 2011).

As only one of the two roundhouses at Tremough was excavated, however, it is not possible to be certain whether both had been used for the same purposes, or if, for example, one was a dwelling and the other a workshop or ancillary building, which has been found elsewhere, as at Penhale Moor (Nowakowski and Johns 2015). We do not know whether Roundhouse 1 was also used as a domestic residence. It was associated with a range of ceramics but these were all derived from abandonment contexts. It is possible that it was the residence of one or more metalworkers who lived with their tools, or that the adjacent Roundhouse 2 was the domestic building and Roundhouse 1 was used solely as a place where metal was worked. Anthropological and historic studies provide evidence that metalworking was often considered to be a magical practice and that it often took place in secrecy, with its practitioners living separately from other members of the community, and this could have been the case at Roundhouse 1 (below).

There were very few external features which can confidently be identified as being contemporary with Roundhouse 1. A few postholes were located outside the roundhouse, but these were devoid of finds. However, running out of the southern side of the stripped area a north east – south west aligned spread of tightly packed stones (105) was uncovered (Figure 2.6). This measured approximately 5.5m wide and 9m long and may represent the ploughed-down remains of a stony bank, perhaps comparable with that found near to the settlement at Trethellan Farm (Nowakowski 1991). Against the eastern side of the feature was a dark clayish silt soil layer (106), measuring 30m long and 2m wide. This perhaps represents a preserved buried soil or possibly a shallow ditch. Sherds of abraded or moderately abraded Bronze Age Trevisker pottery were recovered from both within stony bank (105) and soil layer (106). Like Roundhouse 2, these features were not excavated and were preserved *in situ*. It is, however, reasonable to suggest that the area to the south of the roundhouses was enclosed, and we might envisage either small plots or fields, comparable to those found elsewhere in association with Middle Bronze Age settlements in south west Britain (for example, Nowakowski *et al* 2007; Balaam *et al* 1982; Fleming 1988). It is possible that layer (106) could have been the fill of a shallow ditch, associated with bank (105), but it is also tempting to see it rather as a midden-rich soil which survived in the lee of the bank. Comparable soils have been found in Bronze Age field systems elsewhere, where they have been taken to be produced by manuring and composting with domestic waste (Pryor 1998, 118; Nowakowski 2009). It is also of interest to note that the ceramics within this soil layer were far more abraded than those from Roundhouse 1 (chapter 3), which might again be consistent with a ploughsoil assemblage.

Leaving the roundhouse

As is commonly the case in Cornish roundhouses, most of the artefacts associated with Roundhouse 1 were recovered either from deposits inside postholes or were found in backfill layers which had entered the houses when they were being abandoned. Indeed, as a consequence of this, many of the discussions about roundhouses in Cornwall have focused on the ritualized patterns of roundhouse abandonment, rather than evidence for occupation (for example, Nowakowski 2001; Jones 1998-9a; forthcoming a). At the same time, it has become apparent that roundhouses appear in the archaeological record at the very time that evidence for ceremonial construction and barrow building goes into a decline, and several writers have suggested that the settlement may have become the focus for both formal ritual and ritualized practices as well as other events such as feasting at a community level (for example, Barrett *et al* 1991; Brück 1995; Needham and Spence 1996).

However, as discussed in relation to Neolithic pits above, there has been some questioning of the way in which deposits in prehistoric settlements have been attributed to ritual activity and what is actually meant by terms such as 'structured deposition' and 'ritual'. Brudenell and Cooper (2008), for example, have argued that what have been termed 'ritual deposits', such as artefacts found within pits in settlements, could have been produced through taphonomic processes. They suggest that other practices such as middening may account for the deposits that pottery and other artefacts are found in, as much as their symbolic treatment. It has also been argued (for example, Brück 1999b) that there are problems with the way that many archaeologists define ritual as activities which are out of the ordinary or 'non-functional', and separate it out from what is considered to be 'functional' within the settlement, such as the grinding of grain. Brück suggests that these distinctions are unlikely to have been recognized in prehistory and actions such as the deposition of artefacts would have been viewed as practical actions which produced specific, pre-conceived and sought-after results (even if these were only broadly framed in terms of, say, warding off the potential 'bad luck' which might accrue if the actions were not performed). It is therefore incorrect to see ritualized activity, such as the actions and procedures undertaken at the abandonment of a roundhouse, as being less rational than a task such as planting wheat; both were carried out to achieve desired outcomes.

Following on from Brück's work, Richard Bradley (2003; 2005) has argued that ritual and domestic activities are likely to have been deeply interwoven and not easily separable from one another. Adrian Chadwick (2012) has suggested in relation to later prehistoric settlements that both informal depositing of 'rubbish' and 'special placed deposits' undertaken as ritualized acts were not distinct from each other, but were merely different points on a continuum of practices all influenced to a greater or lesser degree by social and cosmological beliefs. He has stressed the need for archaeologists to develop methodologies to identify and account for all acts of patterned deposition. Seen in this light, Roundhouse 1 could have been used by a metalworker, associated with 'magical practices' and still have been a dwelling.

In addition to the identification of ritualized deposits associated with settlement abandonment, it also apparent that in the South West region traditions which had taken place at cairns and barrows during the Early Bronze Age subsequently informed practices associated with house abandonment (Jones 2008; forthcoming a; Bender *et al* 2007). For example, evidence from recent excavations makes it apparent that many hollow-set roundhouses underwent episodes of transformation at the end of their occupation: they were monumentalised and in many cases would have ended-up looking similar to Early Bronze Age cairns or barrows. At Scarcewater, for example, roundhouse, 1250 became mounded over and another roundhouse 1500 had a substantial cairn-ring built around the edge of the infilled house-hollow (Jones and Taylor 2010, 76-77; Jones, forthcoming a). The resemblances between abandoned houses and earlier ceremonial monuments are likely to have been intentional and drew on earlier Bronze Age ritual traditions (Jones 2008). It should, however, be noted that just as in the Early Bronze Age there were substantive differences in the biographies of creation of barrows and cairns (Jones 2005) specific patterns of house abandonment differed between sites and there were visual differences between the final form of abandoned houses. In other words there was no blueprint for leaving hearth and home.

With these points in mind the abandonment of Roundhouse 1 will be considered. In particular we will seek to establish a 'biography' (*cf* Tringham 1995) for the abandonment process of the house and will consider the contexts within which artefacts were found as well as their condition. Were they old or new and, if old, how might they relate to the biography of the house?

The destruction of the roundhouse follows a pattern which has resonances with other sites across lowland areas of Cornwall, although there is perhaps less evidence for the patterning of artefacts which has been found at some roundhouses. At Callestick (Jones 1998-9a), for example, pottery had been placed behind the wall of the structure and the entrance filled with quartz blocks. There is also rather less evidence for structured deposition than was found at the ceremonial post-rings to the north (Gossip and Jones 2007, 35; and below). Nonetheless, several significant artefacts were recovered from Roundhouse 1 and there is some indication of spatial patterning.

In common with, other hollow-set roundhouses, the destruction of Roundhouse 1 commenced with the removal of the superstructure. Thatch would have been taken off and any walling demolished. As noted above, in some instances walling has been found pushed inside the house-hollow, as at Callestick (Jones 1998-9a). In Roundhouse 1, however, aside from a few stones on the western side of the structure, which could be displaced walling, there was little indication for one. The posts were removed from their sockets. Unlike some other structures, such as the Trevilson roundhouse, near St Newlyn East, there is no evidence for any burning of structural timbers (Jones and Taylor 2004), and it is possible that the posts could have been left to rot off-site or even reincorporated into other structures. Also by contrast with other structures, such as roundhouses 1250 and 1500 at Scarcewater (Jones and Taylor 2010, 74-6), the empty post sockets seem to have been less generally used as receptacles for the formalized deposition of artefacts. There were, however, a few exceptions: two of the three copper-alloy objects recovered, the spiral ring and the pin fragments, were both located in the fills of postholes (Figure 11.7). The spiral finger ring was located close to the entranceway in posthole [705] and the copper-alloy pin diametrically opposite in posthole [785]. The metalwork finds will be discussed in greater detail below, but at this point it worth noting that their distribution creates a north west – south east axis which was also mirrored by finds within several of the ceremonial post-ring structures investigated during previous work at Tremough (Gossip and Jones 2007, 34-5; and below). Interestingly, both of these postholes also contained pottery, although this may have entered the empty postholes accidentally – parts of the same vessels were also recovered from within the general infill layers found across the house, from which most of the pottery and the stonework were recovered (chapters 3 and 4).

It is also noteworthy that, by contrast with other excavated roundhouses in Cornwall, comparatively little worked stone was recovered from the site. Many Middle Bronze Age roundhouses, including those at Trethellan, Callestick, Trevilson and Scarcewater, have produced quantities of worked stone, especially in the form of querns (or fragments of) and mullers used for the processing of grain;

Figure 11.7 Photograph showing the copper-alloy spiral ring which had been placed into the top of posthole [705].

these are often found as 'placed deposits' in pits and postholes (Nowakowski 1991; Jones and Taylor 2004; Jones 1998-9a; Jones and Taylor 2010, 23; Watts 2014, 84-91). The stonework assemblage (excluding the moulds) from Roundhouse 1 includes only one muller fragment, however, and the reminder of the assemblage took the form of heavy-duty cobble hammerstones, suited to the breaking down of ore for metalworking (chapter 4, above), and two whetstones, which may have been used in the final stages of production for sharpening the cutting edges of metal objects.

After the posts had been removed and a few artefacts formally deposited into them, the hollow was backfilled, and the vast majority of the artefacts came from the actual infill deposits which had been spread across the interior of the site (Figure 11.8). The greater part of the finds, including the ceramics, must have entered the hollow without much formal placing of artefacts occurring. Again, however, there is a noticeable pattern with a significant group of finds. All of the moulds were found at the bottom of the infill and were situated at the back of the house in the north-west quadrant close to the hearth. The geochemical analysis (chapter 6) of samples taken from this hearth indicates that it had been used for metalworking and it seems reasonable to suggest that a symbolic connection was being made between the part of the roundhouse where the magical activity of transforming ore into metal took place and the moulds which were a selection of the metalworker's historic working equipment (below).

The majority of the stonework generally, and the pottery from the infill deposits also came from the northern half of the house, although as noted above there was little evidence for careful placing of pottery, and in part the greater number of

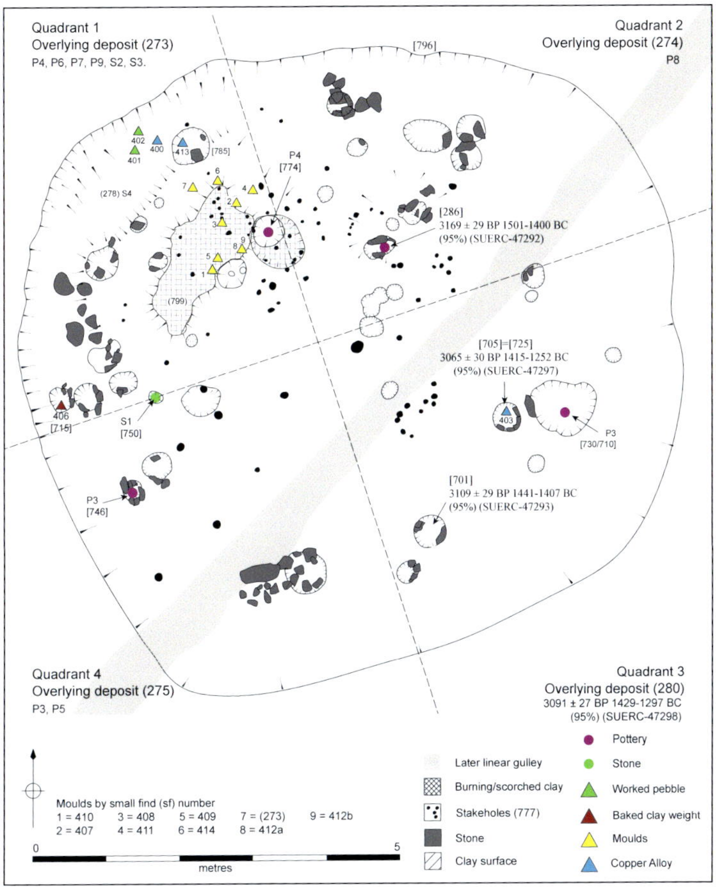

Figure 11.8 Plan showing the distribution of artefacts in Roundhouse 1.

artefacts in this area could be accounted for by the fact that the infill survived to a greater depth over the northern portion of the site.

The infill deposit is itself of interest, as it produced most of the ceramics (Figure 11.9), and therefore raises the question of what it was and its formation. As we have seen, there was some evidence of a surviving soil horizon in the form of layer (106) alongside the remains of stony bank (105). The finds from this layer included abraded sherds of Trevisker pottery, which it was suggested possibly derived from the improvement of the soil with midden-derived material. The majority of the sherds of pottery from cut features in Roundhouse 1 were in a fresh condition but most sherds from the infilling have some varied abrasion, suggesting that they were fresh when deposited but subsequently suffered the effects of groundwater and bioturbation (chapter 3). Sherds from the same vessels were found in both the cut features and the infill deposits, which means that theoretically they should have been in a similar condition. Despite being fresher than those from soil layer (106), the sherds from Roundhouse 1 may also have been derived from a midden deposit. The difference between them may have been that those found within the roundhouse had been in a stockpile which was bound

Figure 11.9 Photograph showing in situ pottery spread in Roundhouse 1.

for use as infill material. Some differentiation between the two assemblages is also suggested by the over-representation of rim sherds in the infill material which could also be indicative of differential storage prior to deposition (chapter 3). It is therefore of interest that the analysis of the pottery from Roundhouse 1 suggested that, despite there being a large ceramic assemblage, comparatively few, perhaps only eight vessels were actually represented. One possible interpretation for this is that particular pots were associated with the roundhouse or its occupants and were stored in a house-associated midden.

Such stockpiles of settlement-generated material could have held their own symbolism and it is possible that particular midden heaps were associated with specific houses, containing residues of occupation strongly connected with events, individuals and the houses themselves. Indeed, Gary Robinson (2013) has suggested that middens beside houses may have been seen as being 'living entities', associated with fertility and reproduction and intimately associated with the biography of the household. If this interpretation is correct, it is again possible to argue that the links between the occupants of Roundhouse 1 and the house itself were made manifest by the deployment of the midden material during the abandonment process.

As we have touched upon above, the most obvious evidence for ritualized deposition in Roundhouse 1 relates to the deposition of copper-alloy artefacts and moulds associated with the production of metal items, including pins and socketed tools. The following section will consider the wider significance of these finds.

Metalworking in the roundhouse and beyond

The likelihood that the building was used for the production of metalwork and had been abandoned with a degree of formality is of particular interest as actual metalworking sites are extremely rare in both the Middle Bronze Age and the Later Bronze Age. A recent survey of 50 sites across the broader South West region (Cornwall, Devon, Dorset, Gloucestershire, Somerset and Wiltshire), Worcestershire and Berkshire (Skowranek 2007), revealed that only a very small number of Middle and later Bronze Age settlements have produced any evidence for metalworking, and in most cases the context was ambiguous. For example, at Bishops Canning Down, Wiltshire, fragments of casting waste were found in plough soils over the area of the settlement but not in direct association with the roundhouses (Gingell 1992, 105-6). At South Lodge, Dorset, a small number of copper-alloy artefacts were recovered from the enclosure ditch around a roundhouse settlement, and a clay mould fragment was recovered from the topsoil over the site (Barrett *et al* 1991, 144-83).

In the South West peninsula (Devon and Cornwall) evidence has been even scantier, despite having both abundant Bronze Age settlement sites and the proximity of sources of tin and copper. There is no evidence for metalworking taking place within Middle Bronze Age settlements in Devon, and with the possible exception of the houses at Trevisker (ApSimon and Greenfield 1972), prior to the excavation of Roundhouse 1 at Tremough, no Middle Bronze Age settlements with a direct association with metalworking were known in Cornwall at all. Where evidence has been recovered it took the form of artefacts which were located away from settlements, or stray stone moulds used in the production of artefacts, as, for example, at Bodwen near Lanlivery (Pearce 1983; Harris 1977).

Indeed, as Stuart Needham (2007a) has pointed out, in Britain generally, there is a distinct lack of correlation between the distribution of settlements and that of metalwork. Metalwork for the most part was deposited in hoards, away from settlements in other parts of the landscape. In southern and eastern England it was often deposited in rivers (Bradley 1991; Pryor 2001; Yates 2007), although in other parts of Britain other forms landscape feature or boundaries were preferred; for example, in the Severn Valley, bogs appear to have been preferred to rivers (Mullin 2012).

Moving back to the South West peninsula, there are further localised trends in the places in which metalwork is found during the later Bronze Age. Susan Pearce (1976, 21), for example, has identified a group of later Bronze Age metalwork finds recovered from hilltop sites which had been enclosed in the Neolithic or subsequently became hillforts, including Woodbury and Hazard Hill in Devon and Hambledon Hill in Dorset. In Devon wet places may also have been significant: near Chudleigh Knighton two complete bivalve moulds for a rapier were found together in a field close to a river (Tucker 1852) and a bivalve mould for a dirk was found during a drainage scheme at Holsworthy (Pearce 1983, 443). Both find-spots could have been associated with the marking of boundaries or with wet places, and it may have been of significance that all these moulds had been made from visually distinctive greenstones. Deliberately deposited Middle Bronze Age metalwork in Devon, however, has also been found in earlier Bronze Age barrows; at the Lovehayne barrow, for example, where copper-alloy palstaves were recovered (Pearce 1983, 438; Jones and Quinnell 2008); more recently copper-alloy palstaves were recovered during excavations of two Bronze Age cairns at Hemerdon (AC Archaeology 2013). This implies that in Devon earlier barrows and cairns had become places of renewed interest to later communities.

By contrast, in Cornwall, only one barrow at Roche has a possible association with later Bronze Age metalwork, in the form of spearheads and possibly palstaves (Pearce 1983, 424). Instead, copper-alloy objects have more commonly been found in other contexts, such as within field boundaries, or at distinctive places in the landscape. For example, a flanged copper-alloy axe and a palstave were found in an old field boundary at Veryan on the Roseland, and the Middle Bronze Age palstave hoard from Mulfra in Penwith, which was found near to the chambered tomb, may have been deposited within a field bank (Pearce 1983, 427, 416). Middle Bronze Age metalwork has also been found within streamworks, and includes two spearheads from Roche and a pin from St Columb (Penhallurick 1986, 196-8). Finds from the streamworks could be seen as propitiatory offerings, or perhaps the streamworks themselves, like field walls and banks, acted as boundaries which needed to be symbolically marked.

Natural landscape features were also marked: for example, hoards of axes were found on Carn Brea near to an outcrop and beside the Giant's Rock, near Polstrong (Mercer 1981; Cornish 1880-81). This strongly suggests that there were certain accepted, localised behaviours or dispositions associated with the discard of metalwork across the landscape. However, in addition to the marking of significant boundaries, small quantities of metalwork and moulds have also been recovered from roundhouses in Cornwall (Table 11.2, below). Interestingly, with the exception of Gwithian, the radiocarbon determinations from roundhouses associated with metalwork or items associated with its production (cassiterite pebbles and moulds) generally fall in the period 1500-1300 cal BC (Figure 10.3).

These deposits take the form of finds which can be argued to have been special deposits, as well as those which are more likely to be accidental losses. The *racloir* mould from Trevalga, which was buried beneath colluvium, represents an almost certain case of accidental loss (Jones and Quinnell 2014). Other finds are much less likely to have resulted from mundane processes associated with the formation of the archaeological record (*cf* Brudenell and Cooper 2008); those from Tremough, Boden and Penhale Moor more probably represent instances where artefacts were deliberately placed into archaeological contexts (Gossip 2008c; Nowakowski 2001; Nowakowski and Johns 2015). As such they require greater contextualization and explanation. The copper-alloy spiral ring from Roundhouse 1, for example, which was found in the top of posthole [405] could not have entered it when the post was

Figure 11.10 Photograph of the copper-alloy knife from a posthole within the roundhouse at Boden Vean.

still standing (Figure 11.7). Likewise, the copper-alloy pin fragments within [784] probably did not enter the posthole when a post was still inside it.

Comparable finds have been made in other roundhouses in Cornwall. The copper-alloy knife from a posthole at Boden (Figure 11.10) was not a casual loss as it had been placed behind the packing stones, and the spearhead which had been driven into the levelling layer at the Penhale Moor roundhouse, structure 1013, required a deliberate thrust which must have been an action beyond casual discarding of an unwanted item. By contrast, at Trevisker two lumps of copper-alloy were found in a posthole within house A and two cassiterite pebbles in another (Greenfield and ApSimon 1972). As discussed above, the placing of these artefacts are likely to belong to the part of the continuum of deposition which is likely to have been highly selective.

More difficult to interpret are those items which are found on the floor of houses, which could have been deliberately placed or casually deposited at the start of the abandonment process. The moulds from Tremough Roundhouse 1 are all parts of bivalve moulds, which are worn, incomplete or broken, and several had been reworked (chapter 5). None are pristine new pieces which were ready to be used and all could have been derived from a midden heap and may not have been deposited with any great formality. The same may be true for the curved fragment of copper-alloy from the gully.

Similarly, at Trevisker cassiterite pebbles and a fragment from a copper-alloy dagger / knife were found in abandonment layers within structure B (ApSimon and Greenfield 1972) and at Gwithian conjoining fragments of the same mould were found in two adjoining structures 724 and 730; copper-alloy objects including three pins were also found in one of them (Nowakowski *et al* 2007; Table 11.2). At Trethellan a copper-alloy wire, possibly a bracelet, was found on the floor of house 2222 (Nowakowski 1991). As was the case at Tremough with the moulds, these objects could have simply reached the end of their lives as moulds or artefacts and have been casually discarded. However, as scholars including Joanna Brück (2001) and Mike Williams (2003) have noted, fragmented items, such as worked stone are frequently found on the floors of roundhouses and, rather than being left over from occupation-related activity, may have been deposits associated with deliberate abandonment.

If it is accepted that metalwork and the moulds used in the production of metal artefacts were deliberately deposited as part of abandonment rites, the question becomes one of how to interpret these items. As noted above, Joanna Brück (1999a; 2001) has argued that most Middle Bronze Age roundhouses in central southern Britain show little sign of renewal and were only occupied for a generation, and she has made links between the life-cycles of roundhouses and their owners, suggesting that they were perhaps abandoned at the death of the head of the household.

As discussed, in Cornwall the situation is rather more complex, as houses frequently show signs of rebuilding and renewal. Nonetheless, as we have also seen, there is good evidence for the ritualized abandonment of roundhouses (Nowakowski 1991; Jones, forthcoming a). The deposition of metalwork within roundhouses was therefore likely to have been part of formalized rites of abandonment. Certain instances, such as the depositing of the spearhead into the base of the Penhale Moor roundhouse, could be interpreted as a deliberate 'killing' of the house (Nowakowski 2001).

However, one of the major things to stand out is that many of the metalwork finds are distinctive, highly personalised artefacts, which probably had individual biographies and associations which would have given them added significance. Anthropological study has showed that the accrued history of personal items can be very significant. For example, when discussing necklaces of sperm whale teeth from Fiji, Gosden and Marshall (1999) described how these items can gain in prestige because of the patina which they have developed through being exchanged and touched by individuals. The idea that artefacts had biographies has been particularly influential in the consideration of Early Bonze Age grave assemblages, where it has been proposed that some artefacts, including beads, pottery and metalwork may have been curated heirlooms (Healy and Harding 2004; Woodward *et al* 2005). However, as Ben Roberts (2007) has argued, Middle Bronze Age ornaments too, including rings, bracelets and pins were personal items which may have been worn for considerable periods of time before being separated from their owners.

Table 11.2 (following page): Copper-alloy artefacts and objects associated with metalworking from Bronze Age house structures in Cornwall and Devon.

Site name	Form	Dating	Context and associations	Principal references
Cornwall				
Tremough, Roundhouse 1.	Copper-alloy spiral ring and pin fragments; nine stone moulds.	SUERC-47292, 3169±29 BP, 1501-1400 cal BC SUERC-47293, 3109±29 BP, 1441-1407 cal BC SUERC-47297, 3065±31 BP, 1415-1252 cal BC SUERC-47298, 3091±27 BP,1429-1297 BC	Spiral ring had been placed in one posthole, pin fragments in another. Part of an unidentified copper-alloy object was found within a gully. Moulds for copper-alloy artefacts of 'ornament horizon' type were found on the floor of the house below infill deposits.	This volume
Boden, roundhouse.	Copper-alloy knife blade.	OxA-14517, 3085±30 BP, 1421-1267 cal BC SUERC-6169, 3055±35 BP, 1411-1223 cal BC SUERC-6170, 3005±35 BP, 1311-1224 cal BC	Copper-alloy knife blade found within a posthole behind packing stones.	Gossip 2008; 2013
Gwithian, structures 724 and 730.	Socketed axe mould and copper-alloy pins.	SUERC-6162, 2835±35 BP, 1110-909 cal BC OxA-14525, 2946±29 BP, 1257-1051 cal BC	Two conjoining fragments of stone forming a socketed axe mould from structures 724 and 730. Two unusual decorated copper-alloy pins and a third lacking its head were found in 724. Structure 724 appeared to have (been) burnt down.	Burgess 1976; Needham 1981, 1-16, fig 3; Nowakowski *et al* 2007
Trethellan, house 2222.	Copper-alloy wire / bracelet.	UB-3114, 3091±20 BP, 1416-1291 cal BC	Plain copper-alloy wire / bracelet found lying on the floor of house 2222 Phase 1.	Nowakowski 1991, figs 54,76
Trethellan, house 142/3022.	Copper-alloy object and mould.	UB-3115, 3091±40 BP, 1491-1265 cal BC	'Trumpet'-shaped copper-alloy object, phase 2 house 142/3022; mould 519 may be related.	Nowakowski 1991, figs 54, 75
Penhale Moor, structure 1013.	Side-looped copper-alloy spearhead and a fragment from a second spearhead.	NZA-32932, 2874+35 BP, 1200-920 cal BC NZA-32931, 2913+35 BP, 1260-1000 cal BC	A side-looped spearhead was embedded at a 45-degree angle into the levelling spread within the roundhouse. A blade fragment from a second spearhead was found in the same levelling layer.	Nowakowski and Johns 2015
Trevalga, roundhouse.	Mould for a racloir.	SUERC-42058, 3105±26 BP, 1434-1312 cal BC SUERC-42059, 3057±23 BP, 1399-1265 cal BC SUERC-42064, 3092±31, 1432-1292 cal BC SUERC-42064, 3092 ±26, 1428-1302 cal BC	Mould was found on floor of house which had been buried beneath colluvium.	Jones and Quinnell 2014, 64
Trevisker, house A, house 3 and structure b.	Fragment of dagger, cassiterite pebbles and mineralized lumps of copper-alloy.	NPL 134, 3060±95 BP, 1509-1028 cal BC	Lumps of copper-alloy, possibly associated with metalworking, were found in one posthole within house A; two cassiterite pebbles were found in another. Cassiterite pebble found in house 3. Further cassiterite pebbles and a burnt fragment of a knife / dagger were found in the badly damaged structure B.	ApSimon and Greenfield 1972, 309-10, 350
Devon				
Dean Moor, hut 5B.	Cassiterite pebble and possible piece of tin-working slag.	Bronze Age pottery found in roundhouses.	A cassiterite pebble was found in 'Hut 5B' and a minute 'bead' of possible tin-working slag was found inside a hearth within 'Hut 7'.	Fox 1957, 30-1

Starting with the metalwork itself, it is noticeable that unlike the material found in hoards during the Middle Bronze Age, which often takes the form of socketed axe-heads or items of weaponry, such as spearheads and rapiers (Needham 1988; Bradley 1991, 123-4), most of the artefacts found in Cornish roundhouses are singular pieces which could be interpreted as personal ornaments or belongings. As can be seen in Table 11.2 the artefacts from roundhouses in the South West include pins, a knife blade, a dagger, a possible bracelet and the spiral ring from Roundhouse 1.

Interestingly, comparable personal copper-alloy items have also been found in roundhouses beyond Cornwall, across southern Britain. At Charlton in Hampshire, a copper-alloy awl, a knife and a palstave were placed on the floor of a roundhouse and a decorative copper-alloy disc was deposited inside a posthole during its abandonment (Cunliffe 1970). At Bestwall in Dorset two copper-alloy bracelets had been placed into features associated with the abandonment of roundhouse 1 (Ladle and Woodward 2009, 72). Metalwork has also been found directly associated with several roundhouses in Sussex (Tapper 2011, 140-43). House 1 at Black Patch produced two spiral rings which are likely to have been deposited during the abandonment process (Drewett 1982, 362; Tapper 2011) and two more of the houses also contained what could be interpreted as personal items, including a copper-alloy razor in house 3.

Although there does not appear to have been any direct continuity in ornament forms between the Early Bronze Age and the Middle Bronze Age (Roberts 2007), there may have been some continuity of ideas relating to their treatment when they came to be deposited. As Needham (1988) made clear, for the Early Bronze Age trinkets or personal items such as pins and daggers are very much associated with round barrows and burial-related contexts. Such items could have been markers of identity or status or have carried symbolic properties (for example, Jones and Quinnell 2013; Fowler 2013); they may have been used to create and express particular ideas about identity or 'personhood' by the community (Fowler 2004, 75). Similarly, in the later Bronze Age items such as pins and bracelets may have helped construct and define individual identity (Sorensen 2010; Davis 2012, 67). It therefore seems likely that such artefacts held symbolic associations and had a role as decorative items during the Middle Bronze Age. Indeed, it is very likely that distinctive items such as spiral rings, bracelets and pins were strongly associated with bodily adornment (Roberts 2007). It is therefore very possible that these items were deposited into abandoned roundhouses because they were linked with their former owners or at least were associated with particular properties which were considered to be redolent of the house and its occupiers. If roundhouses were associated with particular heads of household or family members, then perhaps objects belonging to or resonant of them could have been deposited during the abandonment process.

Seen in this light, it is possible that the personalized character of copper-alloy objects deposited into Middle Bronze Age roundhouses during their abandonment could have had similar connections and served a very similar role as barrow-associated metalwork had done during the earlier Bronze Age.

Moving now to the moulds from Roundhouse 1, these too could have been associated with individuals who occupied the house. However, although these items may have been personal possessions they may have been included because they conveyed information about the biography of the house and the activities which had taken place within it. As noted above, none of these items was fresh but were worn and in some cases reused. Rather like querns, which are often found with abandonment layers and are likely to have been associated with transformation (Brück 2001; Jones and Taylor 2010; Watts 2014, 56-7), moulds are also agents of change, in this case linked with the transformation of molten liquid into cold hard Bronze. Anthropological and historical studies have shown that such processes are often swathed in secrecy, with metalworking considered to be a magical practice often with strict gender divisions associated with it (Budd and Taylor 1995; Herbert 1993; Eliade 1988, 472-4; Helms 1993, 59-60). The actual process of metalworking may also have created social bonds between those engaged in metalwork production (O'Mhaolduin 2014) and potentially with the place where it occurred. Seen in this way, the deposition of the moulds could represent the deliberate deposition of symbolically charged artefacts associated with the 'magical' transformation of stones into metal, which were closely linked to the biography of the roundhouse, its occupants and the arcane activities which took place there.

To conclude, the moulds and copper-alloy artefacts from Roundhouse 1 are unlikely to have been casual losses but instead more convincingly fall at the more formalized end of a continuum of possible ritualized activity associated with the abandonment of the roundhouse. Furthermore, it has been suggested that metalwork was deposited into the roundhouse because it fulfilled a role comparable with that which barrow-associated metalwork had done in the Early Bronze Age. These patterns of deposition are detectable in excavated Middle Bronze Age roundhouses in the south west and more widely across southern Britain.

The setting of Roundhouse 1

The environmental evidence for the wider landscape setting of Roundhouse 1 and the adjacent Roundhouse 2 is, like that of Structure 1, limited to evidence from the plant macrofossils and charcoal assemblages. Although still quite low, greater amounts of cereals are present than in the earlier Bronze Age and there still appears to have been access to mixed woodland (chapters 8 and 9). Interestingly, the quantity of charred grains recovered from Roundhouse 1 was less than from the largest of the timber post-rings identified in previous work at Tremough, which will be discussed below.

There was also little evidence for daily activity outside the roundhouses. Cut features outside the roundhouse hollows were quite limited, and except for the possible buried soil (106), buried land surfaces did not survive. Ditched field boundaries dating to the second millennium cal BC are rare in the south west of Britain, and the stony banks found in upland areas such as Bodmin Moor, or more rarely preserved below colluvium, were more or less absent on the Tremough site (Johnson and Rose 1994; Jones and Quinnell 2014, 135). Two features did, however, indicate that the roundhouses may have been associated with a field system or at least an enclosed plot. In the southern part of the stripped area was what may have been a levelled bank and preserved along the eastern side of this was a soil layer. As discussed above, this could represent a shallow ditch or the remnants of a buried soil which had been protected by the bank. Either way it suggests that the roundhouses lay within or close to an enclosed patch of land.

This is significant because the roundhouse dates to the period around 1500 cal BC when there is widespread evidence for an increase in enclosure and cultivation across southern Britain, from the east of Kent to the Wessex chalklands (for example, Yates 2007, 111; Morigi *et al* 2011, 338-30; Champion 2011, 177; Gingell 1992). In South West Britain major upstanding enclosures which are likely to have been used for pasture are found across the uplands, including Dartmoor and Bodmin Moor (Fleming 1988; Johnson and Rose 1994). Elsewhere, more ephemeral traces of enclosure in the form of stony banks sometimes survive below sand dunes or colluvial deposits (Nowakowski *et al* 2007; Jones and Quinnell 2014, 98).

The somewhat limited environmental data from Tremough therefore indicates a situation comparable to what has been found elsewhere in Cornwall and more generally across southern Britain. This is supported by the charcoal assemblages from both the 2002 and 2011 excavations (Gale 2007; chapter 9, above). On current evidence we might envisage a mosaic, with tree coverage in the wider area, enclosed land closer to the roundhouses perhaps with some cultivation and other

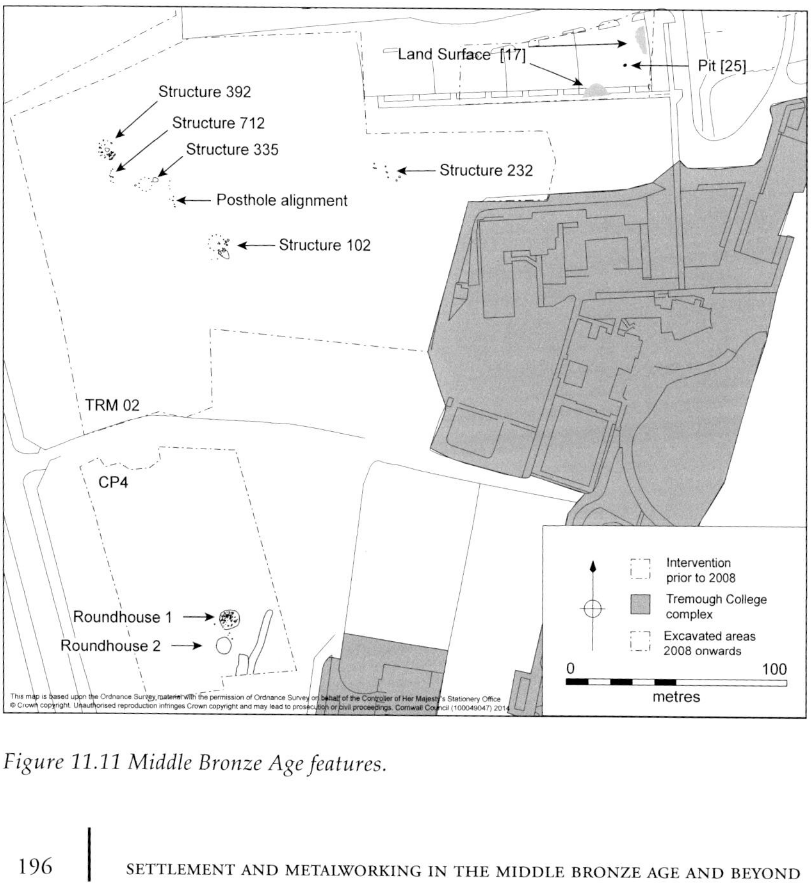

Figure 11.11 Middle Bronze Age features.

areas down to grass. There are also likely to have been extensive tracts of rough ground in the wider area, providing a resource for grazing and a variety of natural resources (Dudley 2011).

Rather more evidence has been gained from past excavation of other sites across the plateau (Figure 11.11). To the north east of the roundhouses there was more ephemeral evidence for broadly contemporary although poorly understood activity. A Middle Bronze Age radiocarbon determination (chapter 10) was obtained from the Iron Age field ditch [30] which cut an old land surface (17) containing Trevisker pottery and fragments from clay loom weights, and the date is likely to be on residual material derived from this layer (Gossip and Jones 2007, 21). A second Middle Bronze Age date was obtained from pit [25], which again contained Trevisker pottery. A sub-rectangular structure, 232, measuring 13m long by 3m wide was also found in this general area. It was not radiocarbon dated but a sherd of Trevisker pottery was recovered from one of the postholes and it is possible that it was also related to the Bronze Age occupation of the area (*ibid*).

If the land to the south and the north east was possibly being used for agriculture, the picture may have been rather different to the north. The roundhouses can be considered in relation to a north west – south east alignment of four timber circles, which lay to the north approximately 160m away (Gossip and Jones 2007, 14-24).

As discussed in relation to Structure 1 above, formal ceremonial activity was identified at the western end of the plateau and dated from the Early Bronze Age onwards (Figure 11.12). Five timber circles were uncovered, one of which, structure 66, dated to the Early Bronze Age. The remaining examples were all of

Figure 11.12 Reconstruction of the Middle Bronze Age landscape showing the timber circles in the foreground and roundhouses 1 and 2 to the south.

Middle Bronze Age date, and this spanned most of the latter part of the second millennium cal BC from, *circa* 1500 to 1100 cal BC (chapter 10). At face value, the radiocarbon determinations from the timber-rings both pre-date and post-date those from Roundhouse 1, suggesting that formal ritual activity in the area to the north lasted longer than the occupation of the roundhouse.

One of the post-rings, structure 102 (Figure 11.13), has very similar radiocarbon determinations to those from Roundhouse 1 and it is entirely feasible that the two were contemporary with one another, occupation of the roundhouse overlapping with that of the post-ring. The structure 102 post-ring formed a circle with a diameter of approximately 7m. It was erected around 1500-1400 cal BC, although a date from an internal hearth-pit fell in the period *circa* 1400-1150 cal BC, suggesting that the structure had been renewed. The post-ring comprised 12 posts. Two additional postholes and a group of pits were located on the south-eastern side, which might have been an entrance. A stony spread was also found to cover these features and it is possible that this represented a closing deposit (Gossip and Jones 2007, 14). Post-ring structure 102 also produced evidence for structured deposition: several pits and postholes, especially those in the entranceway and the posthole directly opposite the entrance, were found to contain artefacts, including two vein quartz pebbles, two beach cobbles and sherds from a minimum of three Trevisker-related vessels.

The pottery assemblage from structure 102 is of interest because although broadly contemporary with that from Roundhouse 1, the two were of a very different character from one another in terms of decoration and vessel form. Indeed, the ceramic assemblage from the post-rings in general was rather different from that of the roundhouse and the term 'Trevisker-related' has been used to describe

Figure 11.13 Photograph of structure 102 taken from the south.

it (Quinnell 2007, 57-9). Given the chronological overlap, these differences are likely to be meaningful, and arguably relate to the biography and contrasting uses of the buildings. Roundhouse 1 may, for example, have been used by a closed group of people, the post-rings by a more extended community. Differences in ceramic forms may therefore have derived from or been used to denote differing contexts of use and users (*cf* Richards 2005, 280).

Despite the differences in the ceramic assemblage, as has already been discussed in relation to Structure 1, there are likely to have been a good many symbolic links between the circular architecture employed at the roundhouses and the post-ring structures. As noted above, both the post-ring within Roundhouse 1 and that embodied by structure 102 had diameters of around 7m. If the timber post-ring supporting the superstructure of the house was believed to embody a cosmological scheme then it is unsurprising that the exposed ceremonial timber post-rings would have had similar associations. The free-standing post-rings may have stood for 'unwrapped' houses (Richards 2014a), with their symbolism laid bare.

As Richard Bradley (2013) has recently argued, circular buildings whether 'domestic' or 'ceremonial', are likely to have embodied the same cosmological ideas, involving relationships between the earth, the sky and the movements of the sun and moon. He also suggests that ceremonial monuments in Western Europe could have taken their form from houses, albeit often on a large scale, so that, for example, a henge could be viewed as a 'big house' (Bradley 2005, 74-5). Likewise, Colin Richards (2014b) has suggested in relation to Orcadian stone circles, that they were the result of an attempt by a 'house society' to construct a community. He argues that at the village level descent and genealogy were materialized monumentally through construction of monumental circles.

At Tremough the building of large-scale monuments does not seem to have been of paramount importance. It is, however, possible that there was again a strong metaphorical link between the post-ring structures and the hollow-set roundhouses and that there was an attempt to create or represent an imagined or fictional community which would link households together and create a genealogy. It is possible that symbolic and metaphorical links between the roundhouses and ceremonial monuments became greater as settlements became more permanent and the house became the dominant expression of the community in the landscape. In this respect it may be significant that the use of the post-rings far outlived that of Roundhouse 1. Individual households of the living, therefore, may have come and gone but the post-rings may, through their construction, maintenance and renewal, have helped to create and maintain community cohesion.

Seen in this way, it interesting that there was evidence for a much more formalized level of ritualized deposition in the post-ring structures, than was found within Roundhouse 1. As discussed above, there was good evidence for the structured deposition within the roundhouse of a small proportion of the overall artefactual assemblage, including the copper-alloy objects and the moulds; however, the majority of the finds were from infilling deposits and had not been carefully placed. This contrasts with the evidence from the post-rings. As we have seen with post-ring structure 102, artefacts were deposited in the entrance,

Figure 11.14 Photograph of structure 392 from the south east.

located in the south west and in the opposing north-east side of the post-ring. This pattern was even more marked in the later post-ring, structure 392 (Gossip and Jones 2007, 35) (Figure 11.14). Items chosen for inclusion within this structure included a minimum of 12 vessels, quartz, and wolframite pebbles, a large broken muller, charred cereals and a possible heirloom in the form of a ripple-flaked flint knife. Interestingly, a cassiterite pebble was also recovered, which again may have been making a metaphorical reference to activities taking place elsewhere on the site. The broken muller and the charred grain are also of interest, for, as Williams (2003) has suggested, the agricultural cycle itself may have become a dominant metaphor in later prehistory, with symbolic links being made between preparing the ground, growing crops and recovering the harvest and the sequence of fertility, death and regeneration.

These finds were strongly patterned, on a south east – north west alignment from the entrance to the opposing side of the post-ring, as was also found in post-ring structure 102 At first glance, the patterning in Roundhouse 1 does not reflect this dominant axis. However, if the two copper-alloy objects which had been formally placed inside postholes are considered by themselves, they maintain this axis, and this may have may have reflected a shared cosmological scheme which was common to the post-ring structures and the roundhouse.

Roundhouse 1, a summary

In summary, Roundhouse 1 can be seen to belong to a wider tradition of roundhouse architecture which has been recorded across lowland areas of Cornwall. It was a component of a small settlement which in part is likely to have been surrounded by fields and agricultural buildings. To the north was a series of timber post-rings

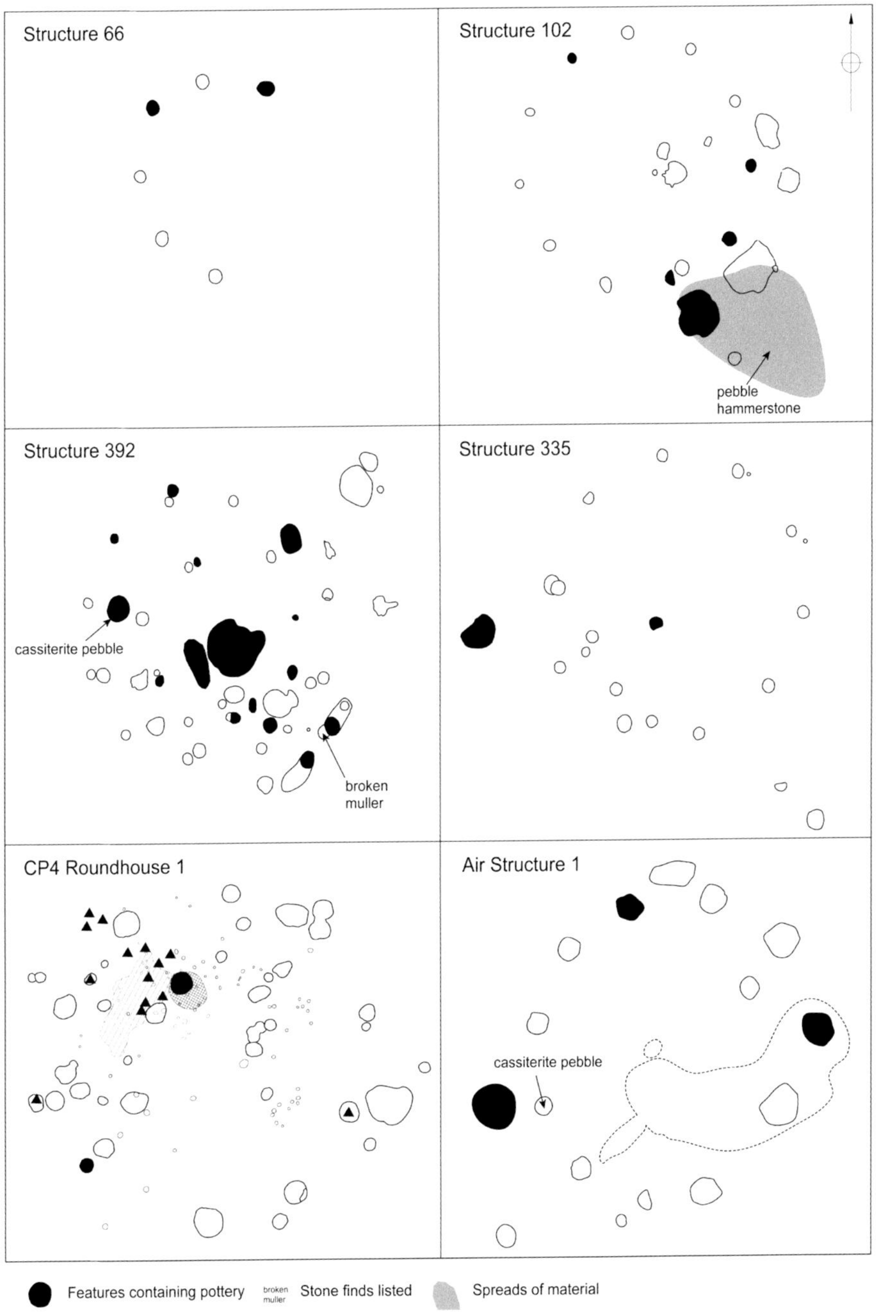

Figure 11.15 The distribution of finds in Middle Bronze Age structures.

which were probably used by the community at times of ceremonial gatherings. Importantly, traces of activities involving metalworking were recovered, and this part of the 'biography' of the house was found to be emphasised during the abandonment process when moulds and copper-alloy objects were deposited. It has been suggested that links between activities in the house and its occupants were made manifest during its closure.

Late Bronze Age Enclosure 1

The wider background

Following the infilling and abandonment of Roundhouse 1, there is a break spanning at least three centuries in the identified settlement record at Tremough, during which the only recorded activity on the site is associated with the last phase of use at the post-rings (Gossip and Jones 2007, 114-16).

Enclosure 1 was not fully exposed, and its western side is likely to have been removed by a service trench. However, its construction, around 1000 cal BC to 850 cal BC, marked a change in the way that space was demarcated on the plateau (Figure 11.15). The layout and features within the enclosure will be discussed below. A second site, the multiple-ditched Enclosure 2, may also date to the Late Bronze Age, although the finds from the limited evaluation work on the site are of Late Iron Age – Romano-British date. Possible relationships between the enclosures are discussed below.

The Enclosure 1 site represents the first evidence for an enclosure at Tremough, and is very significant because it represents one of the earliest securely-dated later Bronze Age enclosed sites in South West Britain. It is likely to have been associated

Figure 11.16 Photograph of Enclosure 1 from the south. The site marks the first formal enclosure of space. Note the burnt stones beside pit [124] in the foreground and the sites of post-built structures in the middle ground.

with changing attitudes to space, as prior to this period both settlement and ceremonial activities were largely unbounded. Up to this point, only certain tasks, such as the metalworking in Roundhouse 1 are likely to have taken place in a closely bounded, well-defined space.

This pattern of change is matched elsewhere and Joanna Brück (2007), for example, has pointed out that across Britain generally the later Bronze Age sees major changes both in the settlement record and in roundhouse architecture. She suggests that greater complexity may have been present in house design with, for example, porches being more commonplace, and in Wessex there is more evidence for the renewal of houses.

Changes also occurred in settlement layout and form as well. Small, fairly standardized Middle Bronze Age settlements made up of relatively unenclosed roundhouses were superseded by a diversity of settlement types, which include comparable open settlements but also a diversity of other site types. Elsewhere in Britain enclosed sites become apparent, with smaller enclosures known as ring-works or ring-forts often encircling roundhouses in the north and east of England and a few larger hilltop enclosures in, for example, the Welsh Marches and the west of England (for example, Brown 1988; Musson 1991; Needham and Ambers 1994; Guttmann and Last 2000; Manby 2007; Brown and Medlycott 2013). Across the Irish Sea, both small and large-scale enclosures began to be constructed (for example, Ginn 2012). Both ring-forts and the Irish enclosures have potential links with Tremough and these will be discussed below.

At the same time there is also increasing evidence for large-scale feasting and the formation of large midden mounds (Parker Pearson and Richards 1994; McOmish 1996). Repetitive social acts at community level appear have led to the formation of very large midden heaps, symbolically linked to consumption, fertility, affluence or success (Needham and Spence 1996, 85). At the same time there is increasing evidence for the production, circulation and deposition of metalwork on a scale which was not evident in the Middle Bronze Age (for example, Bradley 1991, chapter 3; Ginn 2012, 94).

This pattern could be taken to suggest that there was a developing social hierarchy in the later Bronze Age. However, several writers have cautioned against this interpretation (Brück 2007; Davis 2012, 67; Ginn 2012, 310), as although some small groups of people may have enjoyed higher status in the shorter term, there is little to indicate widespread or sustained formation of elite power.

Enclosure 1 and the regional Late Bronze Age settlement context in the south west of Britain

The evidence for Late Bronze Age settlement in the South West peninsula has been rather slighter than has been found in some other parts of southern Britain. Until recently, indications of Late Bronze Age activity have been confined to stray metalwork finds and chance discoveries of isolated features (Pearce 1983; Penhallurick 1986; Miles *et al* 1977). Since the 1990s, however, developer-funded work has led to the discovery of a small but significant number of sites, especially in Cornwall, which although relatively few, represent much more diversity than has been found for the Middle Bronze Age, for which there is a far greater number of sites.

Most of the newly-discovered sites have been post-ring roundhouses. The largest number of these was found at the Richard Lander School site, near Truro (Gossip, forthcoming); four post-ring buildings with diameters of 5-7.7m were uncovered and have been securely dated to the tenth-ninth centuries cal BC. As discussed elsewhere, this form of roundhouse architecture represents a break with the traditional hollow-set houses of the Middle Bronze Age and is likely to reflect contacts with communities to the east (Jones and Taylor 2010, 82). As suggested below, such contact may also have resulted in the construction of Enclosure 1.

Diversity is also evident in the settlement record. At Scarcewater, a post-ring roundhouse approximately 8m in diameter with a porched entrance on the south east was partly encircled by a palisaded enclosure. The palisade was probably not heavily defensive, as it was only wide enough to support split timbers or planks and was open on its western side. The porch and palisade together are likely to have formed a grand façade for the roundhouse when approached from lower ground to the south east (Jones and Taylor 2010, 83). The radiocarbon determinations from the site fell in the range 1130-890 cal BC.

Investigation and radiocarbon dating of stone-walled roundhouses in the uplands has also demonstrated that they could be reused in the later Bronze Age. Recent analysis of the finds from the Middle Bronze Age roundhouse settlement at Bosiliack in Penwith revealed that at least one house was reoccupied in the Late Bronze Age (Jones and Quinnell 2011), and radiocarbon dating of roundhouses 1 and 23 at Leskernick on Bodmin Moor provided evidence for occupation dating to the later Bronze Age and Early Iron Age (Bender *et al* 2007, 88-9). On Dartmoor several sites have also shown evidence for reuse, as at Teigncombe and the nearby Round Pound at Kestor (information S Gerrard and H Quinnell).

A deeply-ditched enclosure, dating to *circa* 1400-850 cal BC, was excavated at Liskeard. Unfortunately truncation of the site made it uncertain whether the ditch encircled a settlement (Jones 1998-9b) and its full extent is unknown; it is likely to be much larger than enclosure 1 and was located on the end of a spur overlooking lower lying ground to the west. As will be discussed in the next section, a series of other enclosures may belong to this period but are undated.

Beyond Cornwall, there are no immediate securely-dated parallels for Enclosure 1 in the wider region. To date no sites are known in Devon but there are a few later Bronze Age enclosures in Somerset. At Norton Fitzwarren the hilltop enclosure was associated with Late Bronze Age metalworking; although no internal features have been identified which relate to the Bronze Age occupation, earlier Middle Bronze Age Trevisker pottery and a hoard of newly-cast Taunton-period bracelets were obtained from the enclosure ditch (Ellis 1989). It was suggested that the site may not have been a settlement but was instead used for ceremonial purposes (*ibid*). Metalworking was also associated with another enclosure at Sigwells, near Cadbury Castle. This enclosure was rectangular and there was a post-built structure at one end associated with a large number of mould fragments.

The site is not is not currently closely dated, although the moulds suggest a Middle to Late Bronze Age date (Tabor 2008, 61-7; Skowranek 2007), and they include a large number of fragments from sword moulds. Interestingly, both of the Somerset enclosures were associated with metalworking and sword moulds, and this point will be returned to below.

Evidence for moulds and metalworking has also been found in non-settlement contexts in the South West. At Dainton in eastern Devon, several cairns were found, one of which was found to cover a pit containing mould fragments from two swords as well as pottery (Needham 1980; Silvester 1980), and at Higher Besore a pit containing part of a Wilburton sword mould was found not far from the Late Bronze Age settlement (Gossip, forthcoming).

Enclosure 1 and its wider relationships to other enclosures

Cornish parallels?

To date, Enclosure I represents the first site of its type to be identified and securely dated to the earlier first millennium in the south west of England. This picture is, in reality, unlikely to be correct, as there are several unexcavated very circular, enclosures and an ever-growing number of cropmark sites which have been located across Cornwall. Most of the latter sites have been interpreted as enclosed farmsteads or 'rounds' and assigned to the Late Iron Age or Romano-British period (for example, Young 2006; 2012), but it is very possible that some will prove to be of earlier date.

Several of the identified sites would happily sit either within the Late Bronze Age or the Early Iron Age. They include Bartinney and the primary phases of Caer Bran and possibly Castle an Dinas west in Penwith, Godolphin Hill, Hay Close at St Newlyn East, the first phase of Castle an Dinas east in central Cornwall, and Trecrogo in east Cornwall (Figure 11.17).

These enclosures are, like Tremough Enclosure 1, located in elevated positions, predominantly on hilltops and spurs. They range in diameter from approximately 60m to more than 100m and include the multiple-ditched enclosure at Trecrogo in east Cornwall (Figure 11.18) and the embanked hilltop site at Bartinney in West Penwith (Figure 11.19).

Several of the sites in this group, including Caer Bran, Bartinney, Castle an Dinas east and possibly Castle an Dinas west contain Early Bronze Age round barrows or cairns, and this raises the possibility that they were constructed to encircle and contain earlier monuments (Jones 2010). It is, however, possible that the barrows and the enclosures are contemporary with one another and the enclosures also belong to the Early Bronze Age (Herring 2011).

Unfortunately, only one potentially early first millennium cal BC enclosure has been investigated, that at Hay Close, St Newlyn East. There the basal fill of the ditch was radiocarbon dated to *circa* 750-450 cal BC, namely the Early Iron Age (Jones, forthcoming b), a few centuries later than Enclosure 1. It is therefore also likely that that not all of these sites are of one period.

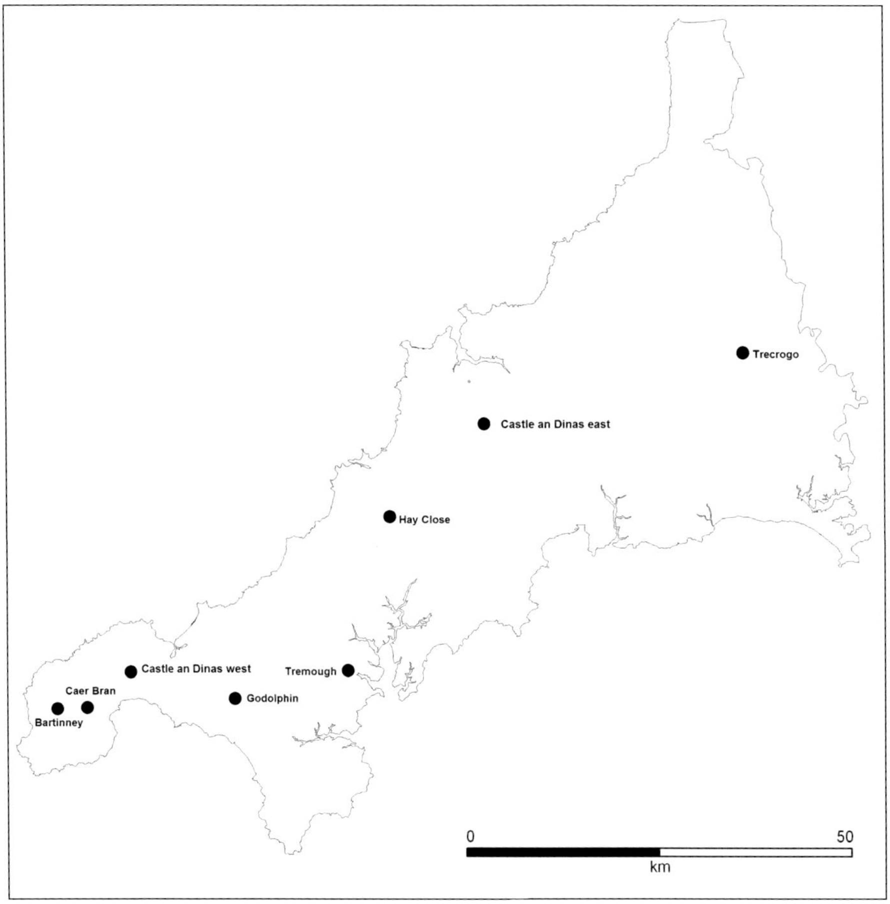

Figure 11.17 The distribution of possible late second – earlier first millennium cal BC enclosures in Cornwall referred to in the text.

The form of Hay Close is worthy of further comment. It had an external bank and prior to excavation had been identified as possible a Late Neolithic henge. This was proved not to be the case but it highlights the issues of dating sites by their morphology. The bank did not survive at Tremough Enclosure 1, which means that its position is unknown; however, Enclosure 2 (see below) appears to have had external banks, which again rendered it morphologically similar to henges. Elsewhere in Britain the circular form of the enclosure has been specifically agued to have derived from earlier henge sites which would have survived as grassed-over earthworks in the landscape (for example, Manby 2007). Indeed, the two Mucking Rings enclosures, for example, were first identified as henges prior to excavation (Jones and Bond 1980). By contrast, at Springfield Lyons the Late Bronze Age ring-fort enclosure was constructed beside an even earlier Neolithic monument, a causewayed enclosure, and the segmented character of the earlier enclosure ditch was adopted by the builders of the Late Bronze Age enclosure. This again has been argued to represent a drawing upon a mythological history or ancestral connections (Brown and Medlycott 2013, 155-9).

Figure 11.18 The multiple-ditched enclosure at Trecrogo from the air (Historic Environment, Cornwall Council).

Figure 11.19 Bartinney from the air with central cairns visible (Historic Environment, Cornwall Council).

The South West region has, however, very few henge monuments and to date, although a few have been recorded in Devon, no causewayed enclosures are known in Cornwall (Oswald *et al* 2001; Jones 2005, chapter 3). In light of this it therefore seems likely that parallels for Enclosure 1 have to be sought further afield, in particular with the ring-forts of southern and eastern Britain and with a variety of enclosure forms found in eastern Ireland.

Ring-forts of eastern England

As discussed above, the Late Bronze Age saw the development of a diversity of settlement types across Britain and Ireland, of which enclosures represent a significant new development. A major element of this enclosure tradition is represented by circular sites, for which the term ring-fort has been adopted to distinguish them from other larger forms of enclosure, such as hillforts (Figure 11.20).

Ring-fort enclosures are predominantly found on the eastern side of England, with most examples being documented in the south-east counties of Essex, Kent and Surrey. Morphologically similar enclosures are, however, also known in western Britain, as at Meillionydd on the Llŷn Peninsula in northwest Wales, although current dating places them in the earlier Iron Age (Alcock 1960; Karl and Waddington, forthcoming).

Most are less than 200m in diameter and occupy eminent positions overlooking valley floors (Needham 1992). They are usually deeply ditched as at Thwing, in the East Riding of Yorkshire (Manby 2007), or Springfield Lyons but sometimes defined by post-rings as at Hornchurch enclosure D in Essex or have palisades set within external ditches as at Cliffs End Farm, Kent (Guttmann and Last 2000; Needham *et al* 2015).

In common with Tremough Enclosure 1, many ring-forts have east-facing entrances (Guttmann and Last 2000). In the case of Tremough this is also of interest as it represents a significant change in orientation from the preference for south-facing entrances found for both 'domestic' roundhouses and ceremonial post-rings during the Middle Bronze Age.

Some ring-forts contain single large buildings inside them, as at Thwing (Manby 2007), or multiple roundhouses as at the Mucking sites. However, the internal layouts of these sites are very variable and, as Richard Bradley (2007, 208-9) has pointed out, they may have served a variety of purposes including defence and communal gatherings involving feasting. Evidence for specialized activity has been found at some sites, including salt production at Mucking (Bond 1988); evidence for metalworking has also been recovered from some, including Springfield Lyons and Mucking North Ring and South Ring, in Essex (Jones and Bond 1980; Bond 1988; Brown and Medlycott 2013), although this is generally of a small-scale nature. The most substantial metalwork deposit recorded from a ring-fort so far, has been the large number of mould fragments from the ditch terminal at Springfield Lyons (Needham and Bridgford 2013, 66). Stuart Needham (1992) has, however, cautioned against assuming that ring-forts were associated with control of metalwork production, and has pointed out that metalworking occurs at many different types of Late Bronze Age site. Likewise, most ring-forts are not

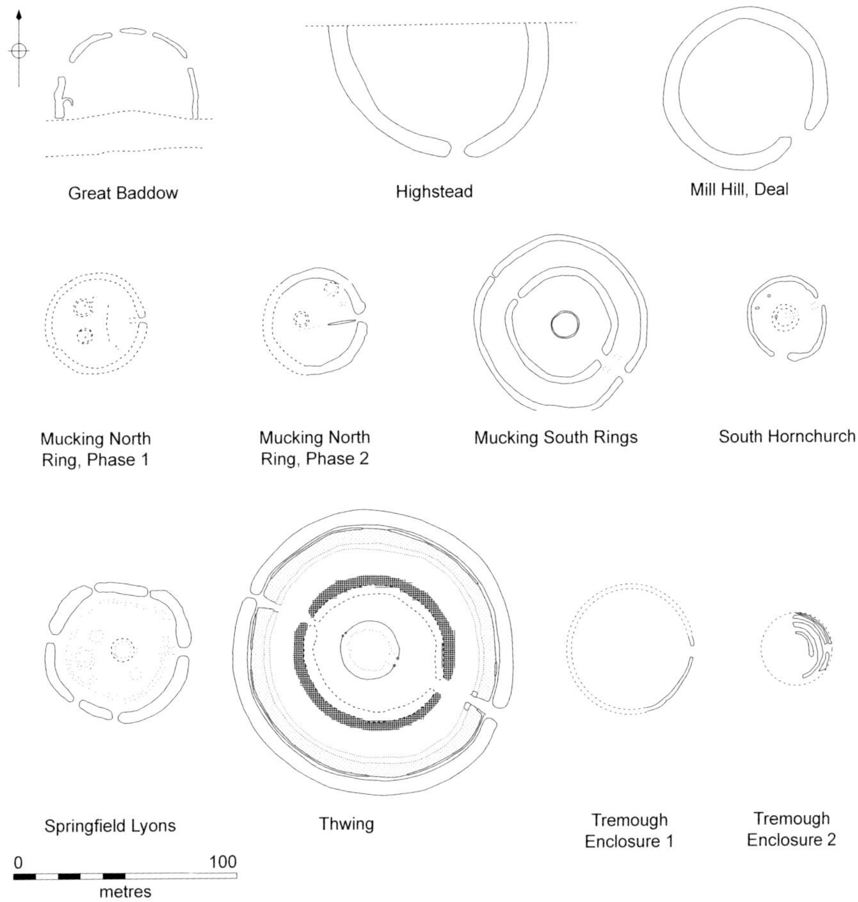

Figure 11.20 Comparative ring-forts and Tremough Enclosures 1 and 2 (After Manby 2007 and Brown and Medlycott 2013).

associated with artefactual assemblages which distinguish them from other forms of Late Bronze Age settlement. Special deposits, such as those found at Springfield Lyons are, however, fairly commonly found, and the terminals of enclosure ditches do seem to have been the foci for special deposits (see below).

By contrast, other enclosures have been found to have very little inside them in terms of coherent structural features, or simply have clusters of pits. For example, at Cliffs End Farm in east Kent two or possibly three palisaded enclosures associated with pits and midden deposits have been interpreted as not being used for settlement but instead possibly having held a ceremonial purpose linked to mortuary rites associated with adjacent Late Bronze Age burials and evidence of feasting (Needham *et al* 2015).

Enclosure form may not therefore have been important in determining function. Some ring-forts are likely to have been used for settlement and others for more specialized purposes such as communal gatherings and high-status activities, and many may have been regarded as special, possibly non-secular places, that lay within settled areas but were clearly separated from the adjacent settlements (for example, Needham 1992).

Returning to the South West, it would seem that ring-fort enclosures of the kind found in the south east of England would provide the most obvious inspiration for Enclosure 1. There is certainly evidence for inspiration from the east influencing a variety of traditions at around 1000 cal BC. As has already been touched upon above, roundhouse forms change from the hollow-set type around the turn of the first millennium cal BC, and the newly adopted post-ring roundhouse form is very likely to have spread from the east into Cornwall.

The same is true of for artefacts. The extraordinarily long-lived regional Trevisker ceramic tradition finally disappears at around 1000 cal BC, with some overlap with use of the simpler forms of Late Bronze Age Plain ware during the eleventh century cal BC (Quinnell 2012). Although Late Bronze Age settlements are still comparatively scarce, excavations of sites at Scarcewater and Higher Besore have shown the establishment of a diverse range of Late Bronze Age ceramics (Jones and Taylor 2010, 81-4; Gossip, forthcoming). These have parallels with some ceramic forms from the south of England (Barrett 1980; Woodward 1990; Fitzpatrick *et al* 1999, 111-12). At the same time, later Bronze Age metalwork hoards and individual finds from various locations across Cornwall, including St Erth in west Cornwall and Mylor, not far to the east of Tremough on Carrick Roads (Department of Culture Media and Sport 2004; 2008), show that either side of the millennium people in the South West were using artefacts which had a far wider currency.

One the other hand, these forms of evidence only point to contacts with southern England generally but not necessarily direct links with the east coast of England, where ring-fort enclosures are found. To date, the most direct evidence for contact with the east of England is a Trevisker-style vessel which was found in a barrow at Monkton on the Isle of Thanet, Kent, which has been radiocarbon dated to 1600-1300 cal BC, the Middle Bronze Age (Bennett *et al* 2008, 61).

Of course given that seaborne movement along the coast and around the Atlantic façade has been documented (for example, Needham *et al* 2013, chapter 5), it is more than likely that seafaring members of communities in Cornwall were aware of enclosures which were found in eastern England and the fact that they were special places in the landscape.

Irish Sea zone

Alternatively, it is possible that the inspiration for Enclosure 1 lies to the west of Britain, across the Irish Sea. Since at least the Neolithic period, the Atlantic seaways have played an important, if intermittent and shifting, role in creating connections between communities around the Irish Sea zone. This can be seen in monument forms such as portal dolmens, in rock art and a range of material culture, including certain forms of goldwork and copper-alloy artefacts including swords and rapiers (Waddell 1991/2; Bradley 1997, chapter 2; 2007, chapter 1; Sheridan 2004; Gibson 2013). It seems unlikely, however, that there was any kind of overarching 'Atlantic' identity (Henderson 2007, 297), as although there is a broad level of archaeologically detectable correspondences in material culture between areas along the Atlantic façade, there are significant differences between them both geographically and temporally, which are likely to reflect changing alliances and exchange networks, as well as the differing localised traditions of far-flung communities.

In Cornwall, the archaeological record provides evidence for at least intermittent seaborne contacts between Cornwall and Ireland throughout the span of the Bronze Age, so it is worth considering the evidence for relationships between these two areas as a potential source of inspiration for Enclosure 1 and more generally for the Cornish enclosures discussed above.

Several waves of contact between these two areas are demonstrated in the later third to middle second millennium cal BC. It is worth noting, however, that as Richard Bradley (2007, 24) has pointed out, the artefacts which have been found represent only the visible remnant of an exchange of personnel which is likely to have taken place to bolster alliances between widely separated communities. To this we may add the perishable goods such as textiles and pelts which, from accounts from ancient history and anthropological study, are likely to have been highly valuable objects but which have only survived in very exceptional conditions (Jenness 1977, 116-7; Randsbourg 2011, 116-8; Jones, in preparation). Connections across the Irish Sea are therefore likely to have been more frequent than the surviving evidence suggests.

The earliest of the Bronze Age contacts, at the start of the second millennium cal BC are demonstrated by four gold lunulae, which were all found in coastal parts of Cornwall, and which are likely to have been made by Irish goldsmiths (Taylor 1980, 40; Mattingly *et al* 2009). Moving forward to the latter half of the second millennium cal BC, a Ballintober-type sword was found at Carnpessack on the Lizard in west Cornwall (Pearce 1983, 412), with one more example from Devon and two from Somerset. The greatest concentration of these swords is found in the Thames Valley. However, numerous examples have also been found in Ireland, and indeed the type takes its name from a site in Mayo (Burgess 1968; Waddell 1998, 204-5). The Cornish find (Figure 11.22) is an outlier, being situated between the two concentrations and as such could have been obtained via contact with communities to the east or the west. Nonetheless, it must have been a valued, status item and shows a connection with wider exchange networks. At this juncture it is also worth noting that a flow of ideas influencing material culture in the opposite direction during the later second millennium cal BC may be demonstrated by Trevisker features on pottery found on Dalkey Island, near Dublin on the east coast of Ireland (ApSimon and Greenfield 1972). This find reveals that the exchanges which took place were not just in one direction. As noted above, it has been suggested that similarities are found between Trevisker Ware and some ceramic assemblages found in Normandy during this period (Marcigny *et al* 2007).

There is also a small group of diagnostic metalwork finds which reflect contact with Ireland during the Late Bronze Age (Figure 11.21). These include the Irish gold penannular bracelets from Morvah in Penwith and a dress fastener from the Lizard peninsula in west Cornwall (Hawkes and Clarke 1963, 230–1; Eogan 1994,

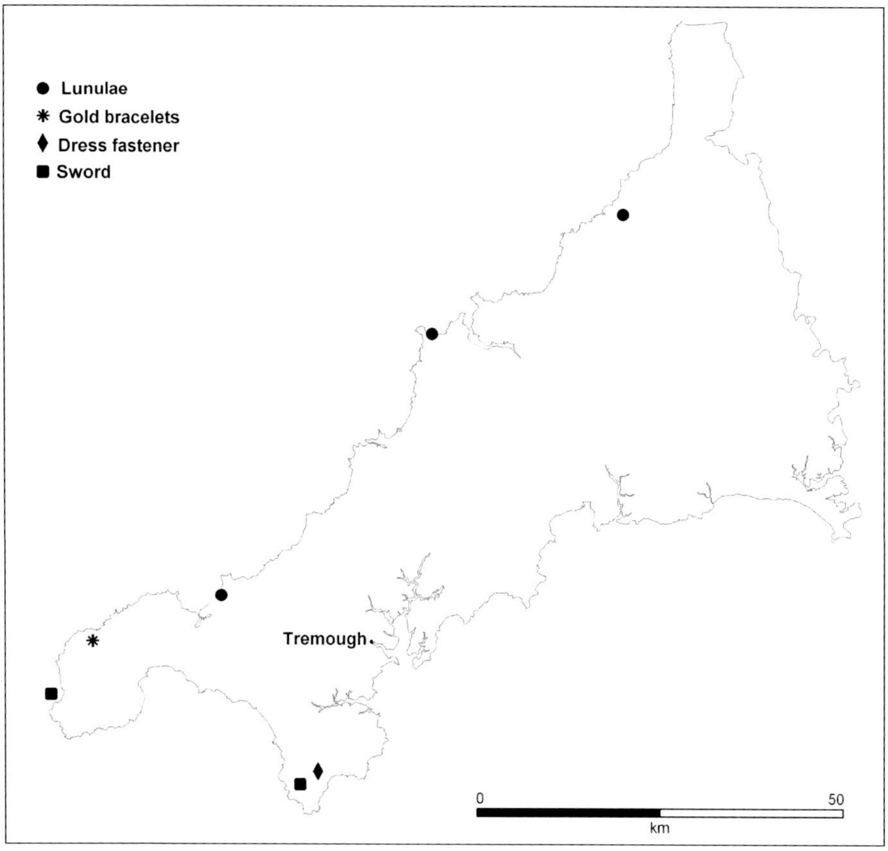

Figure 11.21 The distribution of Irish (or possibly Irish) metalwork in Cornwall.

145, 152; Needham and Hook 1989). In addition to the goldwork finds, there is also the Late Bronze Age Gundlingen-type sword of possible Irish variant which was found in the sea near Sennen Cove, in Penwith (Needham *et al* 2013, 115-6) (Figure 11.22). This sword type is widely found along the Atlantic sea zone and although not necessarily reflecting direct contacts with Ireland is more broadly indicative of the links which existed between Britain, northern France and Ireland in the Late Bronze Age, and of the exchange of prestigious items (Cunliffe 2009).

As with the lunulae, the Ballintober-type sword and the Trevisker-influenced pottery, it is noticeable that all of the Late Bronze Age find spots are in coastal locations, and it may be noteworthy that the bracelets and the Sennen sword are also situated near to the largest concentration of suggested late second early first millennium prehistoric enclosures in Penwith (Fig 11.17). Enclosure 1 and Enclosure 2 at Tremough also, of course, occupy a coastal position overlooking the Fal estuary.

Given the available evidence for long-term contacts, it is reasonable to expect that some individuals or groups would have periodically crossed the Irish Sea throughout the later second and early first millennium cal BC. The likelihood of the eastern seaboard of Ireland providing a potential source of comparanda for

Figure 11.22 Photograph of the Ballintober-type sword from Carnpessack (left) and the Gundlingen-type sword from Sennen Cove (right). (Image by Anna Tyacke, reproduced with permission of the Royal Cornwall Museum). The Royal Cornwall Museum accession numbers for the finds are: Sennen Cove (TRURI: 1992.29); Carnpessack (TRURI: 1923.190).

the Cornish enclosures has been discussed elsewhere (Jones 2010), but it is worth reviewing the potential range of enclosure types in eastern Ireland which could have provided inspiration for Tremough Enclosures I and 2, and other Cornish enclosures.

Morphologically, it is the group of Irish enclosures known as 'royal' sites which perhaps provides the closest parallels with Tremough Enclosure 2. They can comprise single or groups of multiple-ditched enclosures, as at the Tlaghta (Hill of Ward) or the Rath of Synods (Tara) in Co Meath. These sites are located close to the eastern seaboard and therefore may have been encountered by people moving between Ireland and South West Britain. However, they have been found to have their origins in the later Iron Age, and to continue in use into the post-Roman period (Newman 1998; Roche 2002). This extended chronological span means that there is a broad overlap between the ceramic dating from the upper ditch fills of Enclosure 2 and the Irish 'royal' sites, although they would post-date Enclosure 1 by several centuries.

There is, however, evidence for a variety of circular Late Bronze Age enclosures in Ireland, some of which are associated with the production and deposition of metalwork (Mallory 1995; Raftery 1997, 58; Ginn 2012, 188). These include a range of embanked enclosures, including circle-henges under 20m in diameter (O'Brien 2004), to Emain Macha (Navan Fort), with a diameter of 47m, through to very large enclosures, such as Haughey's Fort, which is approximately 150m in diameter (Mallory 1995; Roche 2004; O'Brien 2004) and hillforts such as Rathgall, the outer rampart of which has a diameter of 310m (Raftery 1976). These sites are very much bigger than Enclosure 1 or indeed any of the Cornish enclosures mentioned above. The smaller embanked sites, however, such as Emain Macha or Grange, which has an internal diameter of approximately 47m, are of a similar scale to Enclosure 1 and have distinct morphological similarities to hilltop enclosures such as Bartinney and Caer Bran, which have internal diameters of around 60m. It may be significant that some Irish enclosures, including Grange, in common with both Bartinney and Caer Bran also enclose Early Bronze Age cairns.

It would not be difficult to push the hunt in Ireland for direct parallels for Enclosure 1 beyond the available evidence. It is sufficient to recognise that Late Bronze Age communities in Ireland and Cornwall were engaged in intermittent long-distance interactions which are likely to have led to the sharing of cosmological ideas and architecture.

East or west?

From the foregoing discussion, Enclosure 1 and a number of other Cornish enclosures could be argued to have arisen or been influenced through seaborne contacts with communities along the eastern Irish coastline or through contacts with people along the east coast of England. This raises the question of the character of those connections; namely, were they unidirectional from the east or the west, did they arise through domination by one community over another or were they more subtle interactions over a long period of time?

The low numbers of Irish objects, or artefacts which are specifically from the east coast of England suggests that there was not a wave of settlers from either direction into the South West. Instead it is more likely that, as Stuart Needham (2009) has argued for the earlier Bronze Age, there was a network of interconnected communities around the seaboard who exchanged prestigious items with one another.

Jon Henderson (2007, 297) has suggested that there are detectable similarities between areas around the Atlantic façade but that there is there is little evidence for any kind of overarching 'Atlantic identity' in the later second or first millennium cal BC. Rather, resemblances arose between communities who were linked by the sea and who had engaged with each other and exchanged high-status objects, with one another over several millennia. The biographies of the exchanged objects is also likely to have been important and the swords and the goldwork may have had established 'histories' before they reached their final destinations (for example, Pearce 2013).

There is also a symbolic dimension to exchange. Crossing the sea in search of prestigious metal items may have led to obtaining the gold bracelets from Morvah or the Gundlingen-type sword from Sennen Cove, as well as other forms of material culture, but it is also very likely that, as has been demonstrated by ethnographical studies (for example, Weiner 1987, 154-7) that not all objects were 'equal' and had their own layered biographies. Obtaining these items was probably bound up with shared ideologies and religious beliefs.

The journey itself may have also have enhanced the status of those who braved the unknown danger of crossing the sea. Added to this, Mary Helms (1988, chapter 4; 1993, 81) has also made the case that, at certain times, foreign people and objects, especially those that are valued or have symbolic capital, can be valued over the insular and the traditional, and it is possible that we can see a similar trend in the Cornish later Bronze Age. The mythologization of the journeys involved by those who undertook them may have led some to pursue long-distance voyages in search of exotic and magical items which could be taken home and displayed or used in ritualized contexts.

Portable objects were not the only things which are likely to have held symbolic meaning in the later Bronze Age. As Henderson (2007, 299-300) has argued, the landscape and features within it are also likely to have been embedded with meanings and myths, and they are likely to have been renegotiated through the construction of monuments. With this in mind, it might be possible to add that the circular form of Enclosures 1 and 2 may itself have been making reference to distant special places and a more widely held circular cosmology (*cf* Bradley 2012).

Considered in this way, Enclosure 1 and the diverse range of other enclosures under discussion do not require precise parallels. Their existence could suggest that knowledge of a number of different 'exotic' forms of enclosure emerged from engagement with an east–west flow of ideas. These links could have led to the emergence of circular enclosures, such as those found at Tremough and possibly elsewhere in Cornwall, on the western seaboard of Britain. In other words, widespread contacts resulted in a spread of ideas that were adapted and readapted to fit the traditions and needs of local communities, such as those who occupied the plateau at Tremough.

The organization of space and activity within Enclosure 1

Aside from establishing the possible origins of Enclosure 1, there is also the question of the character of the occupation and activities which took place within it.

The full extent of Enclosure 1 is likely to have been approximately 60m to 65m in diameter, with a 5.5m wide entrance on its eastern side. The ditch was 1.7m wide and deeply cut to a depth of 1.35m. There was no trace of a bank and the tip lines in the ditch layers did not indicate a clear direction from which the infill deposits came (chapter 2). Likewise, there were no signs of any posts around the entranceway which may have supported a gate or gatehouse, and the only trace of any activity close to the entranceway was a very shallow linear deposit which could not be phased. It is therefore probable that the entrance was not gated and that access into the enclosure was not blocked with a barrier.

Maintenance of the enclosure perimeter does, however, seem to have been important as there is evidence that the ditch had been recut, and by so doing the space would have remained well-defined. Most of the finds from the ditch came

Figure 11.23 Photograph of Post Structure 4 taken from the east.

from the upper fills, and it is possible that it had been kept open for some time until the upper layers were finally deposited into it.

No roundhouses were exposed within the enclosure, but it did reveal a number of other structures: two rectilinear buildings were uncovered together with pit groups and features containing burnt stones. In common with many excavated enclosures there were also a large number of pits and postholes which could not be easily assigned to a structure or given a function (Bond 1988, 13-14; Guttmann and Last 2000; Brown and Medlycott 2013, 41-43).

Evidence for residential structures within Enclosure 1 was not immediately obvious; in part this might be due to the fact that the entirety of the interior could not be exposed. Unlike many other Late Bronze Age enclosures, such as Thwing in North Yorkshire and Hornchurch, Mucking South Rings and Springfield Lyons in Essex (Manby 2007; Guttmann and Last 2000; Jones and Bond 1980; Brown and Medlycott 2013), Enclosure 1 was not associated with a large central structure, and there were no certain domestic dwellings. Two of the structures, Post Structure 3 and Post Structure 4, however, were rectangular (Figure 11.23) and were large enough to have been domestic structures or used for other purposes such as storage.

Although less common than roundhouses, rectilinear buildings of later Bronze Age date are known elsewhere in Britain, both on open sites, as at the Tower Works site, Fengate, near Peterborough (Pryor 2001, 35), for example, or within enclosures, such as those at Mucking and Springfield Lyons in Essex (Bond 1988, 14; Brown and Medlycott 2013, 40). Rectangular buildings have often been interpreted as utilitarian grain stores or animal barns, as at Rams Hill in Berkshire and Reading Business Park in the Thames Valley (Bradley and Ellison 1975, 212; Brossler *et al* 2004, 122-3). A centralised storage role was suggested for structure

5050 found within the ring-fort enclosure at Hornchurch in Essex (Guttmann and Last 2000). By contrast, rectangular structure 2 at the Boreham Interchange in Essex was interpreted as a shrine (Brown and Medlycott 2013, 153). Smaller structures referred to as 'four posters' are also known at later Bronze Age and Iron Age sites in southern Britain (for example, Moore and Jennings 1992, 140; Bradley and Ellison 1975, 55-9). These are also usually interpreted as being used for storage (for example, Coles 1973, 62).

However, 'four-posters' and comparable larger later Bronze Age structures are extremely uncommon in the South West peninsula, although a rectangular building, structure [129], was uncovered at Trenowah, near St Austell (Johns 2008, fig 9). This building was 5m long by 3.4m wide and comprised six postholes. It was radiocarbon dated to 980-800 cal BC and was therefore broadly contemporary with activity within Enclosure 1 at Tremough. It was not, however, associated with any artefacts or any other directly related settlement or occupation activity and its interpretation is therefore open to question. A Higher Besore, two possible rectilinear structures were recorded near to the Late Bronze Age roundhouses. However, these were not closely dated and could be of Late Bronze Age or Early Iron Age date (Gossip, forthcoming).

Post Structures 3 and 4 at Tremough, and the possible post structure, contained very little in the way of associated artefacts (chapters 3 and 4), although interestingly Post Structure 4 was associated with larger amounts of charred grain than many of the other features inside the enclosure (chapter 8).

Either of the rectangular post-structures could therefore have been used for domestic occupation, ceremonial activity or storage, but perhaps as we have discussed in relation to the Middle Bronze Age roundhouses it is not necessarily important to make these kinds of rigid distinction. Instead, it is possible that the architecture rather than function is key to their interpretation, and to realise that one role need not negate another. Anthropological study has revealed numerous examples where structures could be used for a variety of purposes, combining both mundane and ritual. For example, Torajan houses in South Sulawesi, Indonesia, embody cosmological schemes and are used for ceremonies, but are also occupied as domestic residences and used for storage (Kis-Jovak *et al* 1988). Similarly, in Papua New Guinea, yam houses, which are used for storage, also have a wider significance: they are associated with marriage and act as a symbol of significant political accomplishment, and their filling is accompanied by rituals and display (Weiner 1987, 91-6).

As we have seen, Richard Bradley (2012) has suggested that in later prehistory the circular architectural form may have embodied widely held cosmological beliefs, and indeed this may have been reflected by the overall form of Enclosure 1. The rectangular buildings inside may therefore have been designed to create a contrast. Evidence for the purposeful use of differing forms of architecture has been noted elsewhere. Adrian Chadwick (2012) has argued in relation to four-post structures that some at least were imbued with greater social significance. For example, at South Elmsall, near the county boundary between South and West Yorkshire, archaeological investigations revealed part of a field system and an unenclosed Middle to Late Bronze Age roundhouse settlement. To the east were at least ten four-post structures, arranged in two north–south rows which may have been constructed on either side of a path. This arrangement was perhaps designed so that they and their contents could be displayed and viewed from the settlement. By constructing rectangular buildings within the circular Enclosure 1, a contrast may have been deliberately designed to create a distinction which would make them visually memorable to onlookers. In this way, their use and / or contents could be bought to the fore. It is perhaps as important to recognize the distinction which was being made between different architectural forms as to assign a domestic or non-domestic role.

The remaining features within Enclosure 1 are more difficult to disentangle. A third possible post structure may have stood near to the entrance but, it is equally possible that this was an unrelated group of features.

The most substantial cluster of features was associated with Pit / Posthole Group 1. It is not possible to make a convincing building from it, and the double L-shaped arrangement of pits is likely to relate to successive rectangular structures and pits. The limited radiocarbon dating, 2822±30 BP, 1071-899 cal BC (SUERC-47288), from pit [114] and 2766±29 BP, 997-835 cal BC (SUERC-47291), from posthole [156], although partially overlapping, might support the suggestion that there was a sequence of structures in this part of the site. To the east of this group of structures, were two linear features, [209] and [213]. These features were not deeply cut, and may in fact have been depressions caused by the weight of objects such as timber beams pressing down into the ground. As such, it is possible that some kind of windbreak, screen or partition had been erected to shield whatever activities were taking place within the area of Pit / Posthole Group 1. This is also implied by the break between the two depressions which might have formed an east-facing entrance into the area. Screens and linear settings of posts are, of course, known from other later Bronze Age enclosures. During phase one of Mucking North Ring (Bond 1988, 14-19), for example, a screen was erected between the entrance of the enclosure and the roundhouses, and it has been argued that the screen was a device to block the roundhouses from view when approached from the east entrance (Parker Pearson and Richards 1994). This could have reinforced distinctions between areas of the enclosure which were associated with different tasks. It is possible that the same was true at Tremough Enclosure 1, with the screen acting to visually separate the structures from people entering the enclosure through the entrance to the east.

The uses to which the structure or more probably structures represented by Pit / Posthole Group 1 were put remains unknown, as there were few finds, only small quantities of charred plant macrofossils and a very small number of burnt bone fragments. The same remains true for the amorphous group of pits forming Pit Alignment 2; although burnt stones were included within some of their fills and this might be suggestive of cooking or other activities involving heating. Mould fragments A-D from metalworking were found in posthole [144]. In fact, the heating of stones was particularly evident in two features located to the south of Pit / Posthole Group 1 and these will be discussed in the next section.

Structured deposition and burnt stone

Evidence for the formalized, structured deposition of artefacts was less than has been found at other Late Bronze Age enclosures, where the ditch terminals, for example, could be focal points for major episodes of deposition. At Springfield Lyons, Essex, the enclosure ditch terminal was the focus for a substantial deposit of sword moulds, and at Hornchurch a ceramic vessel was deposited into the north terminal and cremated human remains found in and near to entranceways. At Mucking North Ring there was a concentration of artefacts in the ditch terminals and two gold rings were found near the entranceway (Brown and Medlycott 2013, 20; Guttmann and Last 2000; Bond 1988; Needham 1992).

By contrast, finds from the ditch of Enclosure 1 were limited to one muller **S1**, two unworked stones (a flint pebble and a vein quartz fragment), and a relatively small quantity of pottery, mostly recovered from the upper fill of the southern ditch terminal (Quinnell, chapters 3 and 4). The fresh condition and large sherd size of this pottery might suggest that it had been placed into the ditch soon after breakage occurred but there did not appear to have been any structuring to this material. Unlike Roundhouse 1, most of the post structures and pits noted above cannot clearly be identified as being associated with the deliberate placing of ritualized deposits either during construction or the abandonment phase.

However, the large sherd size and generally fresh condition of much of the ceramic assemblage found within the pits and posthole structures (chapter 3), suggest the possibility that the pottery entered into these features soon after breakage. Alternatively, it could have been stored elsewhere on site, perhaps in a midden, and the material subsequently used to infill open cut features. This, of course, would have parallels with the main infilling of Roundhouse 1, and could show some kind of continuity with regard to the perceived symbolic properties of midden material and the most appropriate way to deploy it across the site.

Two features, Structure 205 and pit [124] do, however, stand out within the enclosure as foci for specialized activity and structured deposition.

Structure 205 was located on the western edge of the site. It comprised a carefully built cairn of stones, which had been built over a slight depression. Immediately to the east was a very large circular pit [119]. The cairn was made from burnt stones suggesting a burning / heating episode. It is possible that it was constructed from material derived from a burnt mound with an associated pit, although it is likely to have been related to very short-term activity as the mound was quite small and carefully built. A second pit [124] was located to the south. Burnt stones were found within this pit, and during topsoil stripping further burnt stone had also been found in this area, which suggests that a mound of burnt stones had also existed beside it.

One possibility is that both features were associated with cooking, with the heated stones being used to heat water held in the adjacent pits, or for roasting meat in them. Burnt mounds are widely found in Britain and Ireland and examples have been securely dated to the Middle and Late Bronze Age (see papers in Buckley 1990; Ladle and Woodward 2009, 128; Cuttler *et al* 2012, 122-9).

Comparatively few burnt mounds have been identified in the south west of Britain (for example, Wilson-North and Carey 2011) and only one burnt mound has been identified and excavated in Cornwall. This site, at Boscaswell in West Penwith was much older, and associated with Beaker pottery (Jones and Quinnell 2006). In Devon two more sites have been excavated, a burnt mound on Woodbury Common in Devon has recently been radiocarbon dated to the Early Bronze Age (Tilley 2009) and two burnt mounds at Burlescombe in east Devon have been dated to the Middle Bronze Age (Best and Gent 2007). Other sites have been recently identified in the Exeter area (H Quinnell, pers comm.).

Burnt mound sites typically consist of three components: a pit or large trough, a mound of burnt stone and charcoal, and a hearth or fire pit, although as at Tremough, the hearths are not always found. The pits or troughs are frequently well-defined rectangular features, which can be lined with stone or timber, to circular or irregular pits, which do not usually show any signs of heating. The sizes are similarly variable with some measuring more than 2m long and over 1m deep and others under 1m in diameter and only 0.2m deep (Kelly 1992; Beamish and Ripper 2000; Barber *et al* 2006; Best and Gent 2007). Both pits [119] and [124] would fit within this size range.

The associated mounds are made up of large heaps of fire-cracked stones and charcoal and generally lack the careful construction evident in Structure 205. The stones are likely to have cracked by being heated in a fire before being immersed in water within the trough to bring it to the boil (Buckley 1990, 170-2), although heating to high temperatures may itself have also caused stones to fracture. Some sites may have been associated with roasting rather than boiling and in this case stones would not have been placed in water. Excavation has indicated that some sites were used on several occasions and that their use could extend over considerable periods of time (Kelly 1992; Topping 1998). The mound often takes the form of a kidney-shaped arrangement around the trough or pit. This does not appear to have been the case at Tremough, at least in the case of Structure 205, which was carefully built, and this point will be returned to later.

Unlike at Tremough, most burnt mounds are located away from settlement areas and are frequently devoid of artefactual associations (Kelly 1992; Topping 1998; Halsted 2005, 66). This pattern contrasts with Structure 205 and particularly with pit [124], both of which were associated with pottery.

Structure 205 and pit [124] contained a small number of charred cereals and a small amount of burnt bone was also found in the latter pit, which could support the cooking interpretation. However, alternative hypotheses have been put forward for the functions of burnt mound and pit complexes, including their use as saunas, or for tanning or brewing beer (Barfield and Hodder 1987; Drisceoil 1988; Jeffrey 1991; Quinn and Moore 2007). Another suggestion is that some burnt mound sites were associated with metalworking and Skowranek (2007, 28) has noted that metal residues and moulds are frequently found with burnt stone. Examples include Tre-wyn Lllandfydog on Anglesey, where a stone-filled pit was associated with residue from copper working (Lynch 1991, 363-4); at Shorncote Quarry in Gloucestershire mould fragments from a socketed axe were recovered from a large pit which also contained burnt limestone fragments (Herne and Heaton 1994). At the Sigwells enclosure in Somerset (Tabor 2008, 64), mould fragments were found with large amounts of burnt stone, although these were from the enclosure ditch.

At Tremough, pit [124] was found to contain fragments from moulds, including a sword tip and fragments from a probable axe mould (below). The quantity of the mould fragments are, however, quite small, and there is no evidence for large-scale metalworking on the site. There is evidence for deliberate closure at both pit [124] and Structure 205, and this means that the deposits within them may not be directly related to their use and therefore require closer consideration.

Structure 205, which was associated with a deeply cut pit [119], and pit [124] provide the best evidence for formalized structured deposition within Enclosure 1. Both were associated with burnt stones and were comparatively rich in artefacts. Pit [119] did not appear to have been the focus for any structured deposition, although it is worth noting that organic material or unburnt bone placed inside the open cut would not have survived. Instead, the fill may have been associated with its last use: it was full of burnt stone and charcoal. The pile of burnt stones forming Structure 205 beside it was, however, carefully built and had the appearance of a small cairn, with a large flat stone capping it. The stones covered a hollow which produced sherds of Late Bronze Age pottery, including vessels **P14** and **P15**. The former was a large storage vessel, which again may have been associated with cooking. A radiocarbon determination of 2808±29 BP, 1048-896 cal BC (SUERC-47289), from the layer within which the pottery was found is consistent with the date suggested by the pottery. The fact that the stones had been carefully constructed over this layer might suggest that, rather than simply being a burnt mound which had accumulated over time, the intention may have been to mark an area of the enclosure where significant activities, such as communal cooking or other events had taken place.

Pit [124] is also likely to have had a mound of burnt stones beside and very possibly over it as well (chapter 2), but it is not possible to say if it was as well-made as Structure 205. The contents of the pit are, however, unlikely to represent a fortuitous assemblage. This pit had been infilled with burnt stones which are likely to have been derived from activities associated with it. The cut also contained a variety of artefacts, which make it stand apart from all the other features within the enclosure. These finds include the greatest quantity of Late Bronze Age pottery to be recovered from the site, including **P17**, one of the large vessels which may have been associated with communal cooking (chapter 3, above). As discussed above, there were small quantities of charred cereal grains and fragments from moulds associated with metalworking including mould **10**, the sword tip. A cushion / finishing stone **S7**, was also placed into the pit and this too may have been associated with the production of copper-alloy artefacts.

The assemblage from pit [124] therefore represents a collection of materials which was conceivably associated with notable events, including the communal sharing of food and metalworking, although there is nothing to suggest that the pit was directly associated with this transformative process. It is, however, worth noting that the metalworking debris seems to have been more integrated and intermixed with other materials (for example, burnt stone and pottery) than was the case in the Middle Bronze Age Roundhouse 1. Comparable assemblages of mould fragments have been found elsewhere in the South West. At Higher Besore, near Truro (Gossip, forthcoming), part of a Late Bronze Age sword mould was found within a pit and at Dainton in Devon (Needham 1980), mould fragments from two swords and other objects were found within and around a pit which had been covered by a stony mound. This site also produced sherds of pottery; although the assemblage was far richer than that from Tremough the similarities are noteworthy. Later Bronze Age mould fragments from metalworking are, of course, well documented within enclosures and pits across Britain and these have usefully recently been drawn together by Needham and Bridgford (2013, 68-74). Sword mould fragments are relatively frequently found and at Springfield Lyons formed a substantial structured deposit. However, as Needham and Bridgford (2013, 72-3) point out, they are, as at Tremough, usually found with fragments of moulds for other forms of object, and are not found in large quantities. Nonetheless, they may have been redolent of the specific artefact functions which came out of them and of the production of metalwork. As such, they may have been very suitable items for inclusion within ritualized deposits (*ibid*).

As noted above, at Tremough there is no evidence for large-scale metalworking and the mould fragments and cushion / finishing stone in pit [124] are likely to have been associated with a 'one-off' or a very small number of events. Given the incomplete nature of the moulds, and the freshness of the accompanying ceramics, it is probable that the by-products from these activities, together with those from cooking and food storage may again have been set aside, perhaps within a midden mound, until it was time to infill the pit. Not enough is known about any accompanying mound or cairn of burnt stone, but it too could have helped memorialise events in the way that Structure 205 is likely to have done beside pit [119].

The setting of Enclosure 1

There is little evidence for the character of the broader settlement pattern around Enclosure 1. Elsewhere in Britain, as at Hornchurch and Springfield Lyons (Guttmann and Last 2000; Brown and Medlycott 2013), Late Bronze Age enclosures have been found to be situated close to areas of fields and to open roundhouse settlements. At Tremough, to date, evidence for Late Bronze Age occupation outside Enclosure 1 has been limited to the sherds of pottery found in the soil over the infilled hollows for Roundhouse 1 and especially Roundhouse 2 (chapter 3); a Late Bronze Age radiocarbon determination came from residue on one of the sherds of pottery from over Roundhouse 2. This implies that activity in the area of the disused Middle Bronze Age roundhouses might have occurred, possibly in the form of middening, but the extent or location of any contemporary open settlement is unknown.

Enclosure 1 may not, however, have been the only enclosed space in the immediate landscape and it is at this point that we need to consider its relationship with Enclosure 2, which lay to the south (Figure 11.24).

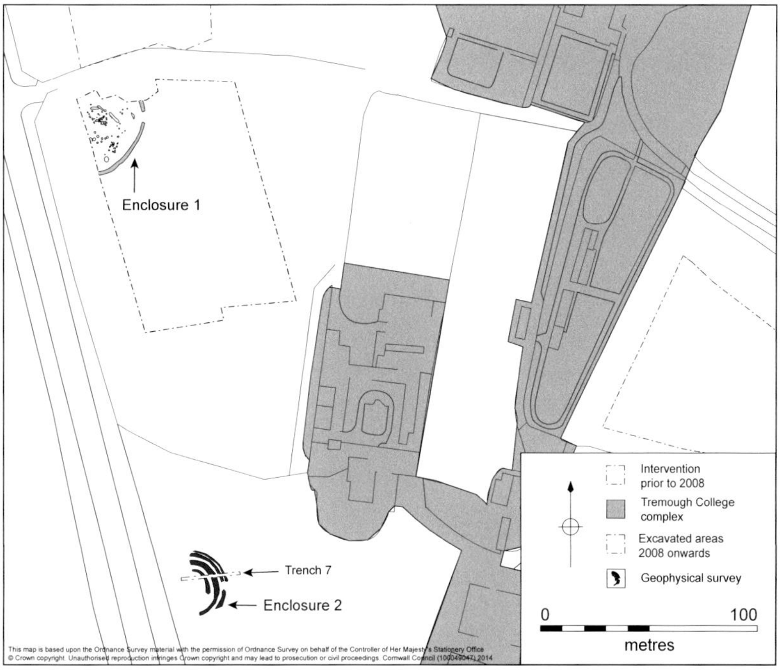

Figure 11.24 Late Bronze Age Enclosure 1 and later prehistoric Enclosure 2.

In other parts of Britain some Late Bronze Age enclosures were constructed in close proximity to one another, as for example at Cliffs End Farm on the Isle of Thanet, Kent, where up to three enclosures may have been built in close proximity to one another. At Hornchurch a timber Late Bronze Age post-ring enclosure may have stood near to the ring-fort (Needham *et al* 2015; Guttmann and Last 2000). More widely spaced are the enclosures at Mucking, although these are likely to have been contemporary with one another and conceived as a pair (Jones and Bond 1980). By contrast, at Springfield Lyons (Medlycott and Brown 2013, 159) the ring-fort enclosure was sited beside a much older Early Neolithic causewayed enclosure, and here the authors suggest that Late Bronze Age communities may have been attempting to draw upon or manipulate a mythological or ancestral past.

At Tremough it is not possible to be certain about the chronology of Enclosure 2. Given the lack of finds from primary fills in its ditches it could be contemporary with or significantly later than Enclosure 1. The small-scale of the evaluation trench on Enclosure 2 meant that activity within it was not well characterised, although a very large hole for a 'totem-pole' sized post was located within the trench and this hints at the possibility of rather different activity to what was found at Enclosure 1. If we hypothesize that the two enclosures were contemporary with one another it is possible that one held structures and features associated with storage, the cooking of foodstuffs, the sharing of food and possibly small-scale metalworking. The other had multiple ditches and a much smaller interior which held at least one massive post. This might imply that one could have been used for communal activity the other was a more bounded space, which was perhaps more rarely entered. Both, however, are likely to have been special places.

Much later activity is, however, certainly apparent at Enclosure 2, from the small amount of pottery of Late Iron Age – Romano-British date which came from the upper ditch fills. It is of interest that there is some evidence for Late Iron Age activity at Enclosure 1 too, where a sherd of Late Iron Age pottery **P19** was recovered (probably from topsoil) from close to the cairn which formed Structure 205. This sherd is likely to have been imported from Brittany and is indicative of long-distance contact between distant communities. It does not, however, appear that Enclosure 1 was a major focus of activity during the Iron Age, and even if there was some overlap in their use Enclosure 2 was certainly used long after Enclosure 1 grassed over.

Although we cannot establish a direct link between the construction or first usage of the two enclosures, it is very likely that Enclosure 1 would have still have been a significant place in the Iron Age landscape. As Stuart Needham (2007b) has pointed out, Late Bronze Age enclosures could have been important foci in the Iron Age, even if their original function had been lost in time, and there is certainly evidence for Iron Age engagement with earlier sites. John Barrett (1999) has suggested that Bronze Age barrows would have had significance in the cultural landscape of Iron Age communities in southern Britain and argued that their monumental forms would have provided physical evidence to support a connection with a mythological past. Likewise, Richard Hingley (2009) has observed the occurrence of Bronze Age artefacts on Iron Age sites and conversely the evidence for Iron Age activity in older enclosures, which he has suggested could have been connected with a desire to establish genealogies. Later activity at older enclosures is also evident in Ireland, where several later earthwork monuments were situated near to Late Bronze Age enclosures, and these sites arguably became ancestral elements within long-lived complexes (Mallory 2005; Raftery 1976). In the centuries after it had passed out of use it is likely that Enclosure 1 survived as a monumental earthwork in the landscape, and as such, in common with other Bronze Age monuments, to have attracted stories and become a mythologized place (Gosden and Lock 1998).

Enclosure 1, a summary

In summary, Enclosure 1 represented a departure from the previous activity which has been uncovered on the Tremough plateau. The architecture was of a type which had not been found in the South West peninsula as a whole before and the enclosure itself represents the first large-scale monument to be constructed on the plateau. Although the site was not fully exposed, it has been argued that the form of the enclosure is likely to have resulted from contacts with other regions, where similar sites dating to the Late Bronze Age are found. These include eastern Britain and Ireland, and it is possible that it was constructed by a group of people who wanted to demonstrate their knowledge and links with distant architectural traditions and wider cosmologies. As such, it was probably an important focal point for the surrounding community.

The special character of the enclosure is perhaps also suggested by the features found inside it. This included rectangular structures that are unusual in south west Britain. Numerous pits were also found and the largest two of these are likely to have been associated with communal events, possibly associated with the cooking of foodstuffs, and this is also implied by the large ceramic vessels which may have been used to store or share food. In addition, other transformative activity was identified involving small-scale episodes of metalworking. Both of the pits appear to have been memorialized, in one case with a well-made cairn of burnt stones. In light of this, it is suggested that it was probably regarded as a special place. If Enclosure 2 is considered to post-date Enclosure 1, it is possible that it lived on as a mythologized earthwork long after it had ceased to be occupied into the Iron Age.

Bibliography

AC Archaeology. 2013. AC Archaeology in Devon; Hemerdon. *Devon Archaeological Society Newsletter* 116, 6-7.

Alcock, L. 1960. Castell Odo: an embanked settlement on Mynydd Ystum, near Aberdaron, Caernarvonshire. *Archaeologia Cambrensis* 109, 78-135.

Aldhouse-Green, M. 2000. *Seeing the wood for the trees: the symbolism of trees and wood in ancient Gaul and Britain*. Aberystwyth: University of Wales.

Allen, M.J. 2005. Beaker settlement and environment on the chalk downs of southern England. *Proceedings of the Prehistoric Society* 71, 219-245.

Allen T, Barclay, A. & Lamdin-Whymark H, 2004. Opening the wood, making the land: the study of a Neolithic landscape in the Dorney area of the Middle Thames Valley. In J. Cotton and D. Field, eds, *Towards a new stone age: Aspects of the Neolithic in south-east England*. London: Council for British Archaeology, 82-98.

Anderson-Whymark, H. 2011. Intentional breakage in the British Neolithic: some comments and examples. *Lithics* 32, 16-21.

Andrefsky, W. 1998. *Lithics: macroscopic approaches to analysis*. Cambridge: Cambridge University Press.

Anon. 2014. The Ockham hoard: unexpected artefacts. *Current Archaeology* 295, 9.

ApSimon, A.M. & Greenfield, E. 1972. The excavation of the Bronze Age and Iron Age settlement at Trevisker Round, St Eval, Cornwall. *Proceedings of the Prehistoric Society* 38, 302-381.

Archaeological Surveys Ltd. 2008. *Tremough Campus, Penryn, Cornwall, Cornwall: survey ref: 235*. Chippenham: Archaeological Surveys Ltd.

Balaam, N.D., Smith, K. & Wainwright, G. 1982. The Shaugh Moor project: fourth report – environment, context and conclusion. *Proceedings of the Prehistoric Society* 48, 203-279.

Barber, A., Pannett, A., Fairburn, N., Cullen, K., Evans, D., Saunders, K. & Thorogood, S. 2006. Archaeological investigations along the Milford Haven to Aberdulais natural gas pipeline: a preliminary report. *Archaeology in Wales* 46, 79-86.

Barfield, L. & Hodder, M. 1987. Burnt mounds as saunas and the prehistory of bathing. *Antiquity* 61, 370-379.

Barrett, J. 1980. The pottery of the Later Bronze Age in lowland England. *Proceedings of the Prehistoric Society* 46, 297-320.

Barrett, J. 1999. The mythical landscapes of the British Iron Age. In W. Ashmore and A.B. Knapp, eds, *Archaeologies of landscape: contemporary perspectives*. Oxford: Blackwell, 253-265.

Barrett, J., Bradley, R. & Green, M. 1991. *Landscape, monuments and society: the prehistory of Cranborne Chase*. Cambridge: Cambridge University Press.

Beamish, M. & Ripper, S. 2000. Burnt mounds in the east Midlands. *Antiquity* 74, 37-38.

Bell, M. 1990. *Brean Down excavations 1983-1987.* London: English Heritage.

Bender, B. (ed). 1993. *Landscape: politics and perspectives.* Oxford: Berg.

Bender, B., Hamilton, S. & Tilley, C. 2007. *Stone worlds: narrative and reflexivity in landscape archaeology.* Walnut Creek: Left Coast Press.

Bennett, P., Clark, P., Hicks, A., Rady, J. & Riddler, I. 2008. *At the great crossroads: Prehistoric, Roman and medieval discoveries on the Isle of Thanet 1994-95.* Canterbury: Canterbury Archaeological Trust.

Benson, D.G., Evans, J.G. & Williams, G.H. 1990. Excavations at Stackpole Warren, Dyfed. *Proceedings of the Prehistoric Society* 56, 179-246.

Bertsch, K. 1941. *Fruchte und samen. Handbucher der praktischen Vorgeschichtsforschung* 1. Stuttgart: Ferdinand Enke.

Best, J. & Gent, T. 2007. Bronze Age burnt mounds and early medieval timber structures at Town Farm Quarry, Burlescombe Down, Devon. *Archaeological Journal* 164, 1-79.

Bond, D. 1988. *Excavation at the North Ring, Mucking, Essex.* Chelmsford: East Anglian Archaeology.

Bonnemere, P. 1998. Trees and people: some vital links. Tree products and other agents in the life cycle of the Ankave-Anga of Papua New Guinea. In L. Rival, ed, *The social lives of trees: Anthropological perspectives on tree symbolism.* Oxford: Berg, 113-132.

Bradley, R. 1970. The excavation of a Beaker settlement at Belle Tout, East Sussex, England. *Proceedings of the Prehistoric Society* 36, 312–379.

Bradley, R. 1991. *The passage of arms: archaeological analysis of prehistoric hoards and votive deposits.* Cambridge: Cambridge University Press.

Bradley, R. 1997. *Rock art and the prehistory of Atlantic Europe.* London: Routledge.

Bradley, R. 2003. A life less ordinary: the ritualization of the domestic sphere in later prehistoric Europe. *Cambridge Archaeological Journal* 13, 5-23.

Bradley, R. 2005. *Ritual and domestic life in prehistoric Europe.* London: Routledge.

Bradley, R. 2007. *The prehistory of Britain and Ireland.* Cambridge: Cambridge University Press.

Bradley, R. 2012. *The idea of order: the circular archetype in prehistoric Europe.* Oxford: Oxford University Press.

Bradley, R. 2013. Houses of commons, Houses of Lords: domestic dwellings and monumental architecture in prehistoric Europe. *Proceedings of the Prehistoric Society* 79, 1-18.

Bradley, R. & Ellison, A. 1975. *Rams Hill: A Bronze Age defended enclosure and its landscape.* Oxford: British Archaeological Reports, British Series 19.

Brossler, A., Early, R. & Allen, C. 2004. *Green Park (Reading Business Park), phase 2 excavations 1995: Neolithic and Bronze Age sites*. Oxford: Oxford Archaeology Unit.

Brown, A. 2000. Flood plain vegetation history: clearings as potential ritual spaces. In A. Fairbairn, ed, *Plants in Neolithic Britain and beyond.* Oxford: Oxbow Books, 49-62.

Brown, L. & Durham, E. 2005. Typologie des vases prehistoriques, tardo-lateniennes et romaines. In B. Cunliffe and P. Galliou, *Annexe C5 online.* www.arch.ox.ac.uk/research_projects/Le_Yaudet.

Brown, N. 1988. A Late Bronze Age enclosure at Lofts Farm Essex. *Proceedings of the Prehistoric Society* 54, 249-302.

Brown, N. & Medlycott, M. 2013. *The Neolithic and Bronze Age enclosures at Springfield Lyons, Essex.* Chelmsford: East Anglian Archaeology.

Brück, J. 1995. A place for the dead: the role of human remains in Late Bronze Age Britain. *Proceedings of the Prehistoric Society* 61, 245-278.

Brück, J. 1999a. Houses, lifecycles and deposition on Middle Bronze Age settlements southern England. *Proceedings of the Prehistoric Society* 65, 245-278.

Brück, J. 1999b. Ritual and rationality: Some problems of interpretation in European Archaeology. *European Journal of Archaeology* 2, 313-344.

Brück, J. 1999c. What's in a settlement? Domestic practice and residential mobility in Early Bronze Age Southern England. In J. Brück and M. Goodman, eds, *Making places in the prehistoric world.* London: UCL Press, 145-166.

Brück, J. 2000. Settlement, landscape and social identity: the Early-Middle Bronze Age transition in Wessex, Sussex and the Thames Valley. *Oxford Journal of Archaeology* 19, 273-301.

Brück, J. 2001. Body metaphors and technologies of transformation in the English Middle and Late Bronze Age. In J. Brück, ed, *Bronze Age landscapes tradition and transformation.* Oxford: Oxbow, 149-160.

Brück, J. 2007. The character of Late Bronze Age settlement in southern Britain. In C. Haselgrove and R. Pope, eds, *The Earlier Iron Age in Britain and the near Continent.* Oxford: Oxbow Books, 24-38.

Brudenell, M. & Cooper, A. 2008. Post-middenism: depositional histories on later Bronze Age settlements at Broom, Bedfordshire. *Oxford Journal of Archaeology* 27, 15-36.

Buckley, V. 1990. Experimentation. In Buckley, V, ed, *Burnt offerings: International contributions to burnt mound archaeology*. Bray: Wordwell, 170-172.

Buckley, V. (ed). 1990. *Burnt offerings: International contributions to burnt mound archaeology*. Bray: Wordwell.

Budd, P. & Taylor, T. 1995. The faerie smith meets the bronze industry: magic versus science in the interpretation of prehistoric metal working. *World Archaeology* 27, 133-143.

Burgess, C. 1968. The later Bronze Age in the British Isles and north western France, *Archaeological Journal* 125, 1-45.

Burgess, C. 1976. Appendix II: The Gwithian mould and the forerunners of the South Wales axes. In C. Burgess and R. Miket, eds, *Settlement and economy in the third and second millennia BC.* Oxford: British Archaeological Reports, British Series 33, 69-81.

Butcher, S.A. 1978. Excavations at Nornour, Isles of Scilly, 1969-73: The pre-Roman Settlement. *Cornish Archaeology* 17, 29-112.

Butler, C. 2005. *Prehistoric flintwork.* Stroud: Tempus.

Butler, J. 1997. *Dartmoor atlas of antiquities, volume 5.* Tiverton: Devon Books.

Butterworth, C. 1999. Long Range. In A. Fitzpatrick, C.A. Butterworth and J. Grove, *Prehistoric and Roman Sites in east Devon: The A30 Honiton to Exeter Improvement DBFO scheme, 1996-9.* Salisbury: Trust for Wessex Archaeology, 138-159.

Campbell, G. & Straker, V. 2003. Prehistoric crop husbandry and plant use in southern England: development and regionality. In K.A. Robson Brown, *Archaeological sciences 1999. Proceedings of the archaeological sciences conference, University of Bristol, 1999.* Oxford: British Archaeological Reports, International Series 1111.

Cappers, R.T.J. Bekker, R.M. & Jans, J.E.A. 2006. *Digital seed atlas of the Netherlands.* Groningen: Barkhuis Publishing and Groningen University Library.

Carruthers, W. 2007. Charred plant remains. In J. Gossip and A.M. Jones, *Archaeological investigations of a later Prehistoric and a Romano-British landscape at Tremough, Penryn, Cornwall.* Oxford: British Archaeological Reports, British Series 443, 100-106.

Cartwright, C.R. 1988. The charcoal from Davidstow Moor. In P.M. Christie, A barrow cemetery on Davidstow Moor, Cornwall, wartime excavations by C K Croft Andrew. *Cornish Archaeology* 27, 27-169.

Case, H. & Whittle, A. (eds). 1982. *Settlement patterns in the Oxford region: excavations at the Abingdon causewayed enclosure and other sites.* London: Council for British Archaeology.

Chadwick, A.M. 2012. Routine magic, mundane ritual: towards a unified notion of depositional practice. *Oxford Journal of Archaeology* 31, 283–316.

Champion, T. 2011. Later prehistory. In P. Booth, T. Champion, S. Foreman, P. Garwood, H. Glass, J. Munby and A. Reynolds, eds, *On track. The archaeology of High Speed 1 Section 1 in Kent.* Oxford: Oxford Archaeology, 151-241.

Challinor, D. forthcoming. The charcoal. In P. Clark and S. Foreman, The archaeology of the A30 Bodmin to Indian Queens road scheme. *Cornish Archaeology.*

Clapham, A.J. & Stevens C.J. 1999. The charred plant remains: Environmental and economic evidence. In A. Fitzpatrick, C.A. Butterworth and J. Grove, *Prehistoric and Roman sites in east Devon: The A30 Honiton to Exeter Improvement DBFO scheme, 1996-9.* Salisbury: Trust for Wessex Archaeology, 196-207.

Clark, P. 2004. The Dover boat, ten years after its discovery. In P. Clark, ed, *The Dover Bronze Age boat in context: society and water transport in prehistoric Europe.* Oxford: Oxbow Books, 1-12.

Clarke, D.V., Cowie, T.G., & Foxon, A. 1985. *Symbols of power at the time of Stonehenge.* Edinburgh: National Museum of Antiquities of Scotland, Edinburgh.

Cleal, R. 1984. The later Neolithic in the east of England. In R.J. Bradley and J. Gardener, eds, *Neolithic studies.* Oxford: British Archaeological Reports, British Series 133, Oxford, 135-158.

Clough, T. & Cummins, W.A. (eds). 1979. *Stone axe studies.* London: Council for British Archaeology.

Cole, R. 1999. *Liskeard to Maudlin pipeline.* Truro: Cornwall Archaeological Unit.

Cole, R. & Jones, A.M. 2002-3. Journeys to the Rock: archaeological investigations at Tregarrick Farm, Roche. *Cornish Archaeology* 41-22, 107-144.

Coles, B. 1998. Wood species for wooden figures: a glimpse of a pattern. In A. Gibson and D. Simpson, eds, *Prehistoric religion and ritual.* Stroud: Sutton, 163-175.

Coles, J. 1973. *Archaeology by experiment.* London: Hutchinson.

Connerton, P. 1989. *How societies remember.* Cambridge: Cambridge University Press.

Cornish, T. 1880-81. Bronze celts. *Penzance Natural History and Antiquarian Society,* 75.

Cornwall County Council. 1996. *Cornwall landscape assessment 1994.* Truro: Cornwall County Council.

Cunliffe, B. 1970. A Bronze Age settlement at Chalton, Hants (Site 78). *Antiquaries Journal* 50, 1-14.

Cunliffe, B. 1987. *Hengistbury Head, Dorset. Vol I; The Prehistoric and Roman Settlement, 3500 BC – AD 500.* Oxford: Oxford University Committee for Archaeology.

Cunliffe, B. 1988. *Mount Batten, Plymouth. A prehistoric and Roman port.* Oxford: Oxford University Committee for Archaeology.

Cunliffe, B. 2009. Looking forward: Maritime contacts in the first millennium BC. In P. Clark, ed, *Bronze Age connections, cultural contact in prehistoric Europe.* Oxford: Oxbow Books, 12-37.

Cunliffe, B. & Galliou, P. 2005. *Les Fouilles du Yaudet en Ploulec'h, Cote-d'Armor.* Oxford: Oxford University School of Archaeology.

Cuttler, R., Davidson, A. & Hughes, G. 2012. *A corridor through time: The archaeology of the A55 Anglesey road scheme.* Oxford: Oxbow Books.

Davis, A. 2012. Beyond the horizon: ornaments in the British Late Bronze Age and Early Iron Age. Unpublished MA Thesis: University of Cardiff.

De la Beche, H.T. 1839. *Report on the geology of Cornwall, Devon and west Somerset.* London: Longman, Orme, Brown, Greene and Longmans.

Department of Culture Media and Sport. 2004. *Treasure annual report 2002.* London: Department of Culture Media and Sport.

Department of Culture Media and Sport. 2008. *Treasure annual report 2005/6.* London: Department of Culture Media and Sport.

Drewett, P. 1982. Later Bronze Age downland economy and excavations at Black Patch, East Sussex. *Proceedings of the Prehistoric Society* 48, 321-400.

Drisceoil, M. 1988. Burnt mounds: cooking or bathing? *Antiquity* 62, 671-68.

Dudley, D. 1956. An excavation at Bodrifty, Mulfra, near Penzance, *Archaeological Journal* 113, 1-32.

Dudley, P. 2011. *Goon, hal, cliff and croft, the archaeology and landscape history of west Cornwall's rough ground.* Truro: Cornwall Council.

Edmonds, M. 1987. Rocks and risk: Problems with lithic procurement strategies. In A.G. Brown and M.R. Edmonds, eds, *Lithic analysis and later British prehistory.* Oxford: British Archaeological Reports, British Series 162, 155-179.

Edmonds, M. 1995. *Stone tools and society. Working stone in Neolithic and Bronze Age Britain.* London: Batsford.

Eliade, M. 1998. *Shamanism, archaic techniques of ecstasy.* London: Routledge

Ellis, P. 1989. Norton Fitzwarren Hillfort: a report on the excavations by Nancy and Philip Langmaid between 1968 and 1971. *Proceedings of the Somerset Archaeological and Natural History Society* 133, 1-74.

Ellison, A.B. 1981. Towards a socioeconomic model for the Middle Bronze Age in southern Britain. In I. Hodder, G. Isaac and N. Hammond, eds, *Patterns of the past -studies in honour of David Clarke.* Cambridge: Cambridge University Press, 413-438.

Eogan, G. 1983. *Hoards of the Irish Later Bronze Age.* Dublin: University College Dublin.

Eogan, G. 1994. *The accomplished art: gold and goldworking in Britain and Ireland during the Bronze Age.* Oxford: Oxbow Books.

Evans, C., Pollard, J. & Knight, M. 1999. Life in woods: tree-throws, 'settlement' and forest cognition. *Oxford Journal of Archaeology* 18, 241-254.

Evans, J.G. 1990. Notes on some Late Neolithic and Bronze Age events in long barrow ditches in southern and eastern England. *Proceedings of the Prehistoric Society* 56, 111-116.

Evans, J.G., Limbrey, S., Mate, I. & Mount, R. 1993. An environmental history of the upper Kennet valley, Wiltshire, for the last 10,000 years. *Proceedings of the Prehistoric Society* 59, 139-196.

Fitzpatrick, A.P. Butterworth, C.A. & Grove, G. 1999. *Prehistoric and Roman sites in east Devon: the A30 Honiton to Exeter Improvement DBFO Scheme, 1996-9.* Salisbury: Wessex Archaeology.

Fleming, A. 1988. *The Dartmoor reaves: Investigating prehistoric land divisions.* London: Batsford.

Fowler, C. 2004. *The archaeology of personhood: an anthropological approach.* London: Routledge.

Fowler, C. 2013. *The emergent past. A relational realist archaeology of Early Bronze Age mortuary practices.* Oxford: Oxford University Press.

Fowler, P.J. 1983. *The farming of prehistoric Britain.* Cambridge: Cambridge University Press.

Fox, A. 1957. Excavations at Dean Moor. *Report of the Transactions of the Devonshire Association* 89, 21-62.

Fox, C. 1959. *Life and death in the Bronze Age.* London: Routledge.

Gale, R. 2006. The charcoal. In A.M. Jones and H. Quinnell, Cornish Beakers: new discoveries and perspectives. *Cornish Archaeology* 45, 31-70.

Gale, R. 2007. Charcoal. In J. Gossip and A.M. Jones, *Archaeological investigations of a later prehistoric and a Romano-British landscape at Tremough, Penryn, Cornwall,* Oxford: British Archaeological Reports, British Series 443, 107-111.

Gale, R. & Cutler, D. 2000. *Plants in archaeology: identification manual of vegetative plant materials used in Europe and the southern Mediterranean to c. 1500.* Otley: Westbury and Royal Botanic Gardens, Kew.

Garrow, D. 2007. Placing pits: Landscape occupation and depositional practice during the Neolithic in East Anglia. *Proceedings of the Prehistoric Society* 73, 1-24.

Garrow, D. 2012a. Concluding discussion: pits and perspective. In H. Anderson-Whymark and J. Thomas, eds, *Regional perspectives on Neolithic pit deposition.* Oxford: Oxbow Books, 216-225.

Garrow, D. 2012b. Odd deposits and average practice. A critical history of the concept of structured deposition. *Archaeological Dialogues* 19, 85-115.

Garwood, P. 2011. Early prehistory. In P. Booth, T. Champion, S. Foreman, P. Garwood, H. Glass, J. Munby and A. Reynolds, eds, *On track. The archaeology of High Speed 1 Section 1 in Kent.* Oxford: Oxford Archaeology, 37-150.

Geological Survey of Great Britain. 2005. *Map sheet 21 and 25.*

Gerloff, S. 2007. Reinecke's ABC and the chronology of the British Bronze Age. In C. Burgess, P. Topping and F. Lynch, eds, *Beyond Stonehenge. Essays on the Bronze Age in honour of Colin Burgess.* Oxford: Oxbow Books, 117-161.

Gibson, A. 1999. *The Walton Basin Project: excavation and survey in a prehistoric landscape 1993-7.* York: CBA Research Report 118.

Gibson, T. 1995. Having your house and eating it: houses and siblings in Ara, South Salawesi. In J. Carsten and S. Hugh-Jones, eds, *About the house: Levi-Strauss and beyond*. Cambridge: Cambridge University Press, 129-138.

Gingell, C. 1992. *The Marlborough Downs: a later Bronze Age landscape and its origins*. Devizes: Wiltshire Archaeological and Natural History Society.

Ginn, V. 2012. Settlement structure in Middle–Late Bronze Age Ireland. Unpublished MA Thesis: University of Belfast.

Ginn, V. & Rathbone, S. 2012. *Corrstown, a coastal community: excavations of a Bronze Age village in Northern Ireland*. Oxford: Oxbow Books.

Gosden, C. & Lock, G. 1998. Prehistoric histories. *World Archaeology* 30, 2-12.

Gosden C. & Marshall, Y. 1999. The cultural biography of objects. *World Archaeology* 31, 169-178.

Gossip, J. 2008a. *An archaeological evaluation report on phase 3 enabling development works, Tremough, Penryn, Cornwall*. Truro: Historic Environment Service, Cornwall Council.

Gossip, J. 2008b. *Penryn College, Penryn, Cornwall: archaeological evaluation and open area recording*. Truro: Historic Environment Service, Cornwall Council.

Gossip, J. 2008c. Excavations at Boden Vean, Manaccan 2008. *CBA Archaeology South-West Journal* 22, 29-31.

Gossip, J. 2009. *Tremough PAC Building, Penryn, Cornwall: Archaeological recording following controlled topsoil strip archive report*. Truro: Historic Environment Service, Cornwall Council.

Gossip, J. 2011. *Archaeological excavations at the AIR Building and Car Park 4 Tremough, Cornwall: Archive report*. Truro: Historic Environment Service, Cornwall Council.

Gossip, J. 2013. The evaluation of a multi-period prehistoric site at Boden Vean, St Anthony in Meneage, Cornwall 2003, *Cornish Archaeology* 52, 1-98

Gossip, J. forthcoming. Life outside the round - Bronze Age and Iron Age settlement at Higher Besore and Truro College, Threemilestone, Truro. *Cornish Archaeology*.

Gossip, J. In preparation. A medieval structure at Tremough, Mabe, Cornwall.

Gossip, J. & Jones, A.M. 2007. *Archaeological investigations of a later prehistoric and a Romano-British landscape at Tremough, Penryn, Cornwall*. Oxford: British Archaeological Reports, British Series 443.

Gossip, J. & Jones A.M. 2008. A Bronze Age roundhouse at Carnon Gate, Feock. *Cornish Archaeology* 47, 101-115.

Gossip, J. & Jones, A.M. 2009-10. Excavations at Tremough, Penryn, Cornwall, 2000-6. *Cornish Archaeology* 48-9, 1-66.

Gossip, J., Jones, A.M. & Quinnell, H. 2012. Early Neolithic activity and an Iron Age settlement at Penmayne, Rock, St Minver. *Cornish Archaeology* 51, 165-190.

Green, S. 1984. Flint arrowheads: typology and interpretation. *Lithics* 5, 19-39.

Greig, J.R.A. 1991. The British Isles. In W. Van Zeist, K. Wasylikowa, & K. Behre, *Progress in Old World Palaeoethnobotany. A retrospective view on the occasion of 20 years of the international work group for palaeoethnobotany*. Rotterdam/Brookfield: A.A. Balkema/Rotterdam/Brookfield, 299-334.

Griffith, F., Healy, F., Jones, A.M., Lawson, A., Lewis, J., Mercer, R., Mullin, D., Nowakowski, J., Pollard, J., Wickstead, H. and Woodward, P. 2008. Neolithic and Early Bronze Age. In C. Webster, ed, *South West Archaeological Research Framework: The archaeology of South West England*. Taunton: Somerset County Council, 75-102.

Guttmann, E.B.A. & Last, J. 2000. A Late Bronze Age landscape at South Hornchurch, Essex. *Proceedings of the Prehistoric Society* 66, 319-384.

Hall, A. 2003. *Recognition and characterisation of turves in archaeological occupation deposits by means of macrofossil plant remains*. Swindon: English Heritage.

Halsted, J. 2005. *Bronze Age settlement in the Welsh Marches*. Oxford: British Archaeological Reports, British Series 384.

Halsted, J. 2007. Bronze Age settlement in Shropshire: research potential and frameworks for settlement studies in the West Midlands. In P. Garwood, ed, *The undiscovered country: The earlier prehistory of the West Midlands*. Oxford: Oxbow Books, 166-181.

Harding, J. 2006. Pit-digging, occupation and structured deposition on Rudston Wold, Eastern Yorkshire. *Oxford Journal of Archaeology* 25, 109-126.

Harris, D. 1977. Bodwen, Lanlivery: a multi-period occupation. *Cornish Archaeology* 16, 43-46.

Harris, O. 2009. Making places matter in early Dorset. *Oxford Journal of Archaeology* 28, 111–124.

Hassan, N.M., Rasmussen, P.E., Dabek-Zlotorzynska, E., Celo, V., & Chen, H. 2007 Analysis of environmental samples using microwave-assisted acid digestion and inductively coupled plasma mass spectrometry: Maximizing total element recoveries. *Water Air Soil Pollution* 178, 323-334.

Hather, J.G. 2000. *The identification of northern European woods; a guide for archaeologists and conservators*. London: Archetype Publications.

Hawkes, C.F.C. & Clarke, R.R. 1963. Gahlsdorf and Caistor-on-Sea: two finds of Late Bronze Age Irish gold. In I.L.L. Foster and L. Alcock, eds, *Culture and environment*. London: Routledge, 193-250.

Healy, F. 1985. And to Cornwall. *Lithics* 5, 18-20.

Healy, F. 1988. *Spong Hill, part VI: 7th to 2nd Millennia BC*. Dereham: East Anglian Archaeology.

Healy, F. 1989. Afterthoughts. In I. Brooks and P. Phillips, eds, *Breaking the stony silence*. Oxford: British Archaeological Reports, British Series 213, 187-198.

Healy, F. & Harding, J. 2004. Reading a burial: the legacy of Overton Hill. In A. Gibson and A. Sheridan, eds, *From sickles to circles: Britain and Ireland at the time of Stonehenge*. Stroud: Tempus, 176-193.

Helms, M. 1988. *Ulysses' sail: ethnographic odyssey of power, knowledge and geographical distance*. Princeton: Princeton: Princeton University Press.

Helms, M. 1993. *Craft and the kingly ideal: art, trade and power*. Austin: University of Texas.

Henderson, J. 2007. *The Atlantic Iron Age: Settlement and identity in the first millennium BC*. London: Routledge.

Herbert, E.W. 1993. *Iron, gender and power; rituals of transformation in African societies*. Bloomington: Indiana University Press.

Herne, C. & Heaton, M. Excavations at a Late Bronze Age settlement in the Upper Thames Valley at Shorncote Quarry, near Cirencester, 1992. *Transactions of the Bristol and Gloucestershire Archaeological Society 112*, 17-57.

Herring, P. 2011. Hilltop enclosures. In P. Dudley, *Goon, hal, cliff and croft, the archaeology and landscape history of west Cornwall's rough ground*. Truro: Cornwall Council, 84-86.

Hills, C. & Lucy, S. 2013. Introduction and background. In C. Hills and S. Lucy, *Spong Hill, part IX: Chronology and synthesis*. Cambridge: McDonald Institute for Archaeological Research, 1–26.

Hillman, G.C. 1981. Reconstructing crop husbandry practises from charred remains of crops. In R. Mercer, ed, *Farming practice in British prehistory*. Edinburgh: Edinburgh University Press.

Hillman, G.C. 1984. Interpretation of archaeological plant remains: the application of ethnographic models from Turkey. In W. van Zeist and W.A. Caspaire, eds, *Plants and ancient man. Studies in palaeoethnobotany.* Rotterdam, A.A. Balkema, 1-41.

Hingley, R. 2009. Esoteric knowledge, ancient bronze artefacts from Iron Age contexts. *Proceedings of the Prehistoric Society* 75, 143-166.

Hood, A. 2009a. *Land adjacent to Tresprison, Helston, Cornwall, post excavation assessment: report 629*. Swindon: Foundations Archaeology.

Hood, A. 2009b. Later Iron Age and Early Roman Settlement at Willand Road, Cullompton, Devon. Swindon: Foundations Archaeology (Unpublished publication proposal).

Jacomet, S. 2006. *Identification of cereal remains from archaeological sites*. Archaeobotany Lab IPAS: Basel University www.ipna.unibas.ch/archbot/pdf

Jeffrey, P. 1991. Burnt mounds, fulling and early textiles. In M.A. Hodder and L.H. Barfield, eds, *Burnt mounds and hot stone technology*. Sandwell: Sandwell Borough Council, 97-107

Jenness, D. 1977. *The Indians of Canada*. Toronto: University of Toronto Press (1st pub 1932).

Johns, C. 2008. The excavation of a multi-period archaeological landscape at Trenowah, St Austell, Cornwall, 1997. *Cornish Archaeology* 47, 1-48.

Johnson, N. & Rose, P, 1994. *Bodmin Moor: an archaeological survey, volume 1: the human landscape to c 1800.* London: English Heritage.

Jones, A.M. 1998-9a. The excavation of a later Bronze Age structure at Callestick. *Cornish Archaeology* 37-8, 5-55.

Jones, A.M. 1998-9b. The excavation of a Bronze Age enclosure at Liskeard Junior and Infant School. *Cornish Archaeology* 37-8, 56-71.

Jones, A.M. 2005. *Cornish Bronze Age ceremonial landscapes, c.2500-1500 BC.* Oxford: British Archaeological Reports, British Series 394.

Jones, A.M. 2008. Houses for the dead and cairns for the living: a reconsideration of the Early to Middle Bronze Age transition in south-west England. *Oxford Journal of Archaeology* 27, 153–174.

Jones, A.M. 2013. Memory, myth, place and landscape inhabitation: a perspective from the south west peninsula. In A. Chadwick and C. Gibson, eds, *Memory, myth, place and long-term landscape inhabitation.* Oxford: Oxbow Books, 55-75.

Jones, A.M. forthcoming a. Ritual, rubbish or everyday life? Evidence from a Middle Bronze Age settlement in mid Cornwall. *Archaeological Journal.*

Jones, A.M, forthcoming b. Hay Close, St Newlyn East: excavations by the Cornwall Archaeological Society, 2007. *Cornish Archaeology.*

Jones, A.M. & Quinnell, H. 2006. Cornish Beakers: new discoveries and perspectives. *Cornish Archaeology* 45, 31-70.

Jones, A.M. & Quinnell, H. 2008. The Farway barrow complex in East Devon reassessed. *Proceedings of the Devon Archaeological Society* 66, 27-58.

Jones, A.M. & Quinnell, H. 2011. Bosiliack: a later prehistoric settlement in Penwith, Cornwall. *Archaeological Journal* 168, 80-117.

Jones, A.M. & Quinnell, H. 2013. Daggers in the west: Early Bronze Age daggers and knives in the south west peninsula. *Proceedings of the Prehistoric Society*, 79, 165-191.

Jones, A.M. & Quinnell. H. 2014. *Lines of archaeological investigation along the North Cornish coast.* Oxford: British Archaeological Reports, British Series 594.

Jones, A.M. & Reed, S. 2006. By Land, sea and air: an Early Neolithic pit group at Portscatho, Cornwall, and consideration of coastal activity during the Neolithic. *Cornish Archaeology* 45, 1-30.

Jones, A.M. & Taylor, S.R. 2004. *What lies beneath . . . St Newlyn East and Mitchell archaeological investigations 2001.* Truro: Cornwall Archaeological Unit.

Jones, A.M. & Taylor, S.R. 2010. *Scarcewater, Pennance, Cornwall, archaeological excavation of a Bronze Age and Roman landscape.* Oxford: British Archaeological Reports, British Series 516.

Jones, A.M., Taylor, S.R. & Sturgess, J. 2012. A Beaker-associated structure and other discoveries along the Sennen to Porthcurno SWW pipeline. *Cornish Archaeology* 51, 1-69.

Jones, A.M. & Tinsley, H.M. 2000-1. Recording ancient environments at De Lank, St Breward, Cornwall. *Cornish Archaeology* 39-40, 145-160.

Jones, J. 1999. Charred plant remains from Bronze Age features associated with the Maudlin to Liskeard pipeline. Unpublished report for Cornwall Archaeological Unit.

Jones, J. 2004. Analysis of the charred plant macrofossil remains. In A.M. Jones and S.R. Taylor, *What lies beneath . . . St Newlyn East and Mitchell archaeological investigations 2001*. Truro: Cornwall Archaeological Unit, 73-81.

Jones, J. 2005. Charred plant macrofossil remains from Boden Vean, St. Anthony-in-Meneage, Cornwall. Unpublished report for Cornwall Archaeological Unit.

Jones, J. 2010. Plant remains. In A.M. Jones and S.R. Taylor, *Scarcewater, Pennance, Cornwall, archaeological excavation of a Bronze Age and Roman landscape*. Oxford: British Archaeological Reports, British Series 516, 142-149.

Jones, M.U. & Bond, D. 1980. Later Bronze Age settlement at Mucking, Essex. In J. Barrett and R. Bradley, eds, *The British Later Bronze Age*. Oxford: British Archaeological Reports, British Series 83, 471-482.

Karl, R & Waddington, K. Forthcoming. Excavations in a Late Bronze and Iron Age double ringwork enclosure at Meillionydd, Gwynedd. In J. Zeidler and S. Junges, eds, *Akten des ersten europäischen Keltologensymposiums in Trier*.

Kelly, R.S. 1992. The excavation of a burnt mound at Graeanog, Clynnog. *Archaeologia Cambrensis* 141, 74-79.

Kis-Jovak, J., Nooy-Plm, H., Schefold, R. & Schultz-Dornburg, U. 1988. *Banua Toraja: Changing patterns in the architecture and symbolism among the Sa'dan Toraja, Sulawesi, Indonesia*. Amsterdam: Royal Tropical Institute.

Knight, J. 1991. Technological analysis of the anvil (bipolar) technique. *Lithics* 12, 57-80.

Ladle, L. & Woodward, A. 2009. *Excavations at Bestwall Quarry, Wareham, 1992-2005, volume 1: The prehistoric landscape*. Dorchester: Dorset Natural History and Archaeological Society.

Lawson, A.J. 2007. *Chalkland: an archaeology of Stonehenge and its region*. Salisbury: Hobnob Press.

Lawson-Jones, A. 2007. Flint. In J. Gossip and A.M. Jones, *Archaeological investigations of a later prehistoric and a Romano-British landscape at Tremough, Penryn, Cornwall*. Oxford: British Archaeological Reports, British Series 443, 88-96.

Lee, K. 2001. Experimental heat-treatment of flint. *Lithics* 22, 39-44.

Leverett, M. & Quinnell, H. 2010. An Early Neolithic assemblage from Waylands, Tiverton. *Proceedings of the Devon Archaeology Society* 68, 1-20.

Loring, D.H. 1991. Normalization of heavy-metal data from estuarine and coastal sediments. *Journal of Marine Science* 48, 115-215.

Lynch, F. 1991. *Prehistoric Anglesey* (second edition). Llangefni: The Anglesey Antiquarian Society.

Lynch, F. 1993. *Excavations in the Brenig Valley: a Mesolithic and Bronze Age landscape in North Wales*. Bangor: Cambrian Monographs 5.

Lynch, F., Aldhouse-Green, S. & Davies J.L. 2000. *Prehistoric Wales*. Stroud: Alan Sutton.

Macphail, R.I. & Linderholm, J. 2004. Neolithic land use in south-east England: a brief review of the soil evidence. In J. Cotton and D. Field, eds, *Towards a New Stone Age: aspects of the Neolithic in south-east England*. London: Council for British Archaeology, 29-37.

Mallory, J.P. 1995. Haughey's Fort and the Navan complex in the Late Bronze Age. In J. Waddell, J. and E. Shee Twohig, eds, *Ireland in the Bronze Age*. Wordwell: Dublin, 97-112.

Manby, T. 2007. Continuity of monumental traditions into the Late Bronze Age? Henges to ring-forts, and shrines. In C. Burgess, P. Topping and F. Lynch, eds, *Beyond Stonehenge, essays on the Bronze Age in honour of Colin Burgess*. Oxford: Oxbow Books, 403-424.

Marcigny, C., Ghesquiere, E. & Kinnes, I. 2007. Bronze Age cross-channel relations. The Lower-Normandy (France) example: ceramic chronology and first reflections. In C. Burgess, P. Topping and F. Lynch, eds, *Beyond Stonehenge, essays on the Bronze Age in honour of Colin Burgess*. Oxford: Oxbow Books, 255-267.

Marshall, W.A. Clough, R. & Gehrels, W.G. 2009. The isotopic record of atmospheric lead fall-out on an Icelandic salt marsh since AD 50. *Science of the total environment* 407 (8), 2734–2748.

Mattingly, J., Marley, J. & Jones, A.M. 2009. Five gold rings? Early Bronze Age gold lunulae from Cornwall. *Journal of the Royal Institution of Cornwall*, 95-114.

McOmish, D. 1996. East Chisenbury: ritual and rubbish at the British Bronze Age-Iron Age transition. *Antiquity* 267, 68-76.

Mercer, R.J. 1970. The excavation of a Bronze Age hut-circle settlement, Stannon Down. *Cornish Archaeology* 9, 17-46.

Mercer, R.J. 1981. Excavations at Carn Brea, Illogan, Cornwall 1970-73. *Cornish Archaeology* 20, 1-204.

Miles, H., Davey, U., Harris, D., Hooper, S., Moreton, P., Padel, O. & Staines, S., 1977. Excavations at Killibury hillfort, Egloshayle 1975-6, *Cornish Archaeology* 16, 89-121.

Moffett, L. 1988. The Archaeobotanical evidence for Saxon and medieval agriculture in central England *circa* 500 AD to 1500 AD. Unpublished Master of Philosophy Thesis: University of Birmingham.

Moore, J. & Jennings, D. 1992. *Reading Business Park: a Bronze Age landscape*. Oxford: Oxford Archaeological Unit.

Morigi, A., Schreve, D., White, M., Hey, J., Garwood, P., Robinson., M., Barclay, A. & Bradley, P. 2011. *Thames through time, the archaeology of the gravel terraces of the Upper and Middle Thames; Early prehistory to 1500 BC*. Oxford: Oxford Archaeology.

Muckelroy, K. 1981. Middle Bronze Age trade between Britain and Europe. *Proceedings of the Prehistoric Society* 47, 275-297.

Mullin, D. 2012. The river has never divided us: Bronze Age metalwork deposition in the west of Britain. *Oxford Journal of Archaeology* 31, 47-57.

Musson, C. 1991. *The Breiddin Hillfort. A later prehistoric settlement in the Welsh Marches*. London: Council for British Archaeology

Needham, S. 1980. An assemblage of Late Bronze Age metalworking debris from Dainton, Devon. *Proceedings of the Prehistoric Society* 46, 177-215.

Needham, S. 1981. *The Bulford-Helsbury Manufacturing Tradition. The production of Stogursey socketed axes in the later Bronze Age in southern Britain*. London: British Museum Occasional Paper 13.

Needham, S. 1988. Selective deposition in the Early British Bronze Age. *World Archaeology* 20, 229-248.

Needham, S. 1992. Special features in the Late Bronze Age Landscape. In C. Mordant and A. Richard, eds, *L' habitat et l'occupation du sol a' l'age du Bronze en Europe*. Paris: Editions du Comité des travaux historiques et scientifiques, 49-69.

Needham, S. 2007a. Bronze makes a Bronze Age? Considering the systemics of Bronze Age metal use and the implications of selective deposition. In C. Burgess, P. Topping and F. Lynch, eds, *Beyond Stonehenge, essays on the Bronze Age in honour of Colin Burgess*. Oxford: Oxbow Books, 276-287.

Needham, S. 2007b: 800 BC, the great divide. In C. Haselgrove and R. Pope, eds, *The earlier Iron Age in Britain and the near Continent*. Oxford: Oxbow Books, 39-63.

Needham, S. 2009. Encompassing the sea: 'maritories' and Bronze Age interactions. In P. Clark, ed, *Bronze Age connections, cultural contact in prehistoric Europe*. Oxford: Oxbow Books, 12-37.

Needham, S. & Ambers, J. 1994. Redating Rams Hill and reconsidering Bronze Age enclosure. *Proceedings of the Prehistoric Society* 60, 225-244.

Needham, S. & Bridgford, S. 2013. Deposits of clay refractories for casting bronze swords. In N. Brown and M. Medlycott, *The Neolithic and Bronze Age enclosures at Springfield Lyons, Essex*. Chelmsford: East Anglian Archaeology, 47-74.

Needham, S. & Hook, D.R. 1989. A compare of recent analyses of British Late Bronze Age goldwork with Irish parallels. *Jewellery Studies* 3, 15-22.

Needham, S., McKinley, J.I. & Leivers, N. 2015. Discussion and concluding remarks. In J.I. McKinley, M. Leivers, J. Schuster, P. Marshall, A. Barclay and N. Stoodley, *Cliffs End Farm, Isle of Thanet, Kent: A mortuary and ritual site of the Bronze Age, Iron Age and Anglo-Saxon period with evidence for long-distance maritime mobility*. Oxford: Oxbow Books, 208-236.

Needham, S., Parham, D. & Frieman, C. 2013. *Claimed by the sea: Salcombe, Langdon Bay and other marine finds of the Bronze Age*. York: Council for British Archaeology Research Report 173.

Needham, S. & Spence, T. 1996. *Refuse and disposal at Area 16 East, Runneymede*. London: British Museum Press.

Newberry, J. 2002. Inland flint in prehistoric Devon: Sources, tool-making quality and use. *Proceedings of the Devon Archaeology Society* 60, 1-36.

Newman, C. 1998. Reflections on the making of a 'royal site', in early Ireland. *World Archaeology* 30, 127-141.

Nowakowski, J.A. 1991. Trethellan Farm, Newquay: the excavation of a lowland Bronze Age settlement and Iron Age cemetery. *Cornish Archaeology* 30, 5-242.

Nowakowski, J.A. 2001. Leaving home in the Cornish Bronze Age: insights into the planned abandonment process. In J, Brück, ed, *Bronze Age landscapes tradition and transformation*. Oxford: Oxbow Books, 139-148.

Nowakowski, J.A. 2009. Living in the sands – Bronze Age Gwithian revisited. In M.J. Allen, N. Sharples and T. O'Connor, eds, *Land and people: papers in memory of John G Evans*. Oxford: Prehistoric Society, 115-125.

Nowakowski, J.A. & Johns, C. 2015. *Bypassing Indian Queens. Archaeological excavations 1992-1994. Investigating prehistoric and Romano-British settlement and landscapes in Cornwall*. Historic Environment, Cornwall Council & The Highways Agency.

Nowakowski, J.A., Quinnell, H. Sturgess, H. Thomas, C. & Thorpe, C. 2007. Return to Gwithian: shifting the sands of time. *Cornish Archaeology* 46, 13-76.

O'Connor, B., Jones, A.M., Quinnell, H. & Taylor, R. 2014. Racloir mould, S7. In A.M. Jones and H. Quinnell, *Lines of archaeological investigation along the North Cornish coast*. Oxford: British Archaeological Reports, 594, 64-65.

O'Brien, W. 2004. (Con)fusion of tradition. In A. Gibson and A. Sheridan, eds, *From sickles to circles: Britain and Ireland at the time of Stonehenge*. Stroud: Tempus, 323-339.

O'Mhaolduin, R. 2014. Saechtain i ndaingean an umha aois (a week in Bronze Age Dingle): A personal experience. *Archaeology Ireland* 108, 40-43.

Oswald, A., Dyer, C. & Barber, M. 2001. *The creation of monuments: causewayed enclosures in the British Isles*. Swindon: English Heritage.

Pannett, A. 2011. Burning issues: fire and the manufacture of stone tools in Neolithic Britain. In A. Saville, ed, *Flint and stone in the Neolithic period*. Oxford: Oxbow Books, 247-255.

Pannett, A. 2012. Pits, pots and plant remains: Trends in Neolithic deposition in Carmarthenshire, South Wales. In H. Anderson-Whymark and J. Thomas, eds, *Regional perspectives on Neolithic pit deposition*. Oxford: Oxbow Books, 126-143.

Parker Pearson, M. 1990. The production and distribution of Bronze Age pottery in south-west Britain. *Cornish Archaeology* 29, 5-32.

Parker Pearson, M. 1996. Food, fertility and front doors. In T. Champion and J. Collis, eds, *The Iron Age in Britain and Ireland: recent trends*. Sheffield: University of Sheffield, 117-132.

Parker Pearson, M. & Richards, C. 1994. Architecture and order: spatial representation and archaeology. In M. Parker Pearson and C. Richards, eds, *Architecture and order, approaches to social space*. London: Routledge, 38-72.

Parker Pearson, M. & Sharples, N. 1999. *Between land and sea: Excavations at Dun Vulan, South Uist*. Sheffield: Sheffield Academic Press.

Pearce, M. 2013. The spirit of the sword and spear. *Cambridge Archaeological Journal* 23, 55-67.

Pearce, S. 1974. The finds of Bronze Age material from Kent's Cavern, Torquay. *Transactions and Proceedings of the Torquay Natural History Society* 16, 176-194.

Pearce, S. 1976. The Middle and Late Bronze Age metalwork of the South-West and its relationship to settlement. *Proceedings of the Devon Archaeological Society* 34, 17-40.

Pearce, S. 1983. *The Bronze Age metalwork of south western Britain*. Oxford: British Archaeological Reports, British Series 31.

Pearce, S. & Padley, T. 1977. A Bronze Age Find from Tredarvah, Penzance. *Cornish Archaeology* 16, 25-41.

Penhallurick, R. 1986. *Tin in antiquity: its mining and trade throughout the ancient world with particular reference to Cornwall.* London: The Institute of Metals.

Pollard, J. 2001. The aesthetics of depositional practice. *World Archaeology* 33, 315-333.

Pope, R. 2007. Ritual and the roundhouse: a critique of recent ideas on the use of domestic space in later British prehistory. In C. Haselgrove and R. Pope, eds, *The Earlier Iron Age in Britain and the Near Continent*. Oxford: Oxbow Books, 204-229.

Pryor, F. 1998. *Farmers in prehistoric Britain*. Stroud: Tempus.

Pryor, F. 2001. *The Flag Fen Basin; archaeology and environment of a fenland landscape*. London: English Heritage.

Quinn, N. & Moore, D. 2007. Ale, brewing and fulachta fiadh. *Archaeology Ireland* 21, 8-11.

Quinnell, H. 2002-3. Early Neolithic pottery. In D. Cole and A.M. Jones, Journeys to the Rock: archaeological investigations at Tregarrick Farm, Roche, Cornwall. *Cornish Archaeology* 41-42, 113-121.

Quinnell, H. 2004-5. The prehistoric pottery. In A.M. Jones, Settlement and ceremony: Archaeological investigations at Stannon Down, St Breward, Cornwall. *Cornish Archaeology* 43-44, 72-87.

Quinnell, H. 2006. Neolithic pottery. In A.M. Jones and S. Reed, By Land, sea and air: an Early Neolithic pit group at Portscatho, Cornwall, and consideration of coastal activity during the Neolithic. *Cornish Archaeology* 45, 5-9.

Quinnell, H. 2007. Prehistoric, Roman and early medieval pottery. In J. Gossip and A.M. Jones, *Archaeological investigations of a later prehistoric and a Romano-British landscape at Tremough, Penryn, Cornwall.* Oxford: British Archaeological Reports, British Series 443, 51-79.

Quinnell, H. 2007. Stonework. In J. Gossip and A.M. Jones, *Archaeological investigations of a later prehistoric and a Romano-British landscape at Tremough, Penryn, Cornwall.* Oxford: British Archaeological Reports, British Series 443, 81-88.

Quinnell, H. 2009. The pottery. In A. Hood, *Land adjacent to Tresprison, Helston, Cornwall, post excavation assessment: Report no 629.* Swindon: Foundations Archaeology, 18.

Quinnell, H. 2010a. Prehistoric and Roman pottery. In A.M. Jones and S.R. Taylor. *Scarcewater, Pennance, Cornwall, archaeological excavation of a Bronze Age and Roman landscape.* Oxford: British Archaeological Reports, British Series 516, 93-112.

Quinnell, H. 2010b. Prehistoric and Roman stonework. In A.M. Jones and S.R. Taylor. *Scarcewater, Pennance, Cornwall, archaeological excavation of a Bronze Age and Roman landscape.* Oxford: British Archaeological Reports, British Series 516, 113-130.

Quinnell, H. 2011. The pottery. In J. Nowakowski and H. Quinnell, *Trevelgue Head, Cornwall: the importance of CKC Andrew's 1939 excavations for prehistoric and Roman Cornwall.* Truro: Cornwall Council, 144-208.

Quinnell, H. 2012. Trevisker pottery: Some recent studies. In W. Britnell and R.J. Silvester, eds, *Reflections on the past: Essays in honour of Frances Lynch.* Welshpool: Cambrian Archaeological Association, 146-171.

Quinnell, H. 2014. ACD667 698 Butts Road, Ottery St Mary assessment of finds. Unpublished assessment report.

Quinnell, H. forthcoming. The pottery and the stonework. In J. Gossip, Life outside the round – Bronze Age and Iron Age settlement at Higher Besore and Truro College, Threemilestone, Truro. *Cornish Archaeology.*

Raftery, B. 1976. Rathgall and Irish hillfort problems. In D.W. Harding, ed, *Hillforts later prehistoric earthworks in Britain and Ireland-studies.* London: Academic Press, 339-357.

Raftery, B. 1997. *Pagan Celtic Ireland: the enigma of the Irish Iron Age.* London: Thames and Hudson.

Randsbourg, K. 2011. *Bronze Age textiles: Men, women and wealth.* London: Bristol Classical Press.

Rathbone, S. 2013. A consideration of villages in Neolithic and Bronze Age Britain and Ireland. *Proceedings of the Prehistoric Society* 79, 39-60.

Reynolds, A. 2006. An Early Bronze Age pit at Trenoweth, Portreath and other results from the Reskadinnick to Portreath transfer pipeline. *Cornish Archaeology* 45, 71-96.

Richards, C. 2005. *Dwelling among the monuments, the Neolithic village of Barnhouse, Maeshowe passage grave and surrounding monuments at Stenness, Orkney.* Oxford: McDonald Institute.

Richards, C. 2014a. Interpreting stone circles. In C. Richards, ed, *Building the great stone circles of the north*. Oxford: Windgather Press, 2–30.

Richards, C. 2014b. Wrapping the hearth: Constructing house societies and the tall stones of Stenness. In C. Richards, ed, *Building the great stone circles of the north*. Oxford: Windgather Press, 64–89.

Richards, C. & Thomas, J. 1984. Ritual activity and structured deposition in Later Neolithic Wessex. In R. Bradley and J. Gardiner, eds, *Neolithic Studies: A review of some current research*. Oxford: British Archaeological Reports, British Series 133, 189–218.

Roberts, B. 2007. Adorning the living but not the dead: Understanding ornaments in Britain *c*. 1400-1100 cal BC. *Proceedings of the Prehistoric Society* 73, 135-167.

Robinson, G. 2013. Re-building memory, identity and place: the long-term re-use of prehistoric settlements on the Isles of Scilly. In A. Chadwick and C. Gibson, eds, *Memory, myth and long-term landscape inhabitation*. Oxford: Oxbow Books, 146-164.

Robinson, M. 1988. The significance of tubers of *Arrhenatherum elatius* (L.) Beauv. from Site 4, cremation 15/11. In G. Lambrick, *The Rollright Stones: megaliths, monuments and settlements in the prehistoric landscape*. London: English Heritage, 102.

Roche, H. 2002. Excavations at Raith Na Rig, Tara, County Meath, 1997. *Discovery Programme Reports* 6, 19-82.

Roche, H. 2004. The dating of the embanked stone circle at Grange, Co. Limerick. In H. Roche, E. Grogan, J. Bradley, J. Coles and B. Raftery, eds, *From megaliths to metals.* Oxbow Books: Oxford, 109-116.

Rogers, W. 1923. The shingles and sands of Cornwall. *Royal Cornwall Polytechnic Society* 5, 45-50.

Rots, V. & Vermeersch, P.M. 2004. Experimental characterisation of hafting traces, In E.A. Walker, F.F Wenban-Smith and F. Healy, eds, *Lithics in action*. Oxford: Oxbow Books.

Rodwell, J.S. 1998. *British plant communities, volume 3: Grasslands and montane communities*. Cambridge: Cambridge University Press.

Rowlands, M.J. 1976. *The production and distribution of metalwork in the Middle Bronze Age in southern Britain.* Oxford: British Archaeological Reports, British Series 31.

Saville, A. 1981. The flint and chert artefacts. In R. Mercer, Excavations at Carn Brea, Illogan, Cornwall, 1970-73 – a Neolithic fortified complex of the third millennium bc. *Cornish Archaeology* 20, 101-152.

Schweingruber, F.H. 1990. *Microscopic wood anatomy: Structural variability of stems and twigs in recent and sub-fossil woods from Central Europe*, Birmensdorf: Swiss Federal Institute for Forest, Snow and Landscape Research (3rd edition).

Sheridan, A. 2004. Neolithic connections along and across the Irish Sea. In V. Cummings and C. Fowler, eds, *The Neolithic of the Irish Sea, materiality and traditions of practice*. Oxford: Oxbow Books, 9-21.

Shotyk, W., Weiss, D., Kramers, J.D., Frei, R., Cheburkin, A.K., Gloor, M. & Rees, S. 2001. Geochemistry of the peat bog at Etang de la Grue`re, Jura Mountains, Switzerland, and its record of atmospheric Pb and lithogenic trace metals (Sc, Ti, Y, Zr, and REE) since 12,370 14C yr BP. *Geochimica et Cosmochimica Acta* 65, 2337–2360.

Silvester, R. 1980. The prehistoric open settlement at Dainton, South Devon. *Proceedings of the Devon Archaeological Society* 38, 17-48.

Skowranek, C. 2007. Random places or organized industry - Middle to Late Bronze Age metalworking in southwest England. Unpublished MA Thesis: University of Bristol.

Smith, G. & Harris, D. 1982. The excavation of Mesolithic, Neolithic and Bronze Age settlements at Poldowrian, St Keverne, 1980. *Cornish Archaeology* 21, 23-66.

Smith, I.F. 1981. The Neolithic pottery. In R. Mercer, Excavations at Carn Brea, Illogan, Cornwall – a Neolithic fortified complex of the third millennium bc. *Cornish Archaeology* 20, 161-184.

Smith, M.A. 1959. The Somerset hoards and their place in the Bronze Age of southern England, *Proceedings of the Prehistoric Society* 25, 144-187.

Smith, M.A. (ed) 1959. *Inventaria Archaeologica 7, Great Britain 42-47. Middle Bronze hoards from Southern England.* London: Garraway.

Smythe, J. 2014. *Settlement in the Irish Neolithic: new discoveries at the edge of Europe.* Oxford: Prehistoric Society.

Soil Survey of England and Wales, 1983. *Soils of England and Wales, Sheet 5, South West England.*

Sorenson, M-L.S. 1996. Sherds and pot groups as keys to site formation process. In S. Needham and T. Spence, *Refuse and Disposal at Area 16 East, Runnymede.* London: British Museum Press, 1-74.

Sorenson, M-L.S. 2010. Bronze Age bodiness – maps and coordinates. In K. Rebay-Salisbury, M-L.S. Sorensen and J. Hughes, eds, *Body parts and bodies whole.* Oxford: Oxbow, 54–63.

Stace, C. 1991. *New flora of the British Isles.* Cambridge: Cambridge University Press.

Straker, V. 1991. Charred plant macrofossils. In J.A. Nowakowski, Trethellan Farm, Newquay: Excavation of a lowland Bronze Age settlement and Iron Age cemetery. *Cornish Archaeology* 30, 162-179.

Straker, V., Brown, A., Fyfe, R., Jones, J. & Wilkinson, K. 2007. Later Bronze Age and Iron Age environmental background. In C.J. Webster, ed, *The archaeology of South West England: South West archaeological research framework, resource assessment and research agenda*. Taunton: Somerset County Council, 103-116.

Tabor, R. 2008. *Cadbury Castle: the hillfort and its landscape*. Stroud: Tempus.

Talon, M. 2012. Trade within the English Channel/North Sea Region. In A. Lehoërff, ed, *Beyond the horizon: Societies of the Channel and North Sea 3,500 years ago*. Paris: Somogy Art Publishers, 74-81.

Tapper, R.Q. 2011. Middle and Late Bronze Age settlement on the South Downs: the case study of Black Patch. Unpublished PhD Thesis: University of Sussex.

Taylor, J. 1980. *Bronze Age goldwork of the British Isles*. Cambridge: Cambridge University press.

Thomas, J. 1991. *Rethinking the Neolithic*. Cambridge: University of Cambridge Press.

Thomas, J. 1999. *Understanding the Neolithic*. London: Routledge.

Thomas, N. 2005. *Snail Down Wiltshire, the Bronze Age barrow cemetery and related earthworks, in the parishes of Collingbourne Ducis and Collingbourne Kingston; excavations 1953, 1955 and 1957*. Devizes: Wiltshire Archaeological and Natural History Society/English Heritage.

Tilley, C. 2009. Jacob's Well, Black Hill: a Bronze Age water shrine on Woodbury Common. *Proceedings of the Devon Archaeology Society* 67, 23-38.

Tingle, M. 1998. *The prehistory of Beer Head: field survey and excavations at an isolated flint source on the South Devon coast*. Oxford: British Archaeological Reports, British Series 270.

Topping, P. 1998. The excavation of burnt mounds at Titlington, Mount, north Northumberland. *Northern Archaeology* 15/16, 3-26.

Townend, S. 2007. What have reconstructed roundhouses ever done for us. *Proceedings of the Prehistoric Society* 73, 97-111.

Tringham, R. 1991. Households with faces: the challenge of gender in prehistoric architectural remains. In J.M. Gero and M. Conkey, eds, *Engendering archaeology, women and prehistory*. London: Blackwell, 113-132.

Tringham, R. 1995. Archaeological houses, households, and housework and the home. In D.N. Benjamin, D. Stea and D. Saile, eds, *The home: Words, interpretations, meanings and environments*. Aldershot: Avebury, 79-107.

Trudgian, P. ApSimon, A.M. 1976. A Trevisker series Bronze Age urn from Largin Wood, Broadoak. *Cornish Archaeology* 15, 112-14.

Tucker. C. 1852. Proceedings at the meeting of the Archaeological Institute, March 5, 1852. *Archaeological Journal* 9, 185-6.

Turner, L. 2010. *A re-interpretation of the Later Bronze Age metalwork hoards of Essex and Kent.* Oxford: British Archaeological Reports, British Series 133.

Turton, A. 1978. Architectural and political space in Thailand. In G. Milner, ed, *Natural symbols in South East Asia*. London: School of Oriental and African Studies, University of London, 113-132.

Waddell, J. 1991/2. The Irish Sea in prehistory. *Journal of Irish Archaeology* VI, 29-40.

Waddell, J. 1998. *The prehistoric archaeology of Ireland.* Galway: University of Galway Press.

Waterson, R. 1997. *The living house: an anthropology of architecture in South-East Asia.* London: Thames and Hudson.

Watts, S. 2014. *The life and death of querns: the deposition and use-contexts of querns in South-western England from the Neolithic to the Iron Age.* Southampton: The Highfield Press.

Webley, L. 2007. Using and abandoning roundhouses: a reinterpretation of the evidence from Late Bronze Age-Early Iron Age southern England. *Oxford Journal of Archaeology* 26, 127-144.

Weiner, A.B. 1987. *The Trobrianders of Papua New Guinea*, Belmont: Wadsworth/ Thomson.

Whittle, A. 1997. *Sacred mounds, holy rings: Silbury Hill and the West Kennet palisade enclosures.* Oxford: Oxbow Books.

Whittle, A., Bayliss, A., Healy, F., Mercer, R., Jones, A.M. & Todd, M. 2011. The south-west peninsula. In A. Whittle, F. Healy and A. Bayliss, eds, *Gathering time: dating the Early Neolithic enclosures of southern Britain and Ireland.* Oxford: Oxbow Books, 476-520.

Whittle, A., Rouse, A. & Evans, J.G. 1993. A Neolithic downland monument in its environment: excavations at the Easton Down long barrow, Bishops Cannings, north Wiltshire. *Proceedings of the Prehistoric Society* 59, 197-240.

Wilkinson, K. & Straker. 2008. Neolithic and Early Bronze Age Environmental Background. In C.J. Webster, ed, *The archaeology of South West England: South West Archaeological Research Framework, Resource Assessment and Research Agenda.* Taunton: Somerset County Council, 63-74.

Williams, C. 2003. Growing metaphors. The agricultural cycle as metaphor in the later prehistoric period of Britain and north-west Europe. *Journal of Social Archaeology* 3, 223–255.

Williams, D. 2005. Analyses petrographiques. In B. Cunliffe and P. Galliou, *Les Fouilles du Yaudet en Ploulec'h, Cote-d'Armor.* In B. Cunliffe and P. Galliou, *Annexe C4 online.* www.arch.ox.ac.uk/research_projects/Le_Yaudet.

Wilson-North, R. & Carey, C. 2011. A burnt mound on Brendan Common, Exmoor. *Proceedings of the Devon Archaeological Society* 69, 9-22.

Woodward, A. 1990. The Bronze Age pottery. In M. Bell, *Brean Down excavations 1983-1987.* London: English Heritage, 121-145.

Woodward, A. & Cane, C. 1991. The Bronze Age pottery. In J.A. Nowakowski, Trethellan Farm, Newquay: the excavation of a lowland Bronze Age settlement and Iron Age cemetery. *Cornish Archaeology* 30, 103-131.

Woodward, A., Hunter, J., Ixer, R., Maltby, M., Potts, P., Webb, P., Watson, J. & Jones, M. 2005. Ritual in some Early Bronze Age grave goods. *Archaeological Journal* 163, 31-64.

Yates, D. 2007. *Land, power and prestige: Bronze Age field systems in southern England.* Oxford: Oxbow Books.

Young, A. 2006. The National Mapping Programme in Cornwall. *Cornish Archaeology* 45, 109-116.

Young, A. 2012. Prehistoric and Romano-British enclosures around the Camel estuary, Cornwall, *Cornish Archaeology* 51, 69-124.